THE GUARDIANS OF DREAMDARK

WINDWITCH

LAINI TAYLOR

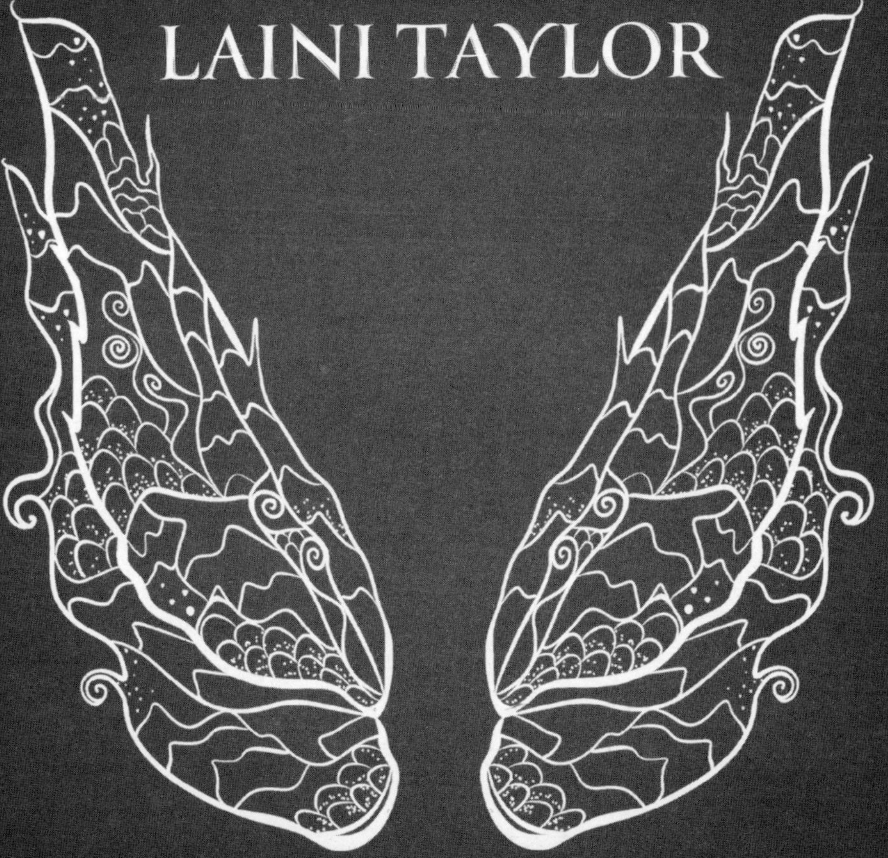

THE GUARDIANS OF DREAMDARK

WINDWITCH

HODDER

HODDER CHILDREN'S BOOKS

First published in Great Britain in 2025 by Hodder & Stoughton Limited
First published in the United States in 2009 by Putnam Publishing Group

1 3 5 7 9 10 8 6 4 2

A CIP catalogue record for this book is available from the British Library.

HB ISBN 978 1 444 95104 2
TPB ISBN: 978 1 444 95276 6

Typeset in Adobe Garamond Pro by Jouve (UK), Milton Keynes
Printed and bound in Great Britain by Clays Ltd, Elcograf S.p.A.

The paper and board used in this book are made from wood from responsible sources.

MIX
Paper | Supporting responsible forestry
FSC www.fsc.org FSC® C104740

Hodder Children's Books
An imprint of
Hachette Children's Group
Part of Hodder & Stoughton Limited
Carmelite House
50 Victoria Embankment
London EC4Y 0DZ

The authorised representative in the EEA is Hachette Ireland, 8 Castlecourt Centre, Dublin 15, D15 XTP3, Ireland (email: info@hbgi.ie)

An Hachette UK Company
www.hachette.co.uk

www.hachettechildrens.co.uk

In gratitude to my parents for a childhood of books
and journeys, and to Jim,
for art and gondola rides and more art,
and always, for love

PRELUDE

THE WOLF TASTED THE BABE'S FACE WITH THE TIP OF HIS tongue and pronounced her sweet, and the fox licked the back of her head to see if it was so. For the rest of her life, when this child grew into a faerie with bright eyes and a laugh as loud and unladylike as a crow's, that spot on her hair would never lie flat. And though she wouldn't remember the night the creatures had gathered round to look at her and taste and smell her, she would call those unruly hairs her foxlick without knowing why.

The branches overhead thrummed with birds. They would wait their turn, but they wouldn't be quiet about it. No matter. The creatures weren't worried about being interrupted by faeries. The imp had smuggled the babe far from home, floating her down Misky Creek on a linden leaf so that this unusual starlight gathering would draw no unwanted notice. The creatures had her for the night, and by morning she would be back snug in her cradle with no one the wiser.

'Shall we begin?' asked the imp, nuzzling the babe's pink cheeks with her whiskers and making her laugh. 'Who'll go first?'

They all clamored to go first. Fur brushed against hide, tusks clashed with horns as they pressed nearer, eager and gentle. Most of these creatures would be long dead by the time this babe had grown up and taken her place in the world. But they would give her their blessings in turn and hope they helped her make her way.

There would never be another chance. So much depended on this tiny faerie whom dreams had at last made real.

1

'DEVILS!' SCREAMED THE FISHERMEN, POINTING AT THE SKY. Magpie Windwitch didn't know many human words, but she knew this one, *devil*, in more than twenty of their languages, though this was the first time she'd been called one herself.

'Foolish mannies!' she scoffed, looking down at them from the sky where she was circling their fishing boat amid a swirl of crows.

'Aieeee!' the humans wailed, dropping to their knees to pray.

Certainly it was strange to see crows this far out over the open ocean, but to call them devils, that was going a bit far. Magpie shook her head and signaled to the crows to turn away. This wasn't the boat they sought anyway. The boat they sought would be empty, forsaken by its fishermen and left to drift.

The boat they sought had met a real devil.

The crows rose up, and the West Wind gathered them again into his arms and surged across the sky. Behind them the fishermen lay slouched and gasping against the rails of their boat, their turbans unwinding in the wind. They were right to fear devils. Magpie had a hunter's respect for fear: it sharpened the senses. But those fishermen, she didn't doubt, for all their prayers and worry, wouldn't hesitate to uncork any strange bottle they fished out of the ocean, just to see what was inside. It happened all the time these days, and the devils were just delighted.

She fixed her eyes fiercely on the sea and scanned its breadth between identical horizons, back and forth. It had been days since her grandfather, the West Wind, had heard the albatross's rumor of an abandoned boat adrift at sea. In the time it had taken him to find her and bring her here, it could have drifted anywhere. The sea was a vast hunting ground, and she was getting nervous. Though the wind held the crows aloft in his airy arms, they weren't made for such long flight and would still grow tired in time. They needed to find that boat.

'How you holding up, my feather?' she asked the crow she rode upon, stroking his sleek head with both hands.

'Like a leaf on a breeze,' he answered in his singsong voice. 'A champagne bubble. A hovering hawk. A cloud! Nothing to it!'

'So you say. But I'm no tiny sprout anymore, Calypso, and sure you can't carry me forever.'

'Piff! Ye weigh no more than a dust mouse, so hush yer spathering. 'Twill be a sore day for me when I can't carry my 'Pie.'

Magpie went back to scanning the sea, her chin resting on Calypso's head. Ever since she was a tiny thing, she'd loved riding him, but as she grew up she did so less and less, generally flying alongside him instead. Her own dragonfly wings were sleek as blades, many-paned like stained glass and as swift as any wings under the sun or moon. But she was tired, still drained from a two-day chase in the desert. That scarab devil had given her a time, to be sure, so she hadn't put up a fuss when Calypso insisted on carrying her.

As far as her keen eyes could tell, the surface of the sea spread out empty all around them. They flew on, deeper into the vastness of it.

An hour passed before at last Magpie spotted a listing, slack-sailed boat. The crows circled, heaving and panting, and dropped out of the arms of the wind to go in for a closer look. Magpie stood up on Calypso's back. She took one step into thin air and plummeted some thirty feet straight down before flicking her wings open like a fan and coming in for a sharp landing on the boat's rail. She crouched, paused, then prowled forward like a creature, ready to spring into the air if surprised.

The boat seemed empty. Magpie waved, and all seven crows came in to land. Seeing nothing amiss on deck, they cautiously descended into the fishing boat's small cabin. There they found signs of recent human habitation: tobacco, dirty tin cups, a backgammon board open on the table. On the same table Magpie found just what she was looking for and had hoped *not* to find. She had hoped this would turn out to be some human mystery of no interest to herself or any of her kind. But that was not the case.

Lying on its side on the table was a tarnished silver flask with a long neck and elegant scrolled handle. Its wax seal had been broken and lay in two pieces beside it. She and Calypso exchanged a somber look.

'Might just be a coffeepot,' the crow offered hopefully. He had a chip in the left side of his beak that made him seem perpetually to grin.

Magpie's eyes swept over the table and settled on the two halves of the seal. She took it up in her hands, and her face paled. 'It's no coffeepot,' she said.

'What is it, 'Pie?' Calypso asked, hopping toward her. The other crows crowded in, curious.

'What ye got, Mags? Eh, Mags?' asked the smallest one, Pup, in a quiver of spasmodic energy.

Magpie held the pieces together. Emblazoned in the wax was a hand in the center of a flame. 'It's the Magruwen's seal,' she said in a hushed voice.

'The Magruwen?' they all squawked, puffing up their feathers.

'The Djinn King?' gasped Pup's brother, Pigeon.

'B-but . . .' Calypso stammered, 'I never heard of him trifling with devils!'

'Nor I.' Magpie was solemn, looking around the small cabin. Aside from the seal, there was no evidence a devil had even been here. The odor was usually overwhelming when a devil had freshly been freed from thousands of years stewing in its own stench, but she smelled nothing. She sat back on her heels.

She'd caught quite a few devils since she got started hunting them eight years ago. The scarab devil had made twenty-three, which was, as far as she knew, twenty-three more than any other living faerie had caught. That was twenty-three ancient bottles fished up by humans and twenty-three broken seals. None of those had borne the sigil of the Magruwen. Magpie knew the legends of the devil wars better than anyone, and in none of them did the great Djinn King himself stoop to wrestling snags into their prisons. That had always been the work of his champion, Bellatrix, the greatest faerie of all legend, and the champions of the other six Djinn.

'What grim beast could need so strong a seal?' Calypso whispered, peering around the cabin. 'Think it's still aboard?'

'Neh,' Magpie said. 'It's gone.' She felt no devilish presence. In fact, but for the missing fishermen there seemed nothing at all wrong. She had seen the aftermath of plenty of devil escapes, and they all had two things in common: blood and stench. Here were neither of those, and yet a shiver gripped her spine. For here was something she had never expected to see: the Magruwen's seal upon a snag's prison. It shivered her to think what could have been inside it.

Something on the floor caught her eye, and she leapt down to it. 'Flummox me . . .' she said. The crows swooped down, too.

Four pairs of battered canvas shoes were arranged around the table with their toes pointed inward, as if the fishermen had gathered here to open the bottle they'd pulled up in their nets. Whatever had been inside, it had been there for a long, long time, and it had come out hungry. Calypso whistled low. 'Snatched 'em right out of their slippers,' he said.

'Why'd they let it out?' Pup wanted to know. 'Why do they *always*?'

'I reckon they heard the story about the wishes,' replied Swig.

Magpie sighed. One devil, just one in all of devil history, had granted three wishes to the human who freed it. Magpie had caught that troublemaking snag five years ago and put him back, but the damage was already done. The mannies had a mania for it now, and every chance they got they freed some wicked thing back into the world, and they surely didn't get wishes for their trouble.

What had these fools gotten? Just their shoes left behind, and no one to spread *that* story. 'Poor dumb mannies,' she muttered.

'Curiosity killed the eejit.' Calypso replied with a shrug.

Magpie frowned at him. Usually pity was the last emotion humans inspired in her, but something about those empty shoes tugged at her heart. She reached toward the frayed fabric of the nearest slipper, forming pictures in her mind as she did so. Glyphs – symbols drawn in one's thoughts – were the basic element of faerie magic. The simplest were mere shapes that every sprout mastered while learning to read. Making light and fire, floating, hiding, protection from trespass, basic healing, and housework: these things were as easy as the alphabet. Real magic came with more complex glyphs and fusing multiple glyphs together in precise ways – being able to conjure them from memory and 'vision' them, hold them burning in one's mind with perfect concentration.

The glyphs Magpie visioned now were for 'memory' and 'touch,' and no sooner had she laid her fingers on the human's slipper than a jolt surged up her arm and she was engulfed in darkness. It went as soon as she jerked her hand away, but the shock drove her to her knees, and she gasped.

''Pie!' squawked Calypso. ''Pie, darlin', what is it?'

Her fingers were still tingling from the jolt. She said, 'Darkness.'

'Eh? That all?'

The mannies' last memory, seared into the last thing they'd touched, was of darkness. This spell for memory touch, learned from faeries in the high Sayash Mountains, had become a valuable snag-hunting tool, more than once showing Magpie the face of the devil she was seeking as glimpsed in its victims' last moments. But these mannies had seen only darkness. Or had there been something else?

She hesitated and touched the shoe again. This time, braced for it, she didn't let it knock her to her knees, but she couldn't stop the gasp it forced from her lips. She drew her hand hastily away and said, 'Hunger.'

'Hunger?'

'Aye. Mad hunger.' She shivered and with one last quick look around said, 'Let's go,' and they flew back up on deck, several crows lugging the devil's bottle between them. 'Rest awhile,' she told them. 'It's a long sky till landfall, and I don't want to feed any crows to the sea.'

Calypso stretched his wings and yawned. 'Just a catnap, then. Wake us when it's time to go, 'Pie.' He tucked his head against his breast and closed his eyes.

Magpie stretched, too, and looked around. Her grandfather had conjured his faerie skin and was waiting for her in the midst of a clump of napping crows, looking just like a jolly old codger with whiskers, broad-chested and lively. Elementals like the winds or the Djinn could put on skins and enjoy a taste of mortal life, which was how Magpie came to have the West Wind for a grandfather. Six hundred years ago, he'd taken one look at a lovely lass named Sparrow, fallen head over heels for her, and gone to craft himself a faerie skin handsome enough to woo her in.

Sparrow had fallen in love back, and he'd swept her off to a life in the sky, to travel always cuddled to his chest as he soared above the world. It was a bold, wild life for a faerie – most never even left their forests – but she was a bold, wild lass, and so were her daughter and granddaughter after her, and their place in the world was everywhere and nowhere, like gypsies on wing. No home had they but their caravans and campfires, and no family but the one they'd cobbled together of crows, creatures, and kindred souls they'd met on their endless journey round and round the world.

'Ach, Grandpa, it's what you thought,' Magpie said, plopping down next to him and resting her glossy head on his shoulder.

'Jacksmoke!' the old fellow cursed, cradling her to his side and absently smoothing down the foxlick that stood up like a tuft from the top of her wind-whipped head. 'Another loose devil? Skiving plague of meddlesome mannies, can't leave a bottle well enough alone!'

'Aye, that's six in as many months. They keep on like this, the world'll be crawling with snags like it was before the devil wars! I can't keep up all on my own.'

'Maybe you shouldn't try, love. Leave 'em free! There are too many mannies anyway, neh?'

'Ach, and what of everyone else? It wasn't mannies that scarab devil killed, but faeries!'

'And what of this one? Got away?'

'Aye.' She scowled. 'And Grandpa, there's something mad strange about this one . . . its bottle, it was sealed by the Magruwen.'

'Eh? Impossible!' he declared. 'That old scorch never dirtied his hands on devils.'

'You never heard of anything, then, during the wars? Some lost story?'

'Neh, and sure I'd remember, no matter it was twenty-five thousand years ago. I remember Bellatrix clear as yesterday. What a sight she was in battle! 'Twas she and the other champions who caught all the snags.'

'Aye, I always thought so, but what of this seal?'

He took it and examined it, frowning. 'Jacksmoke. It's his, all right. Ancient and true.' He handed it back. 'No idea what was in the bottle?'

'Neh, none. There's no smell, no drool, no blood. Nothing at all.'

'And what of the fishermen?'

'Ate them, I reckon.'

'Ate them? I thought you said there was no blood.'

'Nary a drop,' Magpie admitted.

'Ach, there would be! You ever know a devil to chew with its mouth closed?'

'Neh . . .' she said. But she could still feel that hunger tugging at her through the manny's left-behind memory. 'If it didn't eat them, what did it do to them?'

He shrugged. 'Could be they launched a skiff and got away.'

'Maybe,' Magpie murmured skeptically, thinking of the shoes left so suddenly behind. 'But I don't think so.'

'We'll put the word out,' the West Wind said. 'Split up and ask around in the ports. You'll find its trail soon enough. You always do, love.'

'I reckon. But this one . . . it shivers me, Grandpa.'

'Mmm. Always listen to your shivers. They'll save your life sometime.'

When the sun touched the sea, Magpie rousted the crows, and the wind shed his faerie skin and became, once again, a force of nature. Carrying the devil's empty bottle with them, they took to the sky and traveled on through twilight and starlight, back toward land.

2

ACROSS THE WATER IN THE HIDDEN PLACES BENEATH A VAST city, a new thing was taking possession of the darkness. Legions of lesser devils had made their home here for centuries in the underbelly of the human world. Now they fled in panic on their cloven hooves and splayed toes.

A furious wind howled in the underground passages. Those creatures who paused to look back over their shoulders found themselves swept up by a terrible hunger and scarcely had time to wonder what was happening before they ceased to exist. Rats, imps, low devils, and quavering translucent spirits roiled up and out of the sewer grates and made for whatever scraps of shadow they could find in the world above.

Soon the catacombs were empty, and the hungry one prowled on, hunting something far greater than this snack of devils. Dust spun and churned as the wind struggled in his grip, but he dragged it along, merciless. He could feel its panic, but it was powerless against him, for he wielded the one weapon it could never resist: he knew its secret name. He had chanted the elementals' secret names like a song in his prison, plotting this moment. Vengeance had never been far from his thoughts all the thousands of years of his imprisonment, and now his time had come at last.

Doom dawned.

He seeped like a fog through the stacks of skulls lining the corridors. These were the skulls of a species who had not yet walked the world when he had last been abroad in it. So long had he drifted in the sea that in that time, a new species had risen, built cities, fought its own wars, and been dying long enough to overflow its cemeteries. So many years, so many bones. And through the thick stink of dead humans, he scented something else, deeper, older. Faerie bones. He followed the smell and found the way.

Skeletons slumped silent under years of dust, but the hungry one scarcely noticed them. He had found what he sought. He almost couldn't believe it: an ember within a circle of dull stones. A mere ember? How the mighty had fallen! *What had come to pass*, he wondered for the hundredth time since bursting from his bottle, that doom might prove such a simple matter after all?

He savored the moment. As soon as he commanded the wind to expend its final fury in snuffing that dim ember, a new age would begin, an age of unweaving. An age of endings. The hungry one laughed and began to speak.

3

'SKIVE,' MAGPIE CURSED.

'Trail's cold as cold,' said Calypso.

'What trail?' she grumbled. 'If we even found a trail, that'd be something. But unless Maniac and Mingus come back with news, this snag's good and gone.'

They stood on the head of a ruined monument to some long-dead human, eyes sweeping restlessly over the olive groves that sprawled down the hillside from their hunting camp. 'They should've been back this morning at the latest,' said the crow.

'Aye. If it was Pup and Pigeon I wouldn't fret, they dither about so, but Maniac and Mingus are never late. I don't like it.'

'Nor I, pet.'

A devil leaves no footprints upon the ocean, so Magpie and the crows had split into pairs to search the coastlines that touched all sides of the Surrounded Sea. For a week, she and Calypso had questioned gulls, wharf rats, and low snags in the ports of North Ifrit. Had any new devils come to town, fresh from their bottles? Again and again they'd asked, paying in wine and trinkets for this greasy gossip of devil life, but they hadn't learned a thing. Neither had Swig and Bertram or Pup and Pigeon, who had arrived back to their island camp the previous day as arranged.

Only Maniac and Mingus were yet to return, and as the day passed in a slow scorching arc, Magpie paced and cursed.

When the sun sank from sight with no sign of them winging up the hillside, Magpie swooped down from her perch to where the other crows sat smoking. 'Come on, birds,' she told them. 'We got to go find Maniac and Mingus.'

The crows stubbed out their cheroots and rose in unison to follow her.

They left their brightly painted caravans behind on the small island and traveled light, flying high above the masts of ships and later above the towers and battlements of cities. Magpie looked down on the moon-washed rooftops and thought, *This is not my world*. It was some other idea of the world laid atop the geography of her own, smothering it.

It was the humans' world.

In her hundred years, she had seen their towns swell into cities and blacken from the fumes of their foul fires. They dammed rivers, gouged minerals from mountains, built stout ships for murdering whales, chopped down whole forests just to build roofs and cradles for all the new people they daily made.

And the faeries in their wild places knew little of it.

They hadn't paid much attention when the once-monkeys had come down from the trees. They'd laughed at their crude clothing and the fires sparked by sticks instead of spells and gone on dancing, turning their backs on the land outside their forests. When next they peered out and saw how much of the world had been plowed into fields or crushed under cities, it had come as a great surprise. In fact, the word *human* meant 'surprise' in Old Tongue, the language of the ancients. No one knew where they came from, only that the Djinn who made every other creature had not made them. They hadn't even predicted them. And there was the rub.

Many thousands of years ago, when the faeries had at long last won the wars, the seven champions had captured the devils in bottles and cast them into the sea. They had crafted elaborate magicks so that nothing could ever free them from their prisons – nothing then alive in the world, anyway. Not faerie nor dragon, elemental, snag, creature, imp, or finfolk could break those seals. But humans? Humans didn't exist. And then one millennium along they came, fishing the world's oceans, pulling up ancient bottles in their nets and uncorking them to see what was inside.

Now devils were creeping back into the world, faster and faster all the time, but the age of champions was long past, and little Magpie Windwitch found herself alone against them.

Sometime in the night, they met a breeze who carried a message for them. 'Those two crows are waiting for you in Rome,' said the breeze, an air elemental of slight power. 'They're all atwitch and atwitter about the news.'

'What news?'

'There's some telling of a wind gone underground, missy, down where the mannies stack their skeletons.'

'Neh!' Magpie declared.

'I hope it's not true,' said the breeze.

'And I,' Magpie said, knowing how air elementals loathe close spaces. None would ever willingly venture underground. Something strange was at work there. 'I thank you, cousin,' Magpie said. She adjusted her course for Rome, that king of human cities. Beneath its majestic domes and spires it was rotting from the roots, its catacombs and cellars a snug home to multitudes of dim snags. These were the ones faeries had never taken the trouble to capture because they were no more dangerous than dogs. Such creatures dwelled in the dark places wherever there were humans, living off garbage and unwary cats and the occasional stray child, but few cities were as infested with them as Rome.

Magpie and the crows flew most of the night, getting a push from whatever wind or breeze they encountered, and they reached the city before the earliest gleams of dawn. They descended into the catacombs through a grate in a bakery cellar, pausing to steal bread while the baker's back was turned. They had to hop up and down on the loaves to wedge them down through the narrow grate, but after all that trouble they never did get to eat them.

For when Magpie dropped into the underground passage, she knew something was wrong. She peered down the darkened corridor and found no sign of Maniac and Mingus or of anything else. It was utterly silent.

'Where've all the snags got to?' whispered Pup.

'Flummox me . . .' she whispered back.

Their whispers seemed to boom in the unnatural hush of the catacombs.

'Something's mad wrong,' Pigeon breathed with an anxious flutter.

'Aye,' Magpie agreed. There should have been snags here. She had come before to buy their gossip, and though she'd hated the stink of their hidden world, she'd never feared them, as now she feared their absence.

Magpie frowned and began to form glyphs in her mind, but before she was even finished, she was flooded with a powerful memory touch. *Darkness. Hunger.* She stumbled, and each step brought a new burst of the same terrible memory. Many memories, many creatures, suffering the same terrible fate: darkness. Hunger. Again and again. Finally she leapt to her wings, drawing her feet away from the memories seared into the floor. She shook off the visions, her breath coming fast.

'Mags! Ye okay, Mags?' the crows were demanding, crowding round her, unable to feel the magic that had so shaken her. Their bread lay forgotten in the shadows for some rat to retrieve once they'd gone.

Only there were no rats.

There was nothing at all.

'He's been here,' Magpie said. 'The hungry one.'

The crows puzzled over this. 'But there en't any tracks,' observed Bertram.

Magpie looked down at the dirt. Bertram was right. Every time they'd hunted a devil it had left a ripe trail of some kind to follow, be it drool or destruction or at least rooster tracks. It is a strange fact of magic that a devil, no matter what its feet are shaped like, will always leave rooster prints in soft ground, but though Magpie knew a horde of snags had fled this way, there were no tracks at all. The whole corridor seemed swept clean. Violently so, perhaps. 'Looks like that wind came through here, my feathers.'

'Why, Mags?' Pigeon fretted. 'Why would it come down here? It en't natural.'

'Neh, it isn't. We'll keep on this way,' she said, pointing down the passage. They flew along slowly and listened for life as Magpie's light gleamed off the stacks of yellowed skulls. Nothing slunk in the shadows or whispered among the bones. Every word the crows spoke echoed. Every wing beat stirred plumes of dust. Magpie had never felt a place so desolate. Even the forsaken temples of the Djinn, so long ago left to crumble into ruin, had not this feeling of death. Of stolen life. Of absence.

Something profound had happened here, she knew, something far deeper than a wind's rampage or the disappearance of a ragtag population of sad snags. The further she went along the skull-lined passage, the more the feeling stole over her, the sense of a warp in the world where something had been and now was not.

'Mags,' croaked Swig. 'A passage.'

They might easily have walked right past it, for it was barely a passage at all, just a place where the skulls had recessed enough for something to slide past.

'I don't like the look of it,' whispered Pigeon. ''Tis sneaky, like.'

Magpie motioned the crows to fall silent. She listened, sniffed, then moved through the crevice in a sinuous prowl. When Magpie Windwitch was on the hunt, a creature nature awoke in her. She moved like a lynx one moment, a lizard the next, a raptor after that, gliding smoothly between them as if she weren't one creature but all, her faerie self temporarily misplaced in the spaces between. She'd been born to it like a fox kit, a natural tracker with hearing mysteriously sharp, nose unusually keen, and vision clear as a hawk's or owl's, by day or night regardless.

But none of these senses propelled her forward now. She saw no tracks, smelled no scent, heard no sound. As on the fishing boat, there was nothing. No blood, no stink. And still something kept her moving and guided her right or left when the narrow passage began to fork, then fork again. It was a sense she had learned not to speak of, for words failed her and she'd grown tired of the blank stares.

It was an awareness of a force that pulsed beneath the skin of the world, unseen and unknowable but as real to her as the blood under the white skin of her own wrists. Her parents didn't feel it, or her grandmother. No one did. She was alone in it. And sometimes, sometimes . . . the pulse caught her up in its flow and carried her along, and when that happened, the way ahead felt as clear as a path paved with light.

It carried her now, and she went forth on her wings, the crows hurrying behind her until the passage spilled them all into a chamber. The echoes of their wing beats fluttered like living creatures in the high-vaulted space, and they all fell still. Magpie was the first to see what lay in the center of the room.

Skeletons. Faerie skeletons, many, and so old everything had disintegrated but the white bones themselves. The bones, and the knife that protruded from the nearest one's spine.

Magpie didn't linger long over this sight however, for something else caught her notice – a door in the far wall, engraved with a symbol – and her eyes widened in shocked recognition. 'Neh . . .' she whispered, and her wings lifted her toward it, right over the skeletons, her eyes never leaving the symbol. 'Can it really be . . . ?'

''Pie!' squawked Calypso suddenly, and at that moment her senses throbbed a warning and she felt something coming at her, plummeting from the shadowed reaches above. She thrust herself backward, twisting in air and reaching in one fluid motion for the knife handle she'd seen, wrenching it free of its sheath of bone and spilling the skeleton asunder. As she spun toward her attacker all sound was lost in the ruckus of crow squalls and their echoes, and she came face-to-face with . . . the oldest faerie she had ever seen.

Quickly she stayed the knife and hung in the air before him, staring. She had never beheld so ancient a member of her race. The skin of his face sagged like melted wax and his long white beard was woven round him into a cloak that fell to the floor. He wore a crested helm and brandished a sword, and he snarled the word *Devil!* as he lunged at her. She easily dodged him, seeing as she did that his eyes were clouded – probably blind – and sunk deep in bruise-colored sockets, staring and wild. Never had she seen a soul so blighted by terror.

He raised his sword to swing it again.

'Sir!' she cried. 'I'm no devil! I'm a faerie and a friend!'

Hearing her words, he dropped his sword with a clatter and fell to his knees. He reached out gnarled hands, his blind eyes rolling, seeking her. She set aside the knife and stepped forward, placing her palms flat against his in the greeting that had become custom in wartimes when devils had been wont to masquerade as faeries. Their fingers had ever given away their disguise, having either too many joints or too few, and this meeting of hands was proof of kinship – or the lack of it. Though all faeries still used it, few remembered its grim origin. Something told Magpie this one did.

'Blessings . . .' the old warrior whispered, then closed his hands tight over Magpie's. She tried to ease her fingers away, but his grip was surprisingly strong.

Alarmed, she wrenched free and drew back from him. 'Old uncle,' she said warily. 'All these faeries who lie here dead – was it you who slew them?'

He answered in a hoarse voice, 'Nay, 'twas Skuldraig murdered them all. They never learn to leave him lie.'

'Skuldraig? Who—?'

He cut her off. ''Tis of no consequence now. The devil is returned!'

'Which devil, uncle?'

'The worst of them all . . . the hungry one,' he said with a violent shudder.

'The hungry one?' Magpie demanded. 'What is he?'

'I couldn't stop him . . .' he whispered, a look of horror on his face.

'Stop him from what?'

'He should have killed me, too,' he went on.

'Killed? Whom did he kill?'

'He laughed at me . . .' the old faerie whispered, seeming to sink in on himself. 'He left me alive. I outlived my master,' he choked. 'I failed.'

'Who's your—?' Magpie started to ask, but the answer seized her with icy fingers, and she turned back to the door with the symbol engraved on it. 'The Vritra,' she whispered. A numbness came over her mind. 'It's not possible,' she said. 'It's not possible.'

The Vritra was a Djinn, one of the seven fire elementals who had leapt through the blackness of the beginning to light the forge fires of creation. They had wrought the world, every stick and stone of it, each lightning bolt and firefly, aurora and sunrise, firedrake and fox, onyx and oryx, lemon tree and poison frog, and every frizz of Spanish moss. They had even made the faeries.

And four thousand years ago, they had disappeared without a trace.

With one sweep of his great arm, so the legend said, the Magruwen had knocked his temple at Issrin Ev down the mountainside and vanished, and within days the other six had gone from their own temples as well, never to be seen again. If there was a reason, it was lost in the swirling dusts of the past. Generations of faeries had lived and died since then and the Djinn were all but forgotten. Some said they'd never existed at all and others believed they'd returned to the blackness whence they came. But Magpie and her parents and her grandmother Sparrow believed something else, and here was the proof they were right.

Excavating the ruined temple of the Iblis – one of the Djinn – they had uncovered a symbol in an ancient scroll in which the Iblis's sigil intertwined with the glyph for dream. A similar symbol had been uncovered in scrolls at the Ithuriel's temple, and Magpie's folk had come to believe the seven fire elementals had withdrawn deep into the earth to sleep and dream. But though they had searched, they had never yet found the symbols carved in stone. Magpie stared at the inner door. They had never found a Djinn's dreaming place or any sign of a Djinn. Until now.

'Mags!' said Pup at her elbow. 'Listen – Maniac and Mingus!'

Indeed, crows could be heard squawking frantically on the other side of the engraved door, but Magpie barely heard them. She could think only of what else might be behind that door. She darted forward and strained against it. Swig joined her and together they pushed it open. Maniac and Mingus fluttered out, croaking and cawing. Strong, stoic Mingus said only, 'Thanks, Mags, fine to see ye,' but Maniac had worked himself into one of his rages.

'Where's that dastard codger?' he fumed. 'He shut us up in the dark to die! Let me at 'im!'

'Neh,' said Magpie, grabbing his wing tip. 'You don't understand what's happened—'

'Don't I? We came a-hunting that wind and the old prune trapped us here!'

'Maniac!' she said sharply. 'Show some respect to the guardian of a Djinn!'

'Guardian? That gristle?' He paused then, realizing what Magpie had said, and repeated, '*Djinn*?'

'Aye, now hush,' said Magpie, turning toward the inner chamber. With a sickening feeling, she saw it was utterly dark. A fire elemental's cave devoid of fire? She swept past the crows and flared her spelled light. Its orange glow fell over the eight sacred pillars that graced all Djinns' temples, and Magpie knew she was right about this place. On the ground she spotted a small circle of blackened stones. She flew to it and hovered above it. Inside it was nothing but ash.

'I outlived my master,' the old faerie had said. Magpie stared at the pit of ash. A Djinn had been dreaming here.

A Djinn was dead.

Her mind revolted. That old faerie was blind – he couldn't know what had happened, but Magpie could, if she dared. Slowly she stretched out her hand, drew the glyphs in her mind, and ever so gently touched a fingertip to the ashes.

The force of the Vritra's last memory seemed to scour her hollow. She crumpled over, clutching her arms round herself, choking for air that didn't come. She could feel the Djinn's mind screaming inside her as he was unmade. Smoldering flame giving way to a curl of dying smoke. Darkness, and the desperate dying wail of a second creature – a wind – as it was forced to use its own great power to snuff out its creator and spend its own life in the process.

There came a dry crust of a laugh at the very end and a terrible voice that whispered, 'The fire that burns its bellows can only fall to ash. What poetry in a traitor's death!' Then the Vritra knew no more, and Magpie was released from the memory to collapse sobbing to the ground.

It was only after many minutes of crow hugs and rocking and soothing that she began to come back from the depth of unfathomable loss and think about what she'd seen. A wind . . . it hadn't been her grandfather, of that she was sure, but kin nonetheless. The devil had commanded a wind to extinguish the Djinn, and the wind had been powerless to resist. The devil had known its secret name. What devil could wield such power? Only the Djinn knew the elementals' secret names!

The shiver that had gripped Magpie on the fishing boat had long since deepened to dread, and now it deepened further into something approaching despair. What had the humans loosed on the world this time?

'*The devil is returned . . .*' That was what the old faerie had said. He knew what the beast was! Magpie struggled to her feet and returned to the antechamber where she'd left him.

He was still slumped on his knees, but his haggard face was uplifted in a posture Magpie had seen before, and he was muttering words in Old Tongue.

'Wait!' she screamed, darting toward him.

But she was too late. She reached him just as the light left his clouded eyes, and he slumped forward, dead. He had released himself to the Moonlit Gardens, leaving his sad old body behind.

'Neh neh neh . . .' she said frantically, trying to shake him awake, knowing it was futile. 'Not yet, not yet,' she whispered. But he had gone.

The Moonlit Gardens were the faeries' next world, a calm silvered land they traveled to on a day of their own choosing – unless some violence chose the day for them – and from which there was no return. This old warrior – for such he surely was, of the legendary Shadowsharp clan who had guarded the Vritra in ancient days – had long outlasted his life. Faeries could live a thousand years, more if they were stubborn, but never this much more. Magpie had thought the Shadowsharp clan long dead. She couldn't even guess what will had enabled this one to hold on for centuries past his time. He must have been the last of his clan, unwilling to leave his master alone in the world. What a cruel fate then to fail and live on, all those tired, lonely centuries for naught.

This was a new kind of wickedness in a devil, to recognize a fate worse than death and inflict it. But now the old warrior had let go, and so died the last of another great clan. So many bloodlines had ended without heirs – like Bellatrix's, to the world's lasting sorrow. Many others might as well have. With the sad state of magic in this age, faeries bore little resemblance to their glorious forebears. Magpie mourned for bygone days more than most of her folk, because she knew better than they what had been lost. *Much* had been lost, was being lost every day. That loss was the shape of her life: the struggle against it, the hunt, the unending journey, the hollowness of suspecting that ultimately her family's work was in vain. That they were as ants trying to stop a landslide by catching one pebble at a time.

The greatness of her folk was past.

Magpie laid her hand over the wizened fingers of the old warrior, closed her eyes, and blessed him in silence. But she cursed him, too. *A few more moments*, she thought. *If he had only waited, he could have told her what manner of devil this hungry one was!* Whom could she ask now? She could track the invisible trail of death memories until she added her own to it. Or . . .

She began to chew her lip, and a sharp focus gradually came back into her eyes.

'What ye pond'rin', 'Pie?' asked Calypso, who knew her looks.

'Whatever this snag is,' she said, 'it's like nothing we've fought before.'

'Nothing in the world,' he agreed.

'Nor nothing we've heard or read of.'

'Neh.'

'And the only soul we've found that's seen him just took himself where we can't follow.'

'Aye, and hasty.'

'So there's only one thing to do.'

'Aye . . . eh?' He squinted at her. 'What?'

'We got to find the Magruwen, neh? Ask him about it.'

Calypso gaped, his feathers instantly puffing up. 'Find the Magruwen? Jacksmoke, 'Pie! Ye tetched?'

'Neh, feather, listen. Now we know we been right about the Djinn – they're alive, and they're in the world! My parents have been hunting this proof all my life!'

'Let's tell them, then! Let them decide what to do!'

'There's no time for that! They're halfway round the world, and there's a devil on the loose – a bad, strange beast that's eating every low snag in its path and sure every faerie too. How many more will he get whilst I ask my parents' permission? I'm not a sprout anymore!'

'Ye'll be a sprout till I say ye're not!' Calypso cried. 'Look at ye, twig of a lass! Scarce gone a hundred and jaunting off to find the Djinn King? Tetched, I tell ye!'

The other crows had gathered round. 'The Djinn King?' repeated Pup in an excited chirp. 'Mags, ye going to find the Djinn King? Eh, Mags?'

'I'm going to try,' she said defiantly, her eyes not leaving Calypso's.

'But Mags,' worried Pigeon, who had a glorious imagination for doom. 'En't he a fierce old scorch, though? He'll toast ye up like a dragon's hankie!'

'That's if ye can even find him,' added Calypso.

'Aye,' said Bertram, blinking at her through the thick eyeglasses perched on his beak. 'And sure he don't want to be found! Maybe ye don't remember it – ye were just a babe then, but we seen his temple at Issrin Ev, neh? What he left of it, anywhich, and that weren't much. Even Bellatrix's statue got its head knocked clean off, and weren't she his own champion?'

'Aye,' said Calypso. 'Whatever made him leave his temple, it weren't a happy business. And he's stayed gone all these years, 'Pie. He's through with the world!'

'You don't know that!' she protested. 'No one knows what happened then! Ach . . . don't you see, birds?' She gestured toward the Vritra's cave. 'Suppose this is only the start! Suppose he goes after all the Djinn?' The crows blinked at her. She added, 'Who knows whether the world could survive that?'

The crows closed their beaks and shuffled their feet and considered. At last, reluctantly, Calypso said, 'Put it like that, maybe we ought to try to warn him,' and the other crows agreed one by one.

Magpie nodded. 'Right. To Dreamdark, then.'

'Dreamdark . . .' they murmured. 'Been a long old time.'

'Aye, Mags, been scores of years since ye been home.'

'Home? Piff!' she replied. 'You're my home, my feathers. Dreamdark's just some place I was born.'

'Just some place?' repeated Calypso with a short hoot. 'Dreamdark? Been too long since ye seen it, if ye can say that.'

She scowled. 'This is no sightseeing trip. Now come on, let's give this brave codger a decent burial before we go.'

As she turned away, she thought she heard something, a faint pure ringing of crystal, and her eye fell on the knife she had earlier wrenched from the skeleton's spine. She hesitated, knelt, and picked it up. The sound was gone, and she wondered if she'd heard it at all. The dagger showed no signs of all the years it had lain here. Its blade shone like a sunlit mirror as Magpie slowly turned it, seeing faint arabesques and spirals etched into its steel. A pretty, deadly thing. She searched around until she found, strapped to a skeleton's thigh, a fine scabbard equally untouched by age. With a feeling of unease, she loosed it from the bone and strapped it to her own leg.

She didn't recognize the designs engraved in the blade as runes or she would have looked it over more carefully. Most were symbols long fallen from knowledge, but the glyph for curse, at least, would have been familiar. As for the graceful letters that spelled out *Skuldraig*, they were writ in the alphabet of a forgotten time and to her eyes seemed only an elegant design.

4

WITH THE VULTURES EGGING HIM ON, THE IMP THRUST HIS nose out into the world. It was the least ratlike part of him, his nose – flesh while the rest was fur, and quite spectacularly large, with each nostril spacious enough to fit his big toes into, which he frequently did. But though large, it was dainty in its way, and it flushed a delicate crimson as soon as he caught the scent of humans.

He thrust his head further and peered out through the hedge. He saw human lasses leaping about with butterfly nets, dancing near the woods then shying back, fascinated and terrified. Such was the lure of Dreamdark.

The humans had their own name for this most ancient of forests, and their school sat at its very edge, separated from it by only the hedge. But what a hedge! It was an evil bramble, taller than tiptoes and dense as a mermaid's braid, and it encircled the great wood in an unbroken band. Meddling mannies had found their torches wouldn't set it ablaze, and those who tried to chop it down would feel the axe seized from within and wrenched from their hands. They stayed away, called it haunted, claimed beasts and fey creatures lurked within.

They were right.

'Jenny Greenteeth and Nellie Longarms!' chanted the lasses, daring each other near.

'Old Rawhead and Hairy Jack!'

'All the bogeymen together, sitting down to tea!'

Batch Hangnail, the imp, shifted impatiently in the hedge, brambles poking at his meaty backside. Ordinarily the sight of new mannies from whom to scavenge would have excited him, but today he was a pawn in a bigger game.

Once the lasses had raced away in pursuit of a butterfly, he made a crude gesture to the vultures and shoved his bulk through the hedge. He dashed across the rutted path toward the school's formal garden, following his whim to the strange unkempt place at its edge. Though the rest of the gardens were blooming and bonny, pruned and tidy, this spot was dreary, a tree-shaded circle of weedy bricks with a well at its center.

He climbed the mossy stones and peered down into the darkness, feeling a little flutter in his belly. He wasn't afraid of the dark, certainly. The dark was his favorite. And wells, he'd been down many. He'd found his best diamond ring in a well, and a number of gold-capped teeth still clinging to their jaw, and the monogrammed handkerchief he wore tied satchel style over his shoulder. He clutched it against him now to ease his aching heart.

His treasures – ah, his treasures! His wheelbarrow full of treasures was so far away now in Rome, and unless he did just as he was told, he might never see it again! He still had his rings, for he wore them on his bristly tail. But all the eyelashes he'd gathered from the cheeks of sleeping children, the hanks of their unwashed hair, the belly button lint, the baby teeth – ah, the baby teeth! – as good as lost, and why? Because an ill-timed feast of rancid kidneys had made him sleepy, and while others fled the catacombs, he snored, to awaken to the terrible voice . . .

An ancient reek wafted up from inside the well, and Batch breathed deeply, excited in spite of himself. *Perhaps this task would have its own rewards*, he thought. Then, with scuttling grace, he climbed in and began his long descent. Down he went, and down and down. And down some more! 'Munch,' he muttered. ''Tis devious deep.' No ordinary well was this deep, but Batch already suspected this was no ordinary well.

Some time passed, and his little arms and legs grew tired, and the stones became slimier and slipperier. He began to fret. He was already down so deep now he didn't know if he could climb back out. He imagined his wheelbarrow lying unclaimed forever in the dusty pelvis of that human skeleton back in the catacombs. The thought was so wretched it made him twitch just as he reached for a slimy handhold . . . and he missed! His arms windmilled as down, down, down he fell, until with a squelching *thud* he met mud and was buried up to his nose in it, with just those grand pink nostrils poking up. He snuffled deep breaths of rank, sulfurous air through them, letting the good bad smell clear his head. Then he began to fumble about for a toehold in the muck.

By the time he had floundered his way out of it, Batch was a dirtier and richer imp than he had been moments before. Filth-crusted from the top of his head to the tip of his tail, he admired his new silver coins – tossed here, he knew, by silly mannies trying to *buy* wishes – and one old rusty key. He shoved the key into his satchel along with the coins, trusting his gift enough to know that when he found a thing, there was likely a use for it around the bend.

He padded around the pit of the well until he found a deep-set door. A door that had not been opened for centuries. At his push it creaked inward, and the air from the well shaft flowed in and over a lake of smoke, finding and feeding a low smoldering ember in the depths of the cavern.

The ember glowed brighter.

Batch took one slinking step over the threshold.

Suddenly the ember sparked into flame and reared like a waking beast. Salamanders leapt from stalactites and scurried away as it flared and spun and stretched limbs of fire. Its bright dance seared the eyes, too hot to look upon. Batch flung his hands over his face.

He had found what he sought. He always did.

The fire turned slowly toward him. It didn't know how long it had slept. Long. It didn't know if it wanted to wake. The old malice had awoken with it, and also a dull awareness of a new presence in the fabric of the world. Or a new absence. Or both.

'Who comes?' it hissed.

Batch stumbled forward. 'M-m-my Lord Magruwen,' he stammered, eyes downcast. 'Forgive my intrusion. I bring you a riddle!'

Once, the Magruwen had cherished riddles. In the long-gone days of visitors, he had traded treasures for them. There were no more visitors now – he had gone deep where no one would find him. And yet here was an imp, smelling of graveyards and drains. The Magruwen started toward him, then paused. He hadn't worn his head for a very long time. He sucked himself together out of the swirling vapors of his cavern and funneled himself into an ancient skin, buttoning it up and settling the head on last. His eyes burned through vertical slashes in the mask, and where the skin was worn thin, flames could be seen dancing inside it.

'Who are you?' he demanded in a voice to scald the ears.

Trembling, Batch answered, 'I am Batch, Lord. Just a lowly imp. A low creature . . .'

'*Low creature?*' repeated the Magruwen. 'You insult the craft of the Djinn who shaped your kind. We made no creature low. If you are low, it is because you choose to creep. Are you low?'

Batch froze. His master had schooled him in just what to say, and he'd already botched it. What was he to answer? Was he low or wasn't he? No ideas came to him, so he blurted, 'The riddle, it's new!'

Fume hissed from the Magruwen's mask like a sigh. 'Ask,' he said.

With relief Batch straightened up, cleared his throat, and recited:

I have a dozen wings to rake the sky,
a dozen eyes to find the dead,
A thousand souls within my guts,
a single will in many heads.
I've drifted in the ocean's womb,
I've prowled through catacomb and tomb.
I've swept the cobwebs from the clouds,
I've wiped my talons clean on shrouds.
I've soul of shade and heart of smoke,
I'm ink and stain and clot and cloak.
I'm what you've never dreamed about.
I'm tongues gone dumb and fires put out.
What am I?

Fires put out? The Magruwen gave a snort that sent fireworks and salamanders streaming from his eyes and buttonholes. This was an audacious imp, to come before a Djinn and speak of putting out fires! But the Magruwen ceased thinking of the imp when the answer to the riddle brushed his mind like the wing tips of a moth. He flicked it away. It was impossible, just a fancy, and one he was only too glad to ignore. After all, he didn't care about riddles anymore.

The fireworks subsided. He wanted only to fall back to sleep. 'Choose a treasure, imp, and be on your way,' he said wearily.

Batch's eyes lit up. He'd won. He'd won! 'Ha ha HA!' he cackled. He capered about. The Magruwen didn't even ask the riddle's answer but simply cleared the smoke from the floor with a languid sweep of his arm. Batch stopped when he saw what lay beneath it. It was too much, too much for a scavenger to bear.

'You may choose one thing,' said the Magruwen.

Batch swallowed hard. He'd been in treasure chambers before – he was a scavenger imp, after all. He'd wallowed in gold ingots and pried gems from the eyes of icons with a shrimp fork. He'd plundered robbers' caves rigged with booby traps and pyramids riddled with curses. He'd even napped in a mummy's armpit! But nothing had prepared him for this.

The cavern floor glimmered as opals, amethysts, and moonstones caught the glow of the Magruwen's flame and held it burning in their bellies. There were chalices and lyres and mirrors framed in pearls, broadswords and tiaras and bolts of wondrous cloth. Quite forgetting the reason he'd been sent here, Batch flexed his toes and waded in.

He caressed a clockwork hummingbird that could be wound up to collect nectar in a teacup in its belly. He trailed his fingers over a cauldron of sapphires and paused at a ruby-crusted scimitar. The Magruwen watched. That blade had a nasty habit of turning to smoke at the moment of need. Such dark treasures lay among the bright, and one could not always tell from looking which was which. That paring knife lying there so plain beside the scimitar, for example, could cut through any metal ever forged.

Batch moved on, a pendulum of drool swinging from his lower lip. He didn't know what he wanted until he saw it, but as soon as he did, desire gripped him by the guts, and a new obsession began to take root in his soul. There upon stacks of folded lace lay a little pair of silver bat wings, just his size. Of all the absurd dreams an imp can harbor in his secret soul, Batch's was the silliest. He had always longed to fly! To twirl like a faerie in the shimmering forest light. To swoop. To soar! He had a vision of himself fluttering back up the deep shaft of the well and gliding over the world. His fingers reached trembling for the wings.

But he jerked his hand back and wailed. The terrible voice had surfaced inside his head. 'The pomegranate,' it had said, and he remembered why he had come. Snuffling, he turned from the wings and faced the Magruwen.

'My lord,' he said, 'the treasure I desire is not here.'

'What is your desire?' the Magruwen asked.

'Your pomegranate, my lord, is my desire.'

The Magruwen's flames quieted, clenching into a white-hot ball at his very core. 'What did you just say?' he asked in a low, dangerous tone.

'The pomegranate,' cried Batch. 'The pomegranate!'

Belatedly, the Magruwen hissed, 'What was the answer to your riddle?'

'The answer is my master! Escorted through the sky by vultures! He said you must give me what I want if you don't guess it!'

'I *must*? Your master seeks to bind me to the Djinn's honor?'

Batch nodded uncertainly.

The Magruwen laughed. It started low as a cat's yowl but grew to raging, and the old skin burst open and fell away in tatters. Uncloaked, he stood before Batch as a tornado of fire, frenzied and churning, and the imp cringed away from the dazzle. Smoke crept back in like a tide to swallow the treasures.

At last the Magruwen's awful laughter subsided. 'Very well,' he said, 'since honor requires it.' And while Batch crouched with his face in his hands, the Magruwen stretched out long arms of smoke. They grew longer and longer until they disappeared through the ceiling of the cave. Up they reached, across strata of earth and rock and root, through the bleached ribs of a dragon and a dark spring swum by water elementals and their imps, through layers of rabbit warrens and forgotten plague cemeteries, finally reaching the school vegetable garden. Smoke fingers plundered among the roots until they found what they were looking for.

In the garden a human lass sat back with a gasp as a turnip top was tugged right out of her hand to disappear in the soil. *Gophers*, she thought, and moved down the row with a nervous glance at the smoke curling up from the hole.

'Here's your pomegranate,' said the Magruwen, tossing Batch the scorched turnip. 'Send your master my regards.'

Preoccupied by the activities of his tail, Batch missed, and the vegetable skittered into the smoke. He fumbled for it and shoved it into his satchel without a glance. He succeeded in hooking the bat wings and drew them to him beneath the smoke, but just as he made to shove them into his satchel, he saw a salamander clinging to them. It grinned at him before sinking its teeth into his fingers. '*Aiii!*' he shrieked dropping the wings.

'So you'd like to fly, would you?' asked the Magruwen.

Batch brightened. But before he could answer, the Magruwen sucked all the encircling smoke into himself and blew.

A fiery gust somersaulted Batch backward and right out the door. Up, up, up the well he rocketed, until he flew out into the world and landed in the branches of a tree. He lay there, skin singed bald and whiskers sizzled to bristles, unconscious and twitching, for quite some time.

It had not been the kind of flight he'd had in mind.

Down in his cave, the Magruwen paced and muttered. He held a withered, ancient thing, a pomegranate so old the skin was no longer red, but brown and brittle as parchment. As delicate as it looked, however, it was unharmed by the Djinn's fiery grip.

'*I've drifted in the ocean's womb . . .*' the riddle had said. He should have guessed then, but the other clues hadn't matched. The vultures – that was clever, weaving them into the riddle to seem like one creature. It was so clear now. '*Fires put out . . .*' The Magruwen wondered which one it had been, which Djinn, where. This was the world to which he had awakened, a world diminished by one Djinn, a tremendous absence that he should have recognized instantly. One of his six brethren had been extinguished, and more had gone out of the world than that one smoldering fire. And something else . . . something else had come back in.

'So,' he whispered. 'Ocean spit you out? Have this world, then. I don't use it anymore.'

He was so weary. He retreated into the depths of his cave and sank back into oblivion, subsiding once again to a smolder, the pomegranate still tight in his grasp. He dreamed that an immense tapestry was hanging from the eaves of the world. He'd dreamed of it many times, but this time the tapestry shivered and fell to dust and all that remained was the deep black of space with no world spinning in it, graceful and green. No world at all.

5

MAGPIE AND THE CROWS FLEW BY NIGHT, HIGH ENOUGH above the human lands that the jumble of painted caravans they towed wouldn't attract attention. They didn't worry about meeting anyone up here. The pathways of the skies were traveled by winds and white geese, wheeling bats and butterflies, but they never encountered other faeries here, and it had been decades since they had seen a witch silhouetted against the moon.

'Take 'em down, my lovelies!' Calypso croaked, sweeping along the line of airborne caravans. 'The sun, she stirs! Time to fill our bellies and shut our eyes!'

There was a bloom of light on the horizon. Day was coming on. They bade the wind goodbye and dropped down toward the forest far below. This stretch of Iskeri was the last place of safety before the channel they would cross the next night on the way to Dreamdark. They eased through the treetops and set their five caravans down gently in a nook between roots.

The gypsy wagons were a marvel of color in the shady woods. They were carved with sunbursts and stars and painted in jewel tones, with real gems glimmering like mosaic tiles in the designs. The big spoked wheels were radiant red, the roofs were vaulted and the windows round, and each had a bright copper chimney and weather vane, one a dragon, one a whale, a tiger, a phoenix, and a heron with its wings spread wide.

The crows bustled in and out the doors as they set about making camp, and before a half hour had passed they had a fire snapping in a freshly dug pit and were toasting cubes of cheese on the ends of twigs.

Pup caught his cheese on fire at once and took to waving it like a firebrand, while Mingus quietly handed Magpie a chunk that was toasted to perfection. 'Thanks, feather,' she said affectionately, and he just nodded and smiled.

'How ye planning to find where the Magruwen's hid, darlin'?' asked Bertram, dipping his cheese in his brandy and taking a wet bite.

Magpie admitted, 'I don't quite know. It's just a guess and a hope he's stayed in Dreamdark, but if he is, he'll be someplace deep. We'll ask the burrowers and scamperers. Badgers. Hedge imps.'

'Like that old hedgie who took care of ye when ye were wee?' asked Swig.

'Snoshti?' Magpie's face lit up. 'My bossy old nurse! Aye, I'd like to find her, sure, she's a dear soul – but not likely to know much of Djinn.'

'But who is, though?' asked Calypso. 'Not even faeries. Remember them faerie sprouts in the marshland had never even *heard* of Djinn?'

'Aye. That was wretched. Papa says the things faeries have forgotten would fill up a library the size of Dreamdark.'

'If yer father ever found a library like that, we'd never drag him out of it!'

Magpie laughed. 'Aye, for true!'

'All I'm saying, 'Pie,' Calypso went on, 'is don't get yer hopes up.'

'You want me to fly around hopeless?' she asked. 'That what you're saying?'

'Ach,' he sighed. 'Neh. Hope away! And may we be blessed with the luck to find creatures in Dreamdark as nosy as ourselves.'

'Cheers to that,' said Bertram, raising his glass. 'To nosiness.'

'To nosiness!' they all chimed in.

'When we get there,' asked Pup through a beakful of charred cheese, 'we goin' to do the play?'

Magpie groaned. 'Neh, not the play!'

'Course we are,' said Calypso. 'Ye know it's the best way to wriggle into faerie society. They do love a play – next best thing to dancing. And sure ye loved it, too, first time ye saw us.'

'Sure I like to *watch* a play,' she said. 'Just don't put me *in* one.'

'Someone's got to be Bellatrix. You want Maniac playing her?'

'Fine by me!'

'Un-skiving-likely,' Maniac snapped.

'I'll be Bellatrix!' crowed Pup eagerly. 'Let me, let me!'

'Pipe down, runtfellow,' said Calypso. ''Pie'll play Bellatrix.'

'Jacksmoke,' she grumbled under her breath.

Before the crows had been hunters, they had been roving actors. That was how Magpie's family had fallen in with them in Dreamdark and flown away to see the world. It was true there was no better pretext for dropping in on a faeriehold than to pose as players, but that didn't make Magpie like it any better.

'Fearless Magpie Windwitch,' Swig teased. 'Give her devils, give her witches, nary a shiver! But push her out onstage, and she shakes like a twig.'

'A twig!' agreed Pup. 'Just like a scrawny little twig.'

'Ach, would you stop with the twig?' Magpie muttered. Having the crows for companions was a lot like having seven older brothers, the good parts and the bad. So she was a bit of a twig, still a lass at a hundred years. She supposed them calling her a twig was better than what was bound to come later, when she began to . . . no longer *be* a twig. How would they act when she started to get curves and that? Ach. Not that she'd ever turn into some priss. There were other ways to grow up. Like her mother. Or like Bellatrix. In statues, the champion was always wearing a tunic of shed firedrake scales with daggers strapped to both her thighs and her simple gold circlet on her hair. That was the kind of lady Magpie planned to be when the time came: the kind who sharpened her knives beside the fire in a hunting camp filled with crows.

'Never mind them, darlin',' said gentle Bertram, wrapping his wing round her and handing her another wedge of the cheese Swig had swiped off a human's donkey cart. 'Here. Say what you will about mannies,' he declared. 'They have a genius for cheese.'

'For true, my feather,' she agreed, taking a big bite.

Once the crows lit up their stinky cheroots, Magpie hugged them each and took herself to bed. It was full daylight now, but she would have no trouble falling asleep. Her muscles were tired and her belly was full. She entered the gilded door of the stage caravan and squeezed past racks of velvety costumes and prop trunks full of swords and crowns, and past the empty devil's bottle, to her little bunk tucked high in the back. She boosted herself up with her wings and drew closed her patchwork curtain, spelling up a light that would flicker out as soon as her mind relaxed in sleep.

She nestled in under the quilt her grandmother had made for her and pulled a big book into her lap, unspelling the protective magicks she kept on it and hefting it open to a page marked with a green quill. On the page she had written the cryptic words of the devil who had killed the Vritra: *The fire that burns its bellows can only fall to ash. What poetry in a traitor's death!* She uncorked her ink and wrote below it:

Tomorrow we'll arrive in Dreamdark to search for the Magruwen. The crows are mad shivered by the thought of him but my shivers are busy elsewhere, worrying about that snag, wondering where in the world he is and doing what. And there's something else. Like ever, I can't fumble up words to describe it, but the pulse – it's been as strong as I ever felt it, all around me like I could reach my hands into it, and I've even fancied I could see it. Sure, it's just when I'm waking so anyone would say it was the tail of a dream, but I could swear. It's like curls of light at the edges of my vision that fade away when I try to see them, like fireworks into ghosts of smoke. How I wish there was someone I could talk to about it!

The book was her journal and almanac. It was crammed with maps so old their creases had worn white, with brittle leaves and colored feathers and twine-tied packets labeled in strange alphabets, with threads from magic carpets and beaded dreadlocks clipped from the beards of hobgoblins. She flipped to the first page and traced the slanted writing inscribed there.

Our Magpie,

There is a hole in the pocket of the world, and the magic is slipping through it. So much has gone beyond retrieval. Memories have gone slack. Young minstrels disdain to learn the old songs, and the notes pass away with the last old ears to hear them. So much has been forgotten.

Faeries are living upon threadbare magic, and they scarcely know it. It falls to us to preserve what remains in this fading age. May this book come to teem with the spells and songs you will collect in it. The first volume of many. Good luck and happy hunting!

Your loving parents,
Kite & Robin

When they'd written that, Magpie thought, they'd probably envisioned their little daughter jotting down the tea potions and dust magic of old faerie biddies before they passed to the Moonlit Gardens. At most maybe spying on Ifrit witch doctors and rescuing artifacts from the plunder monkeys of Serendip. And Magpie *had* gathered tea potions and such. In her book were no fewer than nineteen dust spells, including one that made its victims ravenously hungry for goat's milk.

But whatever else her parents might have imagined, Magpie knew it hadn't been their only sprout stalking devils across human-infested lands. Not that it should have come as a surprise. Ever since she was wee she'd clamored to hear the legends of Bellatrix, the huntress-princess of Dreamdark. She'd loved to play at tracking and had been surprisingly good at it. Eight years ago, when she came upon her first rooster tracks on a moon-silvered beach, it had seemed like the most natural thing in the world to follow them.

She'd caught that first devil by trapping it in sunlight with only its bottle to escape into or perish in the light. It had been thrilling and even a little easy. Snags were dumb as weevils – no match for a faerie! Not until now had she guessed there could be another sort out there, an unimaginable devil to whom, she had a grim suspicion, the magic of this fallen age would seem but sprout's play.

Weary and worried, she lay down her head and fell asleep with her cheek upon her parents' words. She'd thought she would dream of devils, of darkness and greedy, sucking hunger, and she did, but not right away. First she dreamed of a tapestry, once glorious but now moth-eaten and faded. She'd dreamed of it before and never remembered with waking, but in her dream she somehow knew that, threadbare though it was, it was the only thing holding the darkness at bay, the best and only thing.

Outside, Calypso perched atop a caravan, keeping the watch after the other crows had shuffled off to bed. He puffed smoke rings and turned slowly, surveying the array of shining eyes that peered out at him from the encircling woods. Imps, nightjars, weasels, dryads, toads, all staring in awed silence at the spectacle of the caravans. Calypso noticed a raven who lingered longer than most, and after glancing over his shoulders furtively, he glided down to where the larger bird stood withdrawn in shadows.

'That Algorab?' Calypso croaked in a hoarse whisper.

'Aye, blackbird. Heard ye lot were moving north and had to see for myself. Reckoned it might mean something.'

'Well, it don't. Least, not what ye'd like to think. There's years yet till . . . *that*.'

The raven grunted and scratched his head with his foot. 'Are ye for Dreamdark or neh?'

Calypso nodded. 'We are. Can ye carry a message ahead of us?' he asked.

'I'd be blessed to bring the news.'

'It en't news! She comes to Dreamdark on her own business. It's nothing to do with nothing, got it?'

'Oh, aye? And what is it to do with?'

'Ye wouldn't believe me if I told ye.'

'Sure I would. En't I believed since I was hatched?'

'En't we all? We'll see ye there, Algorab. Meantime, don't get worked up, eh? It en't time.'

'All right, all right. Sure, feather.'

'Blessings fly with you.'

'And with you.' The raven spread his wings and rose into the sky.

6

MAGPIE WOKE AT DUSK TO A SOUND OF CREEPING INSIDE HER caravan. Instantly she came awake and lay rigid, listening, but within a few seconds she relaxed. It was only Bertram. He was moving as quietly as he could – which wasn't very. He'd been something less than stealthy ever since he lost a foot to a croucher devil's second mouth six years back. Magpie heard the faint *thunk* of the ebony peg leg she'd carved for him as he snuck amidst the mess of costume trunks.

He rustled around a bit and then left, and once the door closed, Magpie slipped out of bed. He'd been at her trunk, she saw, and had left it open. On top of her wadded clothes was something new. She lifted it out. It was a skirt of black feathers strung together on a sapphire belt that had likely once been a human's bracelet.

She pulled it on over her breeches and turned slowly in front of the mirror, feeling a lump form in her throat. Bertram had made it, she knew, and out of the crows' own feathers. As she stroked it fondly, she counted one from each bird.

In losing his foot, Bertram had also lost his edge at thieving, and had since had to let the other crows handle all necessary thief work. But to make himself useful, he'd taken up sewing with his good foot, stitching the crow-stolen kerchiefs and bits of parasol lace together into costumes and curtains for their theater. Farsighted as he was, he had a time threading needles, though, so Magpie sneaked into his workbox whenever he was away and did it for him. She always denied it. 'Must be pixies,' she'd say, and lately she'd noticed him sneaking up on his box like he might catch the tiny creatures in the act!

Out the door she went to where the birds were gathering groggily around the ashes of the morning's fire, still in their dressing gowns. 'Bertram!' she cried, hitting him with a flying hug. 'I love it!'

'How fine ye look, lass,' he said, pushing his specs up his beak and looking her over. 'Fine indeed!'

'Aye,' added Pigeon. 'En't ye lovely! Bit o' the crow in ye, sure.'

'That one's mine,' said Pup proudly, pointing at a feather. 'Neh, wait . . . that one! Neh . . .'

'Ach, blitherhead,' grunted Maniac. 'What's it matter?'

Magpie dropped an exaggerated curtsy and drawled, 'Thennnk you sooo much! What a lot of chaaarming birds you are!' in a dead-on impersonation of an Ismoroth clan queen for whom they had recently recovered an amulet from a monkey.

'And ye claim ye're no actress!' said Calypso.

'Actress, piff! Queeens do not act!'

'Ach, drop it, Queen 'Pie, and toss me some brekkie.'

'Brekkie' this evening was cheese. Again. Rubbery-edged from being left out all day and without the benefit of toasting. Maniac griped for coffee but they'd haul out soon – no time for a fire. Mingus brought clear water from a stream and Magpie perched on a stone between Pup and Pigeon, tipped up her tin cup, and drank so the water splashed down her chin. She saved the last gulp to wash her face with and dried it on her sleeve.

*

They flew all night in the arms of the wind and reached Dreamdark with the dawn. By the light of earliest morning, Magpie had her first glimpse in more than eighty years of the forest of her birth. A world of oak and yew, pine and thorn, it seemed to go on forever. Long fog-blurred lakes twisted past knuckles of rock, and creeks meandered out of the dense woods and back in again. There were meadows hither and thither, and rising crags, and an island-dotted river, but mostly Dreamdark from the sky was a tapestry of treetops, as inscrutable as an ocean. Some white owls broke its surface like fish leaping in a sea. All else was still.

No longer fearing human eyes, the crows dipped down from their cloud-high path and skimmed above the crests of the trees. Calypso flew ahead to find the way to the city of Never Nigh, while Magpie zigzagged behind and dropped playbills into the shadowed world below. Thoughts and memories were whirling in her mind. The crows had called Dreamdark home, and she had piffed at the notion. In truth, she barely remembered it. She'd been such a wee babe when they'd left that she hadn't even been flying with her own wings yet. She did have vague fond memories of the house where she was born, a cozy maze of rooms tucked high inside an ancient linden tree by the river. It was the last home she'd had with roots.

And she remembered Snoshti, of course, the bright-eyed imp marm with tickling whiskers who'd rocked her and sung to her in that growly little voice. The only other face that came easily to mind from her time here was Poppy Manygreen's. Her first friend. Magpie had made many friends since: mountain faeries, jungle faeries, selkies, hobgoblins, owls. The world was scattered with friendships she'd begun and left behind when the time came to move on, and the time *always* came.

Once, it seemed, her family's traveling life had been filled with golden seasons. They would find a ruined temple or a remote faerie clan and they'd set down their caravans and stay awhile, collecting glyphs, digging for relics, settling into the rhythm of the native ways. But nowadays Magpie lived a different kind of life, a hunter's life, and there was little time for lingering. The devils gave her no rest. It seemed an age since she'd seen her family or made a new friend. In all of it, the crows were her one constant, her kindred. She'd said they were her home, and she'd meant it. This might be Dreamdark, the navel of the world and her own birthplace, but what of that? Magpie pushed all thoughts of friends and treehouses from her mind. She was looking for a devil and Djinn, not a home.

She and the crows followed the river like a road of poured silver. Each curve they rounded on tilting wings brought them nearer to the hidden city of Never Nigh, until finally Calypso led them toward the trees. The branches reached out to gather them in, and just like that, they passed into another world, one as ancient as the Djinns' first dreams of trees.

Dreamdark.

Here on this very spot in the unimaginably distant past, the Djinn had gathered to dream the world. Here the Magruwen's dragon, Fade, had curled round them while they worked, his serpent shape crushing a great arc in the forest that remained to this day: Fade Hollow, a crescent clearing where nothing grew but blood-red moss. Here, down an avenue of arching branches, lay the fabled city of Never Nigh, where the great faeries of the Dawn Days once had lived. There King Valerian and the ice princess Fidrildi had joined hands in Alabaster Palace and said their vows. And there their daughter, Bellatrix, the greatest of all, had been born and rocked in a cradle of willow.

Spells were woven tight as a basket around Never Nigh, and as the forest closed around her, Magpie gasped and faltered. It was as if she had swum into a current of light. A pattern of radiance flared all around her, weaving and moving, then flickered away into the far reaches of her vision. She alighted upon a branch to clear her head.

'Mags!' cried Bertram, whisking past with a caravan in tow. 'All right there?'

'Fine, feather!' she called back. She blinked and looked around, seeing no more spinning lights but only the dense bower of the forest. *It was the spells*, she thought. Those luminous patterns she'd glimpsed in the air must be the ancient spells of protection the Djinn had spun round Never Nigh so long ago. Somehow she had *seen* them. Ever since she'd felt the Vritra's death with her memory touch, these strange traceries of light had been seeping into her sight, and they seemed to be growing brighter. What new oddity was this, to see what was invisible to other eyes, to *see* magic?

Magpie shook her head and spread her wings, stepping back into the air to follow the crows down the avenue. When she saw the city, thoughts of the lights faded from her mind.

The trees grew wild and strange here, of any shape the Djinn had had a mind to try as they honed their treecraft. The trees *were* the city. Their roots wove across the ground like interlacing fingers and spiraled up into walkways and bridges. Everywhere paths meandered in hidden ways, and from every nook and fissure in the bark sprouted fanciful spires. The massive arms of the yews were festooned with palaces and hanging gardens. Each generation of faeries had added its own flourishes, and the grove was a marvel of towers and domes, balconies and catwalks, chimneys and carved gates and porticos and stained-glass windows. For all the exotic places Magpie had been, no city could hold a candle to Never Nigh for sheer audacious beauty.

The crows and their caravans rocketed beneath soaring bridges and over domes tiled with gold, down the main thoroughfare toward the Ring, the gathering place where they would set up stage. Magpie glimpsed tiny stairways and lamplit courtyards among the branches as she flew. She swooped past a nectar parlor, a haberdasher, a teahouse, and Candlenight's Bookshop, her father's childhood home. As the way widened and branches opened to the Ring, she caught sight of Alabaster Palace gleaming white in the branches above, and her breath caught in her throat.

The crows spiraled in to land, and Magpie eased the floating spells off the caravans and set them gently down on the moss. Then, as the crows shrugged off their harnesses, she turned her gaze up to the treetop palace.

It was white as sugar, its many graceful spires flowing seamlessly into one another as if the whole palace was shaped from one immense block of marble, but with a look of lightness, like it could float into the sky. It stood as a monument to greater times. No one had lived in it, Magpie knew, since that day twenty-five thousand years ago when Bellatrix had announced to the cheering folk that the devil wars at last were at an end.

Dance and rejoice, my friends, my faeries, and my kin,
No longer fear to fly at dusk, no longer hide within.
Come out and feel the pulse of night,
clawless, fangless, free.
The devils are all gone and shall no longer trouble thee.

Looking up at the palace now, Magpie couldn't help wondering, for a thousandth time – a millionth? – what had become of Bellatrix after that. How many libraries and crypts had Magpie searched, how many books and scrolls had she scoured for some word on what became of the Magruwen's champion after that day? The greatest faerie of all legend had simply dropped from history, leaving an empty throne in Dreamdark and no heirs to fill it ever again, and so it had stood empty all these long years since.

Just as her gaze moved on, Magpie caught sight of a figure in the corner of her vision, and she turned. Framed in an arched window of the tallest tower, a lady was peering down at her. She was far away, but Magpie's sharp eyes had no trouble perceiving that her dark hair was crowned by a shining circlet of gold. Crowned? Magpie's eyes widened in surprise, and she thought for an instant that she was seeing a vision of Bellatrix. But that was absurd. The lady in the window was no ghost. But who was she? Alabaster Palace had no tenant, just as Dreamdark had no queen.

'Hoy, Mags!' cried Swig. 'Ye going to brush yer tumbleweed head of hair sometime before the town wakes up?'

Magpie turned to stick her tongue out at him, and when she glanced back up at the tower, the lady was gone.

Down the avenue, Never Nigh was stirring to life. Soon the whole city would be awake, the air vivid with wings as faeries promenaded from their palaces, bejeweled, lacquer-haired, and lovely. Magpie tried to remember when last she'd combed her hair with something other than her fingers and thought it was likely near a week ago. Tumbleweed, indeed. She went zinging back to her caravan to do it.

7

BATCH AWAKENED WITH A GASP TO FIND HIMSELF SLUNG OVER a tree branch. 'Neh, neh, neh!' he said frantically. 'Not sleep, neh!' That was how the master had found him in the first place. He clung tight to the branch and shoved the tip of his tail into his mouth, sucking at it furiously until his terror had subsided to mere panic. When he let it drop from his mouth, it was a spot of shining pink on a lump of filth-caked imp.

Batch moaned. He was bruised and scorched and hungry, and he missed his treasures, but at least he'd done as he was ordered so he could go his own way. He patted his satchel to make sure the pomegranate was still there. It was.

'Stupid fruit,' he muttered, recalling the silver bat wings with a trembling lip. He should have chosen them as his treasure and flown far, far away. Let the master fetch his own fruits. Let the vultures fetch them for him!

The vultures. Batch pulled himself up to a sitting position. They'd have been waiting for him at the hedge all night. Let them wait! Slowly he climbed down the tree and dragged himself back to the well. He peered over the edge. 'Down in the dark, the mudmunching dark . . .' His words twisted into a sob. He knew he couldn't go back down the well. It would be madness. Death.

And yet his thoughts steered back to the wings from second to second. There was a warp in his mind that pulled all thoughts to treasure. Such was a scavenger imp's peculiar genius. Until he had them he'd be able to concentrate on nothing else.

He tried to think what to do. He could find a bird to carry him down the well! But he scarcely spoke their language. He had no reason to talk to birds! Imps generally spoke a pidgin form of Old Tongue in addition to the scamper language favored by those that scurry and slink: beetles, lizards, squirrels, and the like. Rats, of course. Batch had a strong rapport with rats, but that wouldn't serve him now. He needed *wings*.

As if in answer to his thoughts, he heard wings in the sky above him. In the instant before he looked up, a hopeful smile started to shape his snout, but then the shadows fell over him, and the smile died unborn. '*Aieee!*' he shrieked as the vultures bore down on him. '*Neeehhh!*'

Throughout Dreamdark, playbills were being carried in all sorts of hands, furry fox paws and globed frog toes, hooked hawk talons and slippery webbed fingers. All across the forest's many miles, paws and hooves and fins were changing course and heading toward Never Nigh. Faeries weren't the only ones who loved a play.

Kneeling in her garden, Poppy Manygreen knew the crows had come even before the playbill fluttered down to her. The flowers had whispered it to her. She sat on her knees with her head bowed toward the honeysuckle, and its voice was as soft as a feather falling on moss, but she heard it. The forest was a wonderland of voices if only you could hear them, but no one else could, even in her own clan, though plants had always been their lifeblood.

'The crows,' she heard the soft voice say, 'from years ago.' Faeries thought news traveled fast by wind and bird and butterfly, but it was nothing compared with the root-to-root gossip of the green and growing things. 'The noisy crows,' the honeysuckle whispered, and Poppy smiled. She remembered the noisy crows. She remembered them clowning on the stage they set up in the Ring, and she remembered how the lead crow had a cracked beak that made him seem to grin. Most of all she remembered the day they left, because her best friend had flown away with them and had never returned.

She whispered a question to the vine, and the answer came at once. 'Aye,' the voice whispered. 'The trees have seen her. She has come home.'

Poppy leapt to her feet. She didn't spread her wings so much as she unfurled them, the vast red wings of a swallowtail butterfly, iridescent and veined with gold. Fully spread they were twice as large as she was herself. It was a mystery where they'd come from. No one in the whole history of her clan had ever had such wings. She surged into the air, fast as a spark off a firecracker, and sped toward Never Nigh.

It was not uncommon for faeries dawdling in a garden or gossiping under a streetlamp to suddenly notice a hedge imp, where the moment before no hedge imp had been. Sneaks and spies, faeries called them, having a general mistrust of imps, even of hedge imps who were known as fine craftsfolk and cleanly neighbors. That their stealth might be of a magical nature never occurred to faeries. Few creatures looked less magical than hedge imps, and kin though they might be to faeries, faeries were few who would claim them as such.

Snoshti appeared on a small avenue leading into Never Nigh with a twinkle in her eye and a beetle in her arms. It was blue as lapis and mild as a milk cow. She set it down and looked around. Seeing no faeries, she went away again directly. That is, she faded from sight and no sooner had her afterimage glimmered out than she was glimmering in again, this time with a garnet-red beetle in her arms. She set this one down too and repeated the process.

The third time she appeared, she carried an emerald-green beetle under one arm and a shepherd's crook in her paw, and she was whistling. She set off down the avenue, driving her small herd before her. About waist-high to a grown faerie, she was a stout bandy-legged creature with a shiny black nose and whiskers set in a broad, furred face. Her coarse fur was mottled gray and honey, with a touch of white the only hint of her age, and it tufted from the neck and cuffs of her flowered frock. She was sturdy and wide, with a pleasant gentleness in her face and a sparkle of intelligence in her pure black eyes that could turn fierce in an instant.

She whistled her way into the throng of creatures headed toward the Ring. A steady stream of faeries, butterflies, and birds flitted overhead, and the avenue was bustling with toads and crickets, ladybugs and newts, hedgehogs and snakes and badgers and imps, all heading to see the show. Turtles had even come out of the river, some of them with creek maidens riding on their shells, and progress toward the Ring slowed behind their lurching gait.

But Snoshti went on whistling, and why not? Her lass was back. She'd been saving this song for over eighty years.

Talon Rathersting spotted the vultures from the north tower of the castle where he was daydreaming his way through guard duty. Rathersting Castle, peering out from a great hollow yew on the stony east slope of Dreamdark Crag, commanded a view of nearly the entire forest. Every winged thing that swept its way across could be seen from here by those with the eyes for it, and today there were more wings on the wind than usual. The crows had drawn Talon's notice only an hour ago, but they'd made right up the River Wendling for distant Never Nigh. Talon had been there only twice in his life – his folk seldom mingled with those Never Nigh flibbertigibbets with their fancy hair and ribbons and baubles – but well he knew that no unwelcome creatures could slip through the spells that twined round the city. It was the safest place in the world. So after the crows disappeared into the trees, he'd returned to his daydreams, unconcerned.

The vultures were different. Talon leapt atop the tower's crenellations and trained his eyes on them. There were a half dozen, moving with grim purpose just above the treetops, their wings vast, too vast. There were no vultures in Dreamdark. These birds were a long way from home. His daydreams forgotten, he visioned the glyph for the deep chime that would summon his cousins, and he watched to see where the vultures' path would lead.

His cousins arrived on wing almost at once from their own guard posts around the ancient tree. They were a fearsome sight, these Rathersting warriors, lean lads just across the threshold of manhood, their shoulders and sharp cheekbones patterned with coal-black tattoos, no two alike. Talon wore the tattoos, too, though he was yet a lad. And he wore something they didn't: a circlet of woven reeds on his wild pale hair.

'Prince,' said his cousin Shrike, alighting beside him on the tower's high wall. 'What is it?'

'There.' Talon pointed. 'Vultures, from beyond. Monsters. Six of 'em.'

They looked. Wick whistled low. 'Nasty meat.'

'Aye. Fetch the chief,' ordered Shrike, and Wick dived over the edge of the tower, dropping nearly to the rampart before snapping open his wings and whirring away into the deep courtyard of the hollow yew.

By the time the chief came, the vultures had sunk into the forest near the upsweep of the great spine of rock where the Magruwen's temple lay in ruin. 'At Issrin Ev, sir,' Talon told him, pointing. 'They circled and went down less than a minute ago.'

The chief of the Rathersting clan was a formidable faerie. Coming on seven hundred years old, his beard had gone silver but his hair was still white-gold and gleaming, like Talon's. He was thick in the chest and narrow in the hips, and he moved like a peregrine on the hunt, a few fast flicks of his wings launching him into a long deadly glide. He wore a dagger on each arm and each thigh and had slung his crossbow over his back. He looked at his son. 'Good eyes, lad,' he said, and gripped Talon's shoulder hard.

Talon couldn't feel proud, though, because he was already tasting the shame of what would necessarily come next. 'Shrike, Wick, Corvus, come with me. We'll see what we see, neh?' said the chief, his eyes flicking to his son and away. Talon pretended not to notice. He knew the look too well, the look where his father still, after a hundred years, seemed puzzled to have found himself with such a son. 'Keep on the watch, son,' said he, heaving skyward. 'We hunt!' he bellowed, and Wick and Corvus and Shrike launched after him, eager and blooded for danger.

Talon watched them all the way and saw them breach the forest canopy just where the vultures had. At his shoulders his own stunted wings twitched with the yearning to follow them, but he bit his lip. He would keep the watch. He might be a prince of the Rathersting, but with wings too small to lift him in flight, guard duty was about all he was good for.

He watched and watched the distant treetops, waiting for their return. His daydreams had slipped away completely, and he forgot to send word to Orchidspike to tell her he wouldn't be coming today. She would watch the gate all afternoon and frown while she worked, wondering. And Talon would be frowning and wondering, too, and pacing and scanning the treetops with his hawk-keen eyes, watching for the small distant shapes of his father and cousins returning. But the relief and jealousy that usually flooded him when a triumphant war party returned to the castle would elude him today.

His father wasn't coming back, and neither were his cousins. Talon would find their knives that night, abandoned deep in a fissure in the ruined face of Issrin Ev.

8

IN THEIR CARAVANS BEHIND THE STAGE THE CROWS WERE getting into their costumes. Pup looked on as Magpie helped Pigeon with his gown. The crows each played multiple parts in *Devils' Doom*, the epic of Bellatrix. Pigeon would start out as Queen Fidrildi and later change into armor. Pup played assorted devils throughout.

Magpie, as Bellatrix, wore her own battered hunting tunic over breeches, with a circlet on her head that had been an opera singer's earring until Swig swiped it in a daring dive. Strapped to her thigh was the skeleton's knife, partially concealed by the crow-feather skirt she had not yet removed.

She gave Pigeon's flounces a final fluff and slapped his tail feathers. 'There you are, m'lady, pretty as a flower! Do try not to outshine me, if you please.'

Pup squawked, 'Ach! Him? I'm much outshinier than him!' He twirled in his devil costume, got tangled in his tentacles, and sat down hard.

'Careful, meat,' said his brother. 'Ye'll ruin yer costume!'

Magpie laughed and helped Pup stand.

'Come along, ye lot,' called Bertram. 'Curtain's in ten!'

Magpie grimaced and listened to the commotion of faeries

and creatures in the Ring. 'Come on, then,' she said to the brothers. 'Let's do this skiving thing so we can get on with what we came for.'

'Ye'll be great, Mags,' said Pup, tossing a tentacle over her shoulders as he hopped along by her side. They came round the corner of a caravan and nearly collided with a small group of faeries coming the other way. 'Hoy!' cried Pup, swerving to avoid putting out a gent's eye with his beak.

There was a mild commotion as they stumbled over one another, but Magpie had stopped dead in her tracks before a tall young lady, and was staring up at her. It was the same lady from the tower window, the one with the golden circlet. Magpie stared at her and at her crown. Unlike her own circlet, this was no human's earring. It looked exactly like the one Bellatrix wore in all the statues. Then Magpie noticed the lady's tunic and knew from its shimmer it could be naught but real firedrake scales – impossible to come by since the creatures went extinct. Her eyes moved to the lady's face. Exquisite features, a sweet smile with a twist of amusement at each corner.

'Blessings!' said the lady in a rich, musical voice. 'What a small warrior!'

The gents at the lady's sides laughed. 'Aye, Lady,' said one. 'I fear this must be our Bellatrix! A far cry from the huntress.'

'Indeed, it should be you upon the stage, m'lady,' fawned the other gent. 'Then we would all have an excuse to gaze at your loveliness for hours together.'

But the lady smiled at Magpie and said, 'You wrong the pretty child, sirs. She does my ancestress great credit.'

'Ancestress?' repeated Magpie.

The lady said, 'Aye, my great foremother, Bellatrix.'

The gents looked at Magpie as if they expected her to collapse into a curtsy at the revelation, but she only squinted and said flatly, 'Blither. Bellatrix left no heirs.'

Again the lady laughed her lovely tinkling laugh. 'Oh, but she did, as you see.'

One of the gents cut in. 'Hasn't word spread to the world? You can carry the news, when you go away. Tell them Lady Vesper, many-greats-granddaughter of the warrior princess, is come to Dreamdark.'

Magpie snorted. 'Come from where?' she asked. 'And with what for proof?'

The gents, both frocked in frippery to rival the lady's, their hair fragrant with pomade, gaped at Magpie. One managed to say in a voice choked with shock, 'Lady Vesper needn't defend her claim to a ragamuffin!'

Maniac, who'd come to fetch them to the stage, puffed up at once.

'*Ragamuffin?!*' he cried. 'Ye don't call Mags names!'

'Nay, gents. Nay, birds,' said the lady with a look of imperturbable sweetness. 'Don't scuffle on my account. I know how it sounds.' She knelt before Magpie and took her hands in her own. 'It was a shock to me as well when my grande dame told me, just before she crossed to the Moonlit Gardens. She showed me where the ladies of our lineage had long hidden Bellatrix's crown.' She inclined her head, and as the sunlight rippled over the circlet's surface, it had the look of molten gold . . . and there was something else. A pattern like living glyphs sparkled around it then faded again, like a secret. Magpie blinked. There could be no doubt the crown was forged in a Djinn's fire. 'And her tunic,' continued Vesper, brushing her fingertips over the scales. 'These are my greatest treasures, and they belong in Dreamdark, as do I.'

Magpie felt a surprising rush of longing to believe her. She looked at her, so beautiful, so like the warrior princess, and it seemed right that such a lady should exist in this place. She might have stepped from a legend.

There had been a time when the Djinn strode the world in splendor, winking new creatures into being and reaching up to arrange the stars into patterns in the heavens. Faeries had been different then – not only beautiful, but powerful. Magpie's longing for such times was a deep and wrenching ache, and looking into Lady Vesper's eyes she felt the ache begin to give way to a bloom of possibility.

One of the gents was speaking. 'And besides the crown,' he said, 'm'lady has records discovered in the crypts of Chijal Ev showing Bellatrix's descendants back twenty-five thousand years, and the elders of Dreamdark have studied it—'

Magpie blinked. 'Chijal Ev?' she repeated. 'The temple of the Iblis?'

'Aye,' said Vesper fondly. 'Home of my early life.'

'You grew up at the temple?'

'Aye.'

'And you're saying *Bellatrix* lived there after the wars?'

Vesper nodded. 'A long quiet life, until she passed to the Gardens.'

'At Chijal Ev?' Magpie felt the bloom of possibility wilting. The gent had said Vesper possessed ancestral records unearthed from the crypts of Chijal Ev, but Magpie and her parents and grandmother had discovered and excavated those crypts themselves! If there had been even a hint or a runestone that mentioned Bellatrix, they would have found it. There had been nothing of the sort.

'And when did you leave there, lady?' Magpie asked with a frown.

'I arrived in Dreamdark last moon, at long last.'

Magpie squinted at her. 'So recently? Strange we didn't meet in Ismoroth in the snows, then. We performed there for the Stormlash clan at the winter festival and stayed some weeks.'

'Ah, the winter festival, how lovely,' said Vesper, but something cold and hard flickered in her gaze. 'Lords Winterkill and Brambling,' she said without turning to the gents, 'won't you go and find us a seat for the play?'

'Aye, my jewel,' said one.

'Your wish, my sweet,' said the other.

They left, and Vesper turned to Magpie. 'So, you've traveled to Ismoroth, have you? That's far for a little lass to go, is it not? Across oceans? Who are you, sprout?'

'Magpie Windwitch, Lady. But who are you . . . *really*?'

'I am exactly who I wish,' Vesper said gently. 'And irkmeat little lasses would do well to show proper respect while they're in my wood.'

'*Irkmeat*!' hooted Pup, slapping Pigeon with his wing. '*Irkmeat*! I like that!'

'*Your* wood?' said Magpie, incredulous. 'Dreamdark?'

'Mags! Birds!' cried Bertram from the backstage door. 'Get yer feathers over here, now!'

'Calm yer pepper, irkmeat!' Pup called back. 'We're coming!' But Magpie didn't move. 'Come on, Mags,' he started to say, but Pigeon hushed him, seeing the look that blazed between the lady and the lass.

Vesper said in her honeyed voice, 'You heard the bird, little one. Go on, take your phony crown and your preposterous skirt—'

'Eh!' protested Pup, and Magpie's hands flew to her feathers.

'Go and play at Bellatrix,' Vesper went on. 'But remember as you speak her lines who wears her real crown, and practice your curtsies, lass. If we meet again, I shall expect to see the very best you can muster.'

'I'll never curtsy for you,' Magpie said in a low, seething voice.

'And no one will be surprised, will they, if a savage doesn't curtsy for the queen?'

'Savage?' growled Maniac.

'Aye, a little savage who doesn't know herself from a crow and wears their stink as proudly as her own. Really, you reek of cigarillos!' She wrinkled her nose and pretended to fan away a bad smell. 'Surely that's just one hazard of slumming with low creatures.' Her gaze fell with disdain on Maniac, Pup, and Pigeon.

Magpie felt a sudden flash of fury. It tingled like a chill down her arms, and she saw curls of light unwind from her fingertips. They spun with lazy grace toward Vesper and wreathed round her head. Alarmed, Magpie clasped her fingers into fists and shoved them behind her back. The lights faded away, and Vesper seemed not to have noticed them.

Bewildered, Magpie could only think to snap, 'My brothers smoke cheroots, not cigarillos!' as she turned away. But she stopped when she saw the looks on the crows' faces.

'Jacksmoke . . .' whispered Pigeon, still staring at Vesper.

Magpie glanced back over her shoulder and the first thing she saw was the look of confusion on the lady's face. Then she noticed Vesper's hair. 'Oh,' she said.

Vesper's hands fluttered to her head and jerked away. Her hair was writhing. 'There. Are. Worms. In. My. Hair,' she gasped between deep breaths as a look of horror spread over her face.

But she was wrong. Biting her lip, Magpie stared. Where a moment ago had been shining, perfumed black hair, now there were living worms, rooted at the scalp and wriggling. Lady Vesper didn't have worms in her hair. She had worms *instead of* hair.

'Get them off!' she cried.

'Um—' Magpie said.

'*Um?*' Vesper hissed at her. 'Whatever you've done, minx, undo it now, or you'll wish you'd never breathed Dreamdark air!'

But Magpie had no idea what she'd done. She stared at her fists, clasping them tighter to quell the faint tingling, and shrugged helplessly.

The lady spun wildly around. 'I mustn't be seen like this!' she said, and paused to fix Magpie with a vicious glare. 'The day you next look into my eyes will go badly for you, do you hear me, savage?' A worm made an effort to explore her nostril and her hands flew to her face. She cried out in disgust and spread her wings and whirled suddenly away into the shadow of the trees.

Magpie turned to look at the birds, who were still staring, gape-beaked.

'Gorm, Mags, what'd ye do to her?' breathed Pigeon.

She shook her head and looked again to her fingers, wiggling them hesitantly. 'I don't know!'

'Jacksmoke, feathers,' said Calypso, coming up behind them. 'En't ye heard me calling ye? It's curtain time!' He saw the looks on their faces and stopped short. 'What did ye do, 'Pie?' he instantly asked.

'Why do you assume I did something?'

'Well, did ye?'

'Aye,' she admitted in a woeful voice.

'She turned some lady's hair into worms!' Pup broke in breathlessly, hopping from foot to foot. 'Ye should've seen it!'

Calypso's eyes widened.

'It'll be trouble,' said Pigeon, glancing around nervously. 'Trouble!'

'I didn't mean to—' Magpie began, but just then one of the pomaded gents poked his head around the caravan.

'You there, do you know where the queen has gone?'

'Queen?' croaked Calypso, shooting Magpie a quizzical glance. 'Since when has Dreamdark had a queen?'

'Since last moon, crow. Isn't it fine? A new queen in Alabaster Palace! Spread the news when you go. Tell everyone!' cried the gent, ducking away again.

'Ach, 'Pie! Tell me ye didn't—' Calypso began, turning back to her, but where Magpie had been there was only a human earring lying on the moss and a stir in the air from her hasty passage. Magpie had fled.

9

THE EPIC OF BELLATRIX HAD BEEN PUT INTO VERSE BY MAGPIE'S father, Robin, years ago, years even before he had met Kite. In his wildest daydreams as a young poet, he had never imagined that one day it would be performed all around the world. And certainly not in his weirdest fit of whimsy had he imagined it would be performed by crows! But then, nor had he dreamed he would elope with the daughter of the West Wind, but that had come to pass, and many a stranger thing, too.

Besides, crows have a flair for the dramatic.

Calypso, as King Valerian, opened the play: '*The moon whispers o'er the waters, come north and meet thy fate. Daughter, come forth and listen well, for destiny does you await.*'

When a crow hopped out onstage wearing a lady's wig, the audience burst into laughter. Maniac shuffled his feet and glowered out at them, which only made them laugh harder. '*Aye, Father,*' he began, pitching his coarse voice high. '*Destiny is the wind that carries me . . .*'

Hiding on a high branch by the river Wendling, Magpie could hear faint laughter coming from the Ring. Her cheeks burned. Maniac would not be pleased with her! She was ashamed of herself. With a crow as Bellatrix, the epic became a comedy, and in the very shadow of Alabaster Palace, no less. Her hero deserved better, and so did Maniac. But she was still shaking from what had happened. Just thinking of that supposed . . . *queen* . . . brought a new surge of fury.

The vixen had insulted her crows! Magpie fidgeted with the feathers of her skirt. It did smell like cigars, she had to admit, just like the crows did themselves. They also held a hint of wood smoke from their campfires, and the tang of rainy skies, and the strong coffee they favored in the morning. The feathers smelled like her crows, her family, and she felt more comfortable in them than in her own unpredictable skin!

She watched her fingers warily. No more lights, no traceries, but something did shimmer in her peripheral vision, and she squeezed her eyes shut in frustration.

When she opened them again and looked around, she realized she must be near the old linden tree where as a wee babe she had been so cozy. Suddenly she wanted to see her old house very badly, and she gave herself a push with her wings and went drifting slowly along the curve of the river, looking at all the trees, wondering if she would know it when she saw it.

She did. Years were like days to such an ancient being, and it looked just the same: its massive trunk, its canopy of palest green leaves. *Whoever lived here now was sure to be at the Ring with everyone else,* Magpie thought, so with a quick glance around she stole in amongst the leaves, just to get a glimpse of the bright-red door. But when she came to the spot on the trunk where it should have been, she saw nothing but bark. She circled round and found no door and nary a window, and just when she was thinking she'd come to the wrong tree, a small dull glint caught her eye. She looked closer, reached out, and touched the little smooth spot protruding from the wood. It was brass.

It was a doorknob.

Magpie backed away on her wings and sank onto a branch. She understood. When a tree gives itself to be a faerie's home, it expands to make rooms and corridors that flow within its living shape. And as it opens, so can it choose to close. The linden had closed, and the only sign her house had ever been here at all was a small protrusion of brass. Magpie dropped her face into her hands. It had been those little rooms that her mind conjured up to give any meaning to the word *home*, and now it was as if they'd never been.

'Magpie?' inquired a soft voice.

Magpie looked up sharply. A red-haired faerie lass – a *beautiful* faerie lass – stood balanced on the tapered end of the branch, smiling tentatively. 'Who wants to know?' Magpie asked.

'It's me, Poppy,' said the other lass.

'Poppy?' Magpie repeated, staring.

She came closer, knelt at Magpie's side, and tucked her huge wings behind her. 'I looked for you in the play,' she said. 'I thought if you were in it, you'd turned into a crow, though now I see you've turned only halfway.' She nodded to Magpie's skirt and smiled. 'Fine feathers,' she said.

Magpie wondered whether she was being mocked. This faerie was certainly not the type to wear crow feathers! She was beautiful even beyond the usual measure of faerie beauty and as poised as a flower. She wore rose-colored silk, and her hair was upswept in a spiral of braids, each one a different shining hue of copper, bronze, or crimson. Next to her Magpie felt like she was wearing a bird's nest on her head.

'It reminds me of that time,' the beautiful lass said, 'when you conjured yourself imp whiskers so you could look like Snoshti.'

Magpie looked closely at her brown eyes then. They were

warm as a hug, and she knew that it was indeed Poppy and that there was no mockery in her. 'Poppy!' she said, and threw her arms around her earliest friend.

'Blessings, old feather,' Snoshti said, coming up to Calypso behind the stage caravan where he awaited his next cue.

'Ah, madam, we meet again,' he said, sweeping off his crown and bowing low.

'So ye've kept her alive, and that's something,' the little imp said grudgingly.

'Been the pleasure of my long life,' Calypso replied.

'Where is she?'

'Hiding.'

'Eh?'

'Stage fright,' he said with a shrug.

'We *are* talking of Magpie Windwitch?'

'Aye, but don't fret, good-imp. It's pure the only thing that frights her.'

'So she's coming on well?'

'Perfect, just perfect. Clever and kind and mysterious strong.'

Snoshti squinted at him. '*Gifted?*'

'Aye, d'ye doubt it?'

'Does she know it?'

'I haven't told her anything, if that's what ye mean. But someone had better do, soon. She'll start thinking she's tetched.'

'Eh?'

'Not an hour ago she turned the queen's hair to worms—'

Snoshti snorted. 'Worms?'

'Aye, worms. Shivered herself some, I ken. The lass has got magic in her she don't know what to do with.'

'Is that why ye've come now? It en't time. She's still a sprout.'

'Aye, that she is.' Calypso sighed. 'Didn't Algorab tell ye not to get in a fuss?' Pie had her own reason to come. She means to find the Magruwen.'

Snoshti snorted again. 'The Magruwen? She's afraid of the stage but wants to find the Magruwen?'

'That's my 'Pie. Ye wouldn't know where we might find him, now?'

'Neh, bird! And ye know how we've searched!'

'Ach, well, I thought not. Now if ye'll pardon me, madam, my cue. We'll talk more later?' He hopped toward the stage entrance. 'Over scones?' he called back to her.

Snoshti chuffed. Scones! Crow was begging for treats. Well, small price. Her lass was back. She reached out to catch a wandering beetle with her crook. 'The Magruwen, eh, missy?' she murmured, pondering. She drove the beetles back into the forest to find a quiet place to disappear. There was something she'd need to fetch.

'Mad faeries, swooping mad shouty faeries . . .' Batch whimpered as he skittered along the forest floor as fast as his meaty haunches would carry him. He'd never have escaped if the faeries hadn't swooped down like that, too near the crack where master lurked. They didn't know. They only saw the vultures, sure.

They couldn't know.

On wheezed Batch, grateful now he wasn't slowed by his wheelbarrow. He didn't even have the pomegranate to weigh him down anymore. Er, the turnip anyway.

Master wasn't pleased about that.

'Munch turnip, devil!' Batch muttered. A pomegranate, a turnip. How was he to know the Magruwen had tricked him? It occurred to Batch now that master didn't even eat fruits. He ate . . . well, he didn't eat fruits. What did he want a pomegranate for? It didn't matter. Batch was out of it now.

'Scurry scurry, little furry, through the forest, what's your hurry?' he sang low and wheezy, urging himself on.

There had been such a scuffle. The tattooed faeries, swooping in with that war cry. They'd crashed a vulture and Batch had cheered them on. But then out came that liver-colored tongue, long as a lash. It got the old faerie first and the younger ones went wild and threw their knives into the dark. Sure it went quick after that, but Batch was already on his way. No need to stick around for a good look.

Poor faeries.

In the darkness of the catacombs, master had been just a voice to him, a terrible voice. Batch hadn't seen anything then, and he'd scarcely gotten a better look since. Master was hard to look at. The eyes played tricks.

Batch scooted along, wheezing and thinking of the silver bat wings. It was a real puzzle – he needed wings to get his wings, to flap down that horrid well and grab them! He should have ripped the pair off that old faerie chief and used those to fly down the well. Sure the codger didn't need them anymore where he was going, but Batch did. A nasty gleam lit his eyes. There were plenty more wings like those in Dreamdark, sure.

'Eenie meenie minie ming,' Batch sang. 'Catch a faerie by the wing . . . If she hollers, let her sing, the lovely song of a faerie scream!'

10

'HOW DID YOU KNOW WHERE TO FIND ME?' MAGPIE ASKED Poppy, looking around. The thick foliage of the linden enclosed her completely, like a little room.

'I heard from some ivy,' Poppy answered, 'and from a beech sapling just yonder.'

Magpie cocked her head and studied her. 'For true?' she asked. Poppy nodded. 'You can speak with plants and things? That's sharp! What do they sound like? What do they say?'

'Oh, they've all kinds of voices, and they say all kinds of things. Herbs sort of sing, and flowers gossip like biddies.'

'And trees?' Magpie asked, laying her hand on the bark of the old linden.

'Ah, trees, well, you know trees are earth elementals,' Poppy said. 'Some tell tales, but they tell far less than they know.'

'Sure they know a lot.'

'Aye. The ancient ones like old Father Linden here have drunk the dew of the Dawn Days. Think of it, they've been alive in the world for all the lifetimes of faeries stretched end to end, all the way to the beginning! But they keep their secrets close. I rarely hear them speak at all.'

'Oh, aye? Pity. I wonder if he remembers me,' she mused,

glancing at the place where the red door had been swallowed by a skin of bark.

'I'm sure he does! Others do. They told me you'd returned.' Poppy paused and grew serious. 'I missed you so when you left. Why did you? Why did you go?'

Magpie frowned. 'My mother . . . it's the wind blood, I ken. She's never gotten used to being in one spot. They only stayed till I was big enough to travel, and we never stayed anyplace half so long again.'

'But what is it you do . . . *beyond*?' Poppy asked. To the faeries of Dreamdark, leaving the forest was like leaping off the edge of the world.

'Well . . .' Magpie mused, wondering where to start. Not with devils, sure, or chasing witches, or hanging upside down in a monkey king's dungeon. 'We go find faerie clans, and we try to learn their magic. Papa writes it down in books so it won't die out with the old folks. Right now they're with a clan on Anang Paranga that still practices shape-shifting.'

'Shape-shifting?' Poppy marveled. 'And your parents will learn how to do it?'

'Aye. We also search for clues of what happened to the Djinn and try to keep magic relics out of the hands of monkeys and mannies, who're always messing about where they oughtn't.'

'You've seen humans?'

'Piff. Thousands. Mannies are nothing special.'

'But aren't they giant-big?'

Magpie shrugged. 'Not so big. About like a stack of raccoons. There's plenty of bigger things. You should see elephants. Whales!'

'And dragons?' asked Poppy.

'Dragons?' Magpie frowned at her. 'There aren't any dragons left.'

'What?'

'Neh. Humans killed 'em out ages ago! Firedrakes too.'

'All of them?' Poppy asked, aghast.

Magpie knew that faeries lived in isolation, ignorant of the world, but she was still shocked. How could it not be known in Dreamdark that the dragons were extinct? Seeing Poppy's horrified expression, Magpie felt the tragedy anew. She herself had first heard the chronicle of the dragon slaying many years ago, but it still clenched her insides to think of it. Such a frenzy of butchery it had been that even thousands of years could not cleanse humanity of its stain. Magpie chewed her lip. There was no need to school Poppy in the ugliness of the world, was there? She said casually, 'Ach, who knows? There's whole volcanoes a dragon could slip down into like a bubble bath. Sure they're hiding . . . but tell me, what about you?'

Poppy said, 'Nothing to do with mannies and monkeys! Just growing things. Dreaming new flowers. Making potions.'

'Potions?'

'Aye. I've never been great with glyphs,' she admitted with a pretty blush. 'But potions I can see and stir. They make sense to me.'

Potions were a very different art from glyphs, an earthy magic Magpie associated with hearth witches and healers. 'What sort of potions?' she asked.

'Oh, say, for better night vision or a singing voice, or seeing lies or remembering your dreams. And for things like wrinkles and warts—'

'Causing them or curing them?'

Poppy laughed. 'Both! And there are potions for telling if a babe is a lad or lass before it's born. And love magic—'

Magpie snorted. 'Love magic! I don't think you'll be needing any potions to make lads fall in love with *you*.'

'Me?' Poppy grimaced. 'Lads? Echh. Nay, please! But oh, my cousin Kex has been hounding me fierce for a potion to woo the queen.'

Magpie froze and narrowed her eyes. '*Queen?*' she asked.

'Aye! Haven't you heard yet?' Poppy laughed a hard laugh. 'The heir of Bellatrix has been found, blessings be!'

'That fake's nothing to do with Bellatrix!' Magpie snapped.

Poppy looked at her, surprised. 'Oh, *I* know that!'

'You do?'

'Aye. Well . . . I don't *know* it, quite. But I don't *believe* it. It all happened too fast, her showing up here and getting crowned queen.'

'But . . . how *did* it happen?'

Poppy shrugged. 'She had Bellatrix's crown and tunic. She had some scroll proving who she was. And she had . . . well, she had a city full of folk whose legends were worn out. They just wanted to believe her *that* bad. To have a new legend, you ken?'

Magpie remembered how, for a moment, she too had wanted to believe in Vesper. Ashamed, she grimaced and asked, 'Are faeries so bored they got to *invent* legends?'

'Bored, aye, and afraid. I know *I* am. Afraid nothing exciting's ever going to happen again!'

'Not all excitement's good,' Magpie warned. 'Most isn't.'

'Well, boredom's none so fine either. There's only so much dancing a faerie can do. And it's not just faeries,' Poppy said. 'The imps and creatures have a story of their own. They've been waiting for years – so I hear – for the faerie they believe will bring back the Dawn Days.'

'Bring back the Dawn Days?'

'Aye.'

'The creatures got a story about a faerie?'

'A *secret* story,'

Magpie was flummoxed that she'd never heard it herself. The crows couldn't keep secrets to save their beaks. 'But . . . you don't think they mean Vesper, do you?'

'Nay. When first she came I wondered. She does make you want to believe! Wait until you see her; you'll understand.'

Magpie let out a humorless laugh. 'Ach, I've seen her!'

'Oh, aye?'

'And she's not like to forget it soon . . .' Magpie chewed her lip.

'What do you mean?'

'I, er . . . sort of . . . turned her hair into worms.'

Poppy stared at her for a long moment, her face frozen in disbelief. At last she whispered, 'Nay . . .'

'Aye.'

A guffaw erupted from Poppy that threatened to knock both faeries from their branch. Her face turned as red as her hair, and she couldn't stop laughing. Magpie had to start in too, and soon both lasses were clinging to the branch, wheezing with laughter. When she was able to gasp out the words, Poppy asked, 'How did you do it?'

Magpie's laughter died away. 'I don't know! I didn't even vision any glyphs. I don't know what glyphs I'd even use if I was trying. It just . . . happened.'

Poppy looked puzzled. 'Are you sure it was you who did it?'

Magpie shrugged. She knew how it sounded. That wasn't how magic worked. She thought of the curls of light that had wavered off her fingertips. She wasn't about to tell Poppy *that* and get a blank stare in return, so she said, 'Well, Vesper believes it, so I reckon I've made a nice new enemy, my first day back in Dreamdark.'

'Oh, Vesper, she—' Poppy began, but fell suddenly silent. 'Old Father,' she said with surprise, her eyebrows shooting up as she glanced at Magpie. 'Blessings to you and the earth at your roots.' Her head cocked toward the linden tree in an attitude of listening. 'Aye, very pleased she's come back. *Why?* I don't—' She looked at Magpie, wide-eyed, and said, 'Old Father Linden wonders why you've come back to Dreamdark.'

'For true?'

Poppy nodded, seeming stunned that the ancient tree was speaking.

'Well – er . . .' Magpie stammered, caught off guard. 'I . . . I came to find the Magruwen.'

Poppy looked even more stunned. Her expression hovered between disbelief and dismay. 'You're jesting.'

Magpie shook her head. She saw Poppy's eyes go softly out of focus as she listened to the tree for a time before saying, 'Nay, faeries have all but forgotten him. He's only legend now.' She paused. 'The dreamer . . . I like that.' She paused again, then murmured, 'Aye, I never thought of it that way . . .'

There followed a long listening that made Magpie antsy. Poppy's eyes were far away and her brow creased with worry, and Magpie longed to hear what she was hearing. She tried not to wiggle. Long moments passed before Poppy said faintly, 'Aye, old Father, I'll tell her . . .' and blinked her eyes back into focus.

'Poppy!' said Magpie. 'What did he say?'

'Did you know they used to call him the dreamer?' she asked slowly. 'Because he dreamed a world into creation he couldn't even live in.'

'The Magruwen?'

'Aye,' answered Poppy, sadness sweeping over her face. 'He made a world he couldn't even touch. Have you ever thought of that?'

Puzzled, Magpie shook her head.

'Wouldn't you think . . . creatures of *fire* . . . wouldn't you think they'd make a different sort of world? One that wasn't so . . . *fragile*?'

Magpie saw what Poppy was getting at. For fire elementals, spinning through the eternal blackness of the beginning, to come together and make this delicate place, these fern fronds, these woods . . . it was a beautiful dream, but not a sensible one. They could wear skins to keep from setting fire to their creations, but it wouldn't be the same. Magpie's grandfather had said it was like holding hands while wearing gloves. The air elementals could at least dance through the treetops in their true forms and caress the birds they carried in their arms, but the Djinn never could, not without burning everything to cinders. The textures of things, which they'd rendered with such artistry, must always have been a mystery to their own touch.

'Maybe they didn't make it for themselves,' Magpie murmured. 'Maybe they made it for . . . *us*.'

'Maybe. And it's perfect, nay?'

Magpie nodded. It was.

'He's asleep in a deep place now,' Poppy said.

Magpie's stomach flipped. 'Did the tree tell you where—'

'There's a school for humans just outside Dreamdark. In the gardens there's a dry well. That's where the Magruwen dreams, at the bottom of it, alone and forgotten.'

Dazed, the two faeries stared at each other. Magpie realized she'd had only dim expectations of succeeding in her quest. It hit her now that she was truly going to see the Djinn King, and a shiver seized her.

'In a well,' Poppy said, a sheen of tears blurring her eyes. 'The Djinn King! At the bottom of a well in the belly of the world. It isn't right!'

'Neh, it isn't. Did the tree say . . . why?'

Poppy shook her head. 'Nay, but he did say it's high time someone had the nerve to wake him.'

Magpie took a deep breath. 'I reckon it is.'

'But Magpie . . . you don't really mean to?'

'Aye, but I do. Come on, I got to go tell the crows!' She stood and sprang from the branch, shooting out through the tickling leaves. 'Thank you, Father Linden!' she called as she went.

'Blessings, old Father,' Poppy said reverently to the tree, then opened her own wings and followed.

11

MAGPIE AND POPPY SNUCK AROUND THE SIDE OF THE STAGE caravan just as the play ended and cheers erupted in the Ring. They slipped in through the back door to wait while the crows took their bows.

The caravan was even messier than usual. Gowns and tentacles were strewn everywhere from quick costume changes, and every trunk was flung open, so the lasses had to leap over them with a lift of wing. 'It's some fright in here,' Magpie said, but Poppy was taking it all in with shining eyes.

'It's grand,' she said, surveying the glitter of velvets, snakeskins, and manny jewelry that covered nearly every surface. 'Is that where you sleep?' She gestured up at Magpie's little bunk.

'Aye, home sweet . . .' Magpie's words trailed off when she saw that her patchwork curtain was yanked askew. 'What the skive?' she growled, flying to it and not seeing how Poppy's eyes widened in shock to hear her curse. Her book lay out on her quilt. She always put it under her pillow, and she always drew her curtain closed. She thought immediately of Lady Vesper. Her eyes narrowed and she sniffed the air, detecting in it a scent of intrusion. It wasn't faerie, though, but creature. And there was a hint of something else, clean as snow and utterly foreign.

'Magpie,' said Poppy, who'd been watching with curiosity as the huntress awoke in her friend. 'What is it?'

'Someone's been in here,' Magpie answered, reaching for her book. She could feel her protective spells were still intact, so she was startled when a slip of paper dislodged from the pages. It fluttered to the floor at Poppy's feet, a trail of light unfurling behind it like the tail of a comet. Poppy picked the paper up, and Magpie could tell her friend didn't see the blaze-bright aura that hung on it, slower to fade than the brief traceries she'd seen that morning flying into Never Nigh. Poppy handed the paper to her, and she took it and sniffed it like a feral creature.

The strange pure smell was strong on it. Wary, Magpie turned the paper over and read it, and the ferocity left her eyes and was replaced by puzzlement.

'What?' Poppy asked.

'This wasn't in my book before,' she answered.

Poppy moved to her side and looked at the paper, which had elegant writing on it.

<u>Magruwen's Favorite</u>

To a batter of lily flour, oats, honey, and beetle butter, add:

1 half walnut shell of fish's tears
3 strokes of tangled wind
1 shadow of a bird in flight
1,000 years of undreamed life

Stir together with twig from a lightning-struck tree, and bake until a porcupine quill inserted in the center comes out clean. Place in a starling's nest to serve.
B.

'Magruwen!' exclaimed Poppy. 'But . . . who put it there?'

'Flummox me,' Magpie said. 'I haven't told anyone but you and the tree why I've come!'

'Could the crows have put it here?'

'Neh. They'd just give it to me.'

'A mystery, Magpie!' Poppy said, excited. 'And a riddle! What can it mean, a thousand years of undreamed life?'

Magpie puzzled on it. 'Undreamed life? A life that hasn't started yet, that hasn't even been dreamed up . . .'

'But something you can bake into a cake?'

'Like an egg? There's a life inside that hasn't been dreamed up yet.'

'And will never be life, if you crack it into a cake.'

Magpie shook her head. 'I don't know,' she said, looking at the strange recipe card. She suddenly squinted and looked closer. 'Jacksmoke!'

Again, Poppy looked startled by Magpie's cursing. Magpie caught her look this time and blushed. 'I mean, skiffle . . .'

'What is it?' Poppy asked.

Magpie opened her book and leafed through it until she found a page marked with an iridescent snakeskin. Her eyes shifted rapidly back and forth between the book and the recipe. 'Poppy, look.' Pasted to the page was a scrap of parchment gone sepia with great age, once ripped in half and carefully seamed back together. It read:

Hurry home, love, through the dream-dark glade,
Where moontime beasts lurk in darkling shade.
Never linger, love, where the shadows grow.
The Blackbringer hunts where the light fears to go.

'The Blackbringer?' said Poppy. 'That old bogey? My mum used to scare me with tales about him so I wouldn't stay out past dark.'

'Aye, that's just an old nursery story. But look, see on the recipe here, the initial *B*? Now look at the big *B* on *Blackbringer*.'

Poppy looked back and forth between them. 'It's the same,' she said. 'Sure! And look at the *h* on *half* and *home*. These were written by the same hand!' She glanced up at Magpie.

But Magpie was chewing her lip and shaking her head, bewildered. 'Sure looks like, but skive, it's impossible!' Her voice had an edge of suspicion to it as she said, 'Poppy, this parchment? I found it in the ruins of Shaith Ev, the temple of the Ithuriel. It's part of a letter from the age of the devil wars.'

Poppy's mouth dropped open. 'For true? That's old . . .'

'Twenty-five thousand years. And that's not all.' Magpie traced the *B* on *Blackbringer* with her fingertip. 'It was written by Bellatrix!'

The two lasses fell silent and stood looking at each other in disbelief.

'Ach, there y'are, ye treacherous twitch!'

Magpie and Poppy both swung toward the door to see Maniac in his lady wig, glowering in at them. 'Feather . . .' Magpie said sheepishly. 'I'm sorry—'

He jerked his head so the wig sailed off and landed in a hairy heap at her feet. 'Where ye been? Sure ye come back once it's all over, neh? Sneaky as an imp!'

'Glad to hear she's not all crow,' said a growly little voice out of sight.

Maniac turned his head. 'Good-imp,' he croaked, 'ye mistake me. She's crow straight through. 'Tis only when she's wicked that she's imp.'

'Then may she always be wicked!'

'Snoshti?' Magpie leapt over the prop trunks to get to the door and peered around for the imp marm. She saw her there, so small and quizzical, surrounded by beetles, and her heart swelled. She dropped to her knees before her and flung her arms round the little creature. 'Snoshti!' she cried. Her whiskers tickled just the same after all these years.

'How wild ye look!' Snoshti declared, holding Magpie at arm's length to examine her. 'Brown as an acorn and skinny—'

'As a twig,' Magpie finished. 'I know! And you look just the same as always. I missed you fierce, Snoshti! You should have come away with us when we went. We needed you!'

'Blessings!' Snoshti cried. 'The world's too big for the likes of me, and flying gives me a flutter. Where can ye hide in the sky? Neh, sky's no place for an imp.' She eyed Magpie's feather skirt. 'Ach, but look at ye, lass! Ye'll have a beak on next and be squawking like a crow!'

'She squawks as good as any of us!' said Maniac gruffly. 'And curses too.'

'Mags!' cried Pigeon, landing with a flutter beside her. 'Where'd ye go? I was fierce shivered that queen would get ye!'

'Piff!' Magpie said. 'I'd like to see her try!'

'She will,' said Snoshti.

'What?' asked Magpie, surprised.

'She will try, make no mistake. Better ye lot come away now, caravans and all, than stay right under her nose.' Snoshti jerked her head toward the palace. They all looked up and saw a figure silhouetted in the tower window, standing perfectly still. They shifted uneasily, feeling themselves watched.

'That lady's one mean twist,' said Pigeon in a low voice. 'Sure she's no match for ye, Mags, but maybe the imp's right. We en't come to tangle with faeries. We got any reason to stay in Never Nigh?'

'Neh, none,' Magpie said. 'I already found what we're looking for.'

'What?' croaked Maniac. 'When?'

'While *not* on the stage, as a matter of fact!' she said. 'So thank you!' She planted a smooch on his beak.

'Ach,' he grunted. 'Don't be thinking that gets ye off the hook!'

The rest of the crows gathered round, tossing their crowns and capes into the caravan. Magpie introduced them all to Poppy and quickly whispered what they'd learned from the ancient tree. They were suitably impressed, with the news and with Poppy both.

'Gorm,' said Pup, still wearing a pair of devil horns. 'Ye can talk to trees? How fine!'

'Thank you.' Poppy blushed.

'Poppy Manygreen!' called an imperious voice from overhead, and they all looked up to see a gent hovering above them on smoke-gray wings. It was one of the two who'd earlier been fawning over the queen. Magpie narrowed her eyes.

'My cousin,' Poppy muttered. 'What is it, Kex?'

'The queen calls for you. Come at once,' he said, looking down his nose at the crowd of crows.

Poppy frowned. 'The queen? Tell her I'm busy—'

'At once!' He cut her off.

'Now, there's no call to be barking at the lass,' Calypso interjected.

'It's fine,' said Poppy, turning to them with a twinkle in her eye. She whispered, 'This is sure to be about her hair, nay? She's always demanding potions for this or that. Sure she wants me to undo your spell.'

'Can you?' Magpie asked.

'I'd have to want to, first. And though I haven't seen it yet I'm fair certain I'll find it suits her.'

'Cousin!' hollered Kex.

'Calm yer pepper!' squawked Pup.

'Magpie, the cake recipe,' Poppy whispered quickly, unfurling her wings to fly. 'Do you think we could make it?'

'I don't know where it came from! It could be a trick.'

'Meet me in the morning at old Father Linden.'

Magpie nodded. 'Sure.'

'Good!' Poppy curtsied to Snoshti and the crows and said, 'I'd best go, then. Lady Vesper awaits. I can't wait to see this!' And with a wink she flew up to meet her cousin.

'She seems a fine lass,' Calypso said, watching her go. 'Could be mad handy, talking to trees.'

'Aye,' Magpie agreed. 'She hears things. And one thing she heard? That the creatures have this story, right, about a faerie who's supposed to bring back the Dawn Days.' She chuffed a laugh. 'You haven't heard that, have you?'

Calypso scratched his head with one talon. 'Eh? Maybe, sure,' he said vaguely. 'Creatures got nursery stories, same as faeries got.'

'Aye,' agreed Bertram. 'Like that one about how a rain shower on a sunny day means a fox's wedding?'

'Ach,' said Snoshti. 'That one's true. Ye never been to a fox's wedding? They do make a fuss.'

In the Ring, tunes shivered across fiddle strings and Magpie turned to look. Faeries were dancing in air, jewel-bright and shimmering in their gowns and frock coats. She glanced up at the palace. The queen was gone from the window. To the crows she said, 'Where to, birds?'

‘Come on,’ Snoshti said. ‘There’s a green near my village. My kin would be pleased to host ye.’

Leaving the stage props in disarray inside, the birds slipped into their harnesses and towed the caravans out of the city.

12

DAYLIGHT TWINKLED INTO TWILIGHT AS THE LAST SLANTING rays of sunset withdrew from the treetops. Darkness came, and the forest's moontime citizens awoke, glittery-eyed and hungry. Wolves slunk to the edge of the river and dipped their pink tongues in. Foxes jackknifed on scurrying voles. The hag Black Annis crouched naked on a high branch and shot her tongue at bats who flew too near.

In the southern reaches of the great wood, Magpie and the crows sat around a fire with a clan of hedge imps, trading wind songs for scamper ballads and sipping spiced wine.

Far across Dreamdark in the tiny hamlet of West Mirth, a certain darkness was gliding down the white road out of town. It was a formless thing, unfixed, the edges of it bleeding into the night like watercolors on wet paper. There was no one to feel the desolation it left in its wake. The sentry tower was empty, and in front of its dying fire a rocking chair was slowing to a halt as if someone had stood and stretched and gone to bed. But all the beds in all the cottages were empty. The coverlets were drawn up as if tucked beneath the chins of sleepers, but sleepers there were none. Nothing had been disturbed. The dray pigeons snoozed in their stables and beetles dreamed in their pens, but the faeries were gone. Every one. Even the cradles were empty.

The faerie healer Orchidspike, out foraging in the Deeps for night-blooming flowers, stopped suddenly and straightened up. She was the oldest faerie in Dreamdark, older by an entire lifetime than the next oldest, but her senses were creature-sharp, and she knew the currents of the forest like no other. She looked around, feeling an alien chill riding the air, and shivered. Pulling her shawl tight around her, she picked up her basket of flowers and hurried home.

At the ruin of Issrin Ev, Talon Rathersting discovered what the search parties had failed to find: his kinsmen's knives abandoned in a shadowed cleft in the cliff. He gathered them up and brought them out, laying them carefully on a flat rock. There were fourteen in all. That was all of them: Wick had been wearing only two; the others had worn four each. All were bare of their sheaths. They'd been drawn and thrown at something sunk in that crevice. The point of one blade was nicked off where it had met rock, hard and fast. None of the knives seemed to have hit flesh or drawn blood, and whatever had been in the crevice, it was gone now, as were the vultures and the warriors who'd gone hunting them.

When several hours had passed yesterday with no sign of their return, Talon had summoned the rest of the Rathersting warriors, his uncles, more cousins, and his sister, Nettle, and they'd sent out rotating search parties all through the day. Talon had stayed behind at the castle keeping the watch, his heart clenched like a fist in his chest as their wings flashed away over the treetops. The shame and yearning boiled into a kind of fury as he watched and waited, feeling the relentless tug of the sky as his feet stayed firmly on the rampart.

Days were long this near the summer solstice, and there had been light well into the evening, but the search parties had returned with nothing but haggard faces. Talon and Nettle had stayed up in the tower watching owls hunt over the silent forest, and when the moon was high, he'd turned to look at her. She was taller than he, being a half century older, but with nearly identical tattoos and the same royal circlet on the same pale hair. Her eyes were copies of his, too, and her heart knew his heart, and she met his gaze evenly, understanding. She put a hand on his arm and said, 'Be careful.'

And Talon went over the wall and into the woods, alone.

He stood now in the courtyard of Issrin Ev with the Rathersting daggers laid out at his feet and the moon-cast shadows of broken statues swaying around him. Headless, wingless, toppled, split, and shrouded in moss, the statues made the Magruwen's temple seem like a monument to suffering and battles lost. It wasn't. It had been a place of the highest glory until the very day the Djinn himself destroyed it. Bards and scribes and kings had hurried along these paths, their hearts and heads full of great magic. Now it was hard to imagine any but ghosts coming up the long, crumbling stair in the rock face or anything arriving on wing but vultures.

Talon had found bones and feathers down the slope. A vulture had been devoured. Not enough remained of it to tell whether his father and cousins had killed it, but he suspected so. As for what had eaten it, it could only have been its five fellows. Cannibals. Talon's lip curled in disgust.

They were gone now.

Talon couldn't carry all the bare daggers, but he took his father's favorite and turned west. There was only one faerie he wanted to talk to. He headed for Orchidspike's cottage, starting down the ruined stair at a loping gait and gathering speed. Soon he was hurtling through the gloom of the Deeps, the long, wooded basin gouged between two rocky plateaus. The sun penetrated here only a few hours each day when it was directly overhead, and the rest of the hours were just a slow fade from dark to dusk and dusk to dark again.

He raced along, launching himself off roots and spiraling airborne so fast he blurred. He would run half up a tree trunk and dive for the next one, never even slowing as he came to land between wild leaps and kept on, powerful and thrilling, explosive, acrobatic. But he always touched down between leaps. He'd launch, push off, hurtle toward the canopy of the forest, and never quite break through to the sky.

His feet touched down and he pushed on.

He found Orchidspike awake when he arrived, and she hurried to open the door for him. 'Lad,' she said, relieved, taking his head in both her hands and looking straight into him through his eyes. Her relief was short-lived, for she saw the trouble in his heart. 'What's happened?' she asked.

'My father's gone. And Shrike, Wick, and Corvus. Gone.' Talon's young face was somber under the ink of his ferocious tattoos, but Orchidspike knew him well, knew to look past the warrior and into his eyes, which were the eyes of a lad, and frightened.

She took his hands and led him into the cottage. This place had been Talon's sanctuary since he was wee. His clan had long worked closely with Orchidspike and her foremothers, for she and her kind were the healers of Dreamdark, and the Rathersting were its guardians. Besides protecting the forest from intruders and keeping a close eye on its unfriendlier residents like Black Annis, the Rathersting launched regular raiding parties into the drear

Spiderdowns, the nastiest place in all of Dreamdark. There they gathered the silken skeins of web the healer required for her intricate magic of knitting torn faerie wings back together.

Orchidspike had been ancient all Talon's life, ancient and marvelous. When the shame of his wings had become at last undeniable, when he was still small and his cousins had started calling him 'Prince Scuttle,' Orchidspike had been the light in his darkness. He had come here to her cottage every day after his lessons. She had never taken an apprentice, a lass who would become healer in her place when she made her journey to the Moonlit Gardens, so he had done what an apprentice would have done: the garden work, the transcribing, the spinning and winding of the spidersilk onto bobbins. He had even learned how to knit, though never, never had he breathed a word about it to anyone in his clan.

Orchidspike's knitting needles were ancient, djinncraft, passed down through generations of Dreamdark healers. They sang to the fingers and were capable of mysterious things. And using them, Talon had found himself capable of mysterious things too. In the privacy of the healer's cottage, he had stumbled upon an art form he believed no faerie had ever undertaken before, a secret art, and it had become a fascination for him. No instructions existed in any book, not even the slightest hint. He had to invent it for himself as he went along, stitch by stitch, but he didn't feel himself alone in it. There was something that guided him, a sense he could not put into words. It was like being swept into a current of magic and carried along, even as he sat still and knitted. His heart pulsed with the pulse of some unseen force, glyphs came together in his mind, and his hands knew just what to do. It was almost like a trance. He had tried explaining it to Orchidspike and her eyes grew bright and sharp but she said little. And because it involved knitting needles he could never mention it to anyone else. Who ever knew a warrior prince to knit?

Orchidspike put on a kettle and gathered leaves from a half-dozen little jars, mixing a tea for Talon. Then she sank back into her rocker and said, 'Tell me.'

'Yestermorn on the watch I spotted six vultures,' he told her. 'Monstrous big beasts. My father and cousins went out to see to them. They never came back. I found their knives at Issrin Ev.'

'Issrin?' she asked, and nodded to herself. 'Aye, near the mouth of the Deeps. Lad, I was in the Deeps this night and I felt a dark presence, and it wasn't vultures, I can tell you.'

'But what was it?'

'It grieves me to say I've no idea. Some dark power has come to Dreamdark, and we need to learn what it is.'

'I'll go search the Deeps,' he said, rising to his feet.

'Nay, you will not,' she said, her eyes ablaze. 'There's something out there, lad, and it might only be luck you made it through the Deeps once tonight. Come. You've some hours till dawn and work to do. You can finish in that time, I think.'

'Finish? But—'

'It's time, lad,' she said. She opened a workbox that sat near the hearth and lifted from it her knitting needles and a long streamer of shimmering threads.

Talon took them from her very gently. Light skittered across the fabric and couldn't seem to fix a color to it. It looked frail as a cobweb adrift on a breeze, insubstantial as a veil knit of moonbeams. Holding the needles in his hands he felt the familiar pulse catch him up like a current. Glyphs filled his mind, and the work began to flow from his fingers.

Just before dawn he looked up from it and his eyes were shadowed with sleeplessness but bright with excitement.

'It's ready,' he said.

Orchidspike looked it over closely. 'It's more than ready. You've done something true here, lad. It's perfect.'

Talon glowed with pride.

Orchidspike said, 'Once the sun's full, I want you to go to the hamlets on the Sills and see how they fare there. If anything seems awry – anything – shepherd the folk to the castle for safekeeping, you ken?'

He nodded and shook out the skin – for that was what he had made – and stepped into it, visioning the glyph that would awaken it. After that, even Orchidspike couldn't have distinguished him from a real falcon.

The clot of darkness had returned to Issrin Ev. Before sunrise it slipped into a deep fissure in the rubble of the temple, and five vultures hunkered down on branches to wait out the day, restless and hungry. They'd eaten nothing since their brother's corpse, a whole day past. And though their master had hunted through the night, he had left them no bones to pick over. He never did.

13

Magpie woke half buried in pillows in a blanket nest on the floor. She stretched like a cat and rolled over, blinking up at the root-ribbed ceiling of Snoshti's burrow. It smelled sweet in the close space, of tea and earth and spice. 'Up and greet the day!' Snoshti called, and Magpie got to her feet and ambled down a low corridor to the kitchen, where hot scented water awaited her in a copper tub.

'Ach,' grumbled Magpie, for whom a bath was a dip in a pond or a quick shine with the last gulp in her cup.

'Sure even crows bathe sometimes,' Snoshti told her, frowning at the feather skirt – for Magpie had slept in her clothes same as she always did. As she stepped out of them she unstrapped her new knife from her leg and laid it aside. It caught Snoshti's eye, and the imp did a double take behind her back. A little later, when Magpie's head was underwater, she looked closer, sucking in her breath when she saw the knife's runes, but when Magpie surfaced, Snoshti didn't say a word about it.

She lathered Magpie's chestnut hair with pear-scented soap and watched fondly as the lass used magic to float a scone across the room from the stove to her mouth, leaving it suspended in the air before her face and taking great bites without the use of her hands. Crumbs cascaded into the bathwater. 'Little barbarian,' Snoshti chuckled.

A dozen families lived in the hedge imp village, an intricate warren beneath the earth with wide tunnels for avenues, and passages that Snoshti said reached all the way to other villages. Glossy gemhued beetles milled about as Magpie made her way topside, and impkins darted up to touch her shyly and giggle, never having had a faerie visit them underground before nor ever having met one so ready to smile at them or carry them into the air on short flights.

The crows were up and smoking in their dressing gowns, and Mingus poured Magpie a cup of sludgy coffee.

'So, 'Pie,' said Calypso. 'When are we for the Magruwen, eh? First thing? Or ye going to make that cake?'

Magpie took the recipe out of her pocket and chewed her lip. She'd have been certain the writing belonged to Bellatrix but for the one thing that made it impossible: The paper wasn't ancient. It could have been written yesterday. 'What if it's a trick?' she asked.

'A trick? Ye mean, like, if it's not really his favorite cake?' puzzled Pup.

Magpie smiled. It seemed such a silly notion in itself, that the great Djinn had a favorite cake at all. She looked at the ingredients. Oats, honey, the usual things, and what else? Tears, wind, lightning . . . Magpie cocked her head to one side and took a swig of her coffee, thinking. Tears, wind, and lightning. Water, air, and fire – that was three of the four elements.

She thought of what she and Poppy had talked of, how the Djinn had dreamed a world he couldn't even touch. He couldn't wade in a stream and feel the rush of water without boiling it, couldn't sleep beneath a tree without burning it, or ride a bird, or feel the wind, or lay his cheek on a sun-warmed stone. It began to seem like just the kind of cake that *would* be his favorite.

And what of the thousand years of undreamed life? What was a life not yet begun? A cocoon, sure. But no butterfly or moth lived a thousand days, let alone years. And Magpie had an idea that this last ingredient would somehow represent the fourth element: earth. Rich earth, steady, solid earth, the element that anchored all the rest, like roots in soil.

Suddenly she had it. She clapped her hands. 'An acorn!'

'Eh, 'Pie?' Calypso asked.

'A tree lives a thousand years!' she said, and the idea settled in her mind with the *snick* of a puzzle piece fitting into place. What was an acorn if not the perfect expression of life, a millennium of it and more, curled up tight and just waiting for the proper encouragement to begin?

She would make the cake. Wherever it had come from, whoever had written it out, it was made of such things as could have only good in them. 'I'm going to meet Poppy,' she told the crows.

She went back down into the imp village to borrow a half walnut shell from Snoshti, then she set out.

Fringed by a circle of willows, Lilyvein Pond was the largest of a string of spring-fed ponds on the outskirts of Never Nigh. Faerie weddings were often held here in the spring when white narcissus bloomed round it thick as snowbanks, and in winter it was the favorite spot for ice-skating. Magpie flew quietly over the glassy water and, hovering just above the surface, began to sing. Poppy watched and listened from the air.

The strange words, sung low in a language not often heard above the waves, rippled over the water, and sleek shapes began to gather beneath.

Magpie was singing the ballad of Psamathe, fiftieth of the fifty daughters of the sea, and it was a tale of despair sure to bring tears to the eyes of fish, eel, and creek maiden, and any other creature who knew their language. Magpie couldn't speak the fin tongue fluently, but she knew a good number of their ballads by heart as a result of a long winter some twenty years earlier spent trapped in an ice cave with selkies. She'd become quite a good ice sculptor that winter, too, a skill she hadn't since had to call upon, but who knew but that one day she might? Little had she suspected then, sharing a selkie's seal pelt for warmth, that the day would come when she'd need to bring a fish to tears. But here that day was.

And all clad in sea foam
she clung to the waves,
singing her love to the sky.
He swept o'er without stopping,
that tempest, by moonlight,
ne'er heeding her heart-rending cry . . .

The tricky fin verses trilled off her tongue, and as the last notes rippled across the pond, the fish wept like babes. Hanging like a dragonfly over the green water, Magpie gingerly scooped the walnut shell in and filled it to brimming with their tears.

'What was that song about?' Poppy asked as they flew slowly away, trying not to slosh the tears. Not understanding a word of it, she'd still felt a tug at her heart, so mournful had been the sound.

'Lost love,' replied Magpie with all the feeling of a child to whom such a thing is mere words. 'Woe and heartache. The usual.'

The Manygreen lands sprawled across a varied terrain of speckled meadows and scrubby rises laced with tree cover. As they were growers and plant mages, they lived where the trees were sparse and the sun could dip down and kiss their growing things to life. Poppy guided Magpie to a soft landing atop a tangle of wild plum roots at the edge of a garden in riotous summer bloom. There were checkered heads of drooping fritillary mixed into swaths of bird cherry and cloudberry, kiss-me-quick and creeping jenny, primrose and bee orchid and yellow archangel. Fuchsia and wild peony tumbled over rocks, and fiddleheads unfurled among stalks of honey daphne. From tree to tree rolled carpets of wood anemone, and above it all a fringe of whitebeam and flowering plum waved its plumage in the wind.

'Oh, Poppy . . .' Magpie breathed, taking it all in. 'It's wonderful here . . .'

Poppy beamed. 'There's my workshop,' she said with a flourish of her arm. Emerging from a nook between roots was a many-gabled roof bristling with copper chimneys. Poppy led Magpie through a covered porch into a single large room. Herbs and blossoms hung upside down from the ceiling to dry, and the walls were hidden entirely by shelves and glass-fronted cabinets. A pair of big slab worktables were covered in a tumble of kettles, crucibles, and cauldrons, bubbling vials, interconnected tubes, beakers, shining instruments, and books.

Magpie looked at it all, wide-eyed. 'Skive,' she murmured. 'I've never seen the like!'

Poppy pulled a bowl down from a shelf and emptied the tears into it.

Magpie read from tiny labels on earthen jars: 'SONGBIRD TISANE, LOVER'S POSEY – A CURE FOR HICCUPS AND NIGHTMARES. MOONLIGHT MIST . . . What's that do?'

'That helps you remember your dreams.'

'Sharp! Does it work?'

'Aye, sure. Here.' She poured some of the blue cordial into a little metal flask and screwed the cap on tight. 'For later. Just a sip before bedtime.' She handed it to Magpie.

'Thanks!' The flask had a ring on its cap that Magpie threaded through her belt. 'How'd you make it?'

'You've got to collect full moonlight all night long in a mirror, set out someplace no shadows will fall over it from dusk to dawn, and at first light tip it, and pour the moonlight through a sieve of mist into a jug with a sprig of lavender and then distill it for a moon's time.'

'There's one for my book!' Magpie said. 'How'd you think that up?'

'Sometimes,' Poppy said with a bashful glance at Magpie, 'I just sort of . . . *feel* what to do, like the magic's already there, all around, and I just have to sort of let my mind open – like a flower – and then . . . I don't know, I . . . find it.'

Magpie stared at her and Poppy blushed, looking back down at the bowl in her hands as she said quickly, 'It's just a fancy, really.'

'Neh,' said Magpie, a push of her wings carrying her half across the room. 'Poppy,' she said earnestly, 'is it like . . . a pulse?'

Poppy looked up sharply and said, 'Aye . . .'

'Like . . .' Magpie went on. 'Like invisible blood pulsing through the veins of the air?'

Poppy nodded eagerly. 'Like if you could feel the roots of things alive under the ground, twisting and living and growing, even though you can't see them, but it's not just underground, it's everywhere, all around, and it's faster than roots growing and bigger, bigger than anything—'

'And it's warm and alive and—'

They spoke the next words in unison – 'and it carries you along with it' – and stood staring at each other.

Tears suddenly sprang to Poppy's eyes. 'Magpie, I've never . . . no one else has ever understood . . .'

'I know,' said Magpie. 'Me too!'

'Have you always—?' Poppy started to ask, but just then a crow poked his head through the window.

'Mags,' he croaked. 'C'mere a secky, darlin'.' It was Swig. He had a hunched, serious look about him that Magpie knew could mean nothing good. She went to the window at once. Beyond, she could see Maniac and Mingus in close conversation with a raven so large he made the crows look like hatchlings.

'Who's that feather?' she asked.

'Algorab's his name,' said Swig. 'Dreamdark bird. He's heard something, Mags.'

'What?'

'Little hamlet called West Mirth? There's bats who hunt bugs round the pigeon stables there by night. They say last night something came through.'

'What kind of something?'

Swig shook his head. 'Don't know. Bats said their echo sense went right through it. Just *darkness*, they said.'

Magpie's stomach lurched. 'Darkness? Not the hungry one! Not in Dreamdark!'

'No one came out of those houses this morning, Mags, and Algorab says it's some eerie kinda quiet.'

'Quiet,' Magpie repeated, remembering the terrible hush of the catacombs. 'Neh . . .' she said, leaning heavily on the window ledge, her head spinning. It was mad. Dim as devils were, they'd always known to steer clear of Dreamdark in their day. If the beast had come here, then she'd been right about one thing, one awful thing: it had come for the Magruwen. 'Where's Calypso?' she asked Swig.

'Pup went for him.'

She glanced at Poppy, who was watching them, puzzled. 'All right,' she told Swig, 'I'm coming.' To Poppy she said, 'We'll go gather up the rest of the ingredients. The shadow and wind and that? You got the oats and flour and all?'

'Aye, sure my mum has it at home.'

'Good, then, I'll meet you back here.'

Poppy watched with a slight frown as Magpie flew out the window to join the birds. After they'd flown away, she stepped out into her garden and pondered what she'd overheard. Then she knelt beside a patch of crimson primroses. 'Good morning, beauties,' she said. 'What gossip in the wood?'

14

A FALCON HUNG WEIGHTLESS IN THE UPDRAFTS THAT ROSE along the rocky Sills. Suddenly it plunged into a harrowing dive, spiraling hard groundward before swooping into a long, smooth upward glide. There was something joyful in the sight of it, a wild, bracing freedom that the flightless could only dream of. After a hundred years of standing on heavy feet watching other wings rise, Talon felt as if a flare had been lit over the world, revealing all new colors. He'd never felt so alive.

He came to perch in a pine above Pickle's Gander, the smallest of the three hamlets on the Sills. Inside his skin he was winded and grinning. No other faerie had to work this hard to fly, sure. They didn't have to learn to knit, and they didn't have to operate false wings with their arms. But no faerie had ever done what he'd done. Not ever. Skin-making was the work of elementals and none other. Until now.

It was washing day in Pickle's Gander. In the creek below his perch the sprouts were splashing their feet while the biddies taught the lasses glyphs for cleaning linens. He knew everyone. These were the Ratherstings' nearest neighbors, and several of his cousins were courting here. He spotted Shrike's lass, Lyric, laughing and tossing her long yellow hair, and his grin subsided. She hadn't yet heard the news. He remembered the sight of the fourteen knives at Issrin Ev, and his joy turned cold. Just because East Mirth and Pickle's Gander were carrying on as usual didn't mean the trouble wasn't real. He would just go check on West Mirth before he flew the skin back to Orchidspike for safekeeping, then he'd return to the castle.

He was prince of the Rathersting. On a day such as this, with the chief missing and a dark presence abroad in the realm, his place was with his folk. He was ashamed of himself, of his grin, his joy, his pride. He lifted his arms, shaking open the wings of his skin, and leapt into a long tilting glide that would carry him all the way over the Deeps to the Western Sill and West Mirth.

On the way, the joy returned unbidden. There was nothing he could do about it.

While the other crows foraged for cake ingredients, Magpie and Calypso followed the raven Algorab across the vastness of Dreamdark toward the rocky rises in the west. The Dreamdark Deeps were sunk between two ridges, the Crag and the Spine. Where these faced each other across the sunken forest long horizontal ledges of igneous rock extruded on both sides, looking quite like windowsills. Calypso pointed down with his wing as they passed above the devastation of Issrin Ev, and soon they were circling the cleft boulder into which West Mirth was tucked.

Long ago the boulder had split clean and fallen open, and inside it the hamlet was founded, a row of sweet cottages on either side of a white lane. Their rear gardens backed up to the rock face, billowing with fragrant herbs, and Magpie came in to land on the brink of the cliff above. Looking down, she thought this was the kind of place that belonged in a painting, a place that should never know of devils.

It was far too quiet.

Magpie walked off the cliff as if it were a mere step and fell fast, flicking open her wings just in time to move lightly forward in an animal prowl. The birds dropped down beside her. Cautiously she went in the back door of a cottage. All was neat as a pin within and there was nothing amiss but the beds. She prowled around them, looking, smelling. Of scent there was nothing that didn't belong. Honeysuckle, rosemary, and soap. But the puzzling way the covers were arranged, as if tucked around sleepers who'd simply melted into the night; it shivered her. It brought to mind the fishermen's shoes left so suddenly behind in the world when the mannies themselves were whisked, somehow, out of it.

She visioned the glyphs for memory touch, gritted her teeth, and laid her hand upon a pillow, but there was no jolt of darkness. She saw only fragments of dreams. Whatever had happened here, the faeries had slept through it, up until the very last.

All the cottages were the same.

It was only the rocking chair in the sentry tower that gave her what she still hoped not to find. A blast of darkness, hunger, and hatred. Going outside again, Magpie nodded once to Calypso, her eyes hard.

'Jacksmoke!' he croaked.

Passing the stables, Magpie heard sounds within, beetles lowing to be milked and the bleat of hungry dray pigeons. The prowl went out of her step, and her faerie self returned to her with the recognition of this simple task to be performed, the care and feeding of livestock. Saddened and shaken, she walked into the stable.

She froze in the doorway.

There was never any reason to find a bird of prey in a pigeon stable. Especially when traceries of light shimmied and wove round it, tracing its falcon shape and glinting off its feathers before sliding into the dim outskirts of Magpie's vision; when it wasn't a falcon at all, but a disguise. Magpie saw it all in an instant, and that instant slammed into the next instant, in which she found herself hurtling at the imposter with her dagger drawn, knocking the bird to the ground and kneeling over it, the edge of the blade against its false throat.

'Shed it,' she growled.

It didn't speak or move, and she said, 'The skin. Shed it now!'

The bird lay silent as a dead thing, without even a rise and fall of ribs to give a hint of the creature hidden inside. But there was a sound. Magpie shifted uneasily in her crouch and glanced around the stable. The pigeons were bleating louder in their agitation, but that wasn't it. She could hear a sound like the pure ring of crystal against crystal, a fluid and melodious chime that seemed to surround her. It was only when she shifted the knife slightly away from the falcon's throat that the sound began to ebb and she felt the figure shift beneath her.

'Wait,' it said in no birdlike voice.

She thrust the knife edge again to its throat and again the falcon fell still and the strange chime grew louder. Magpie looked at the blade and saw runes agleam on it. She realized with a jolt that it was the knife that was singing. Her eyes widened, and her gaze shifted rapidly back and forth between the blade and the falcon. A magic blade! There was many a story in legend of strange weapons that mastered their masters, having wickedness and will forged into them by their makers.

In a fluid movement she drew it off the falcon's throat and backed quickly away, staying crouched and ready to spring. The blade fell silent, and the falcon moved.

A ripple went through it, a rift appeared in its belly, and it sort of split apart and fell away, its feathers transforming as it did into a strange membranous sheath that looked like little more than a stocking. Inside it was a faerie like no faerie Magpie had ever seen. She'd seen tattoos on witch doctors, savage jungle faeries, but not like these. The black patterns on his face had grace and reminded her of only one thing: the mysterious whirls of light that had of late been spinning across her vision. She stared at him. Looking closer, she saw the features of a lad and eyes like crystals with the sky dancing through them.

'What did you do to me?' Talon gasped, falling on his side and clutching his throat.

Magpie looked at the blade in her hand, confused. It was silent. 'Are you okay?' she asked, her voice wary.

'Okay?' Still clutching his throat, he rose to his knees and said, 'Now that I'm not paralyzed and suffocating, aye, I'm right as rain.'

'Paralyzed and suffocating? How—?'

With narrowed eyes he looked at her and at the knife. 'Djinncraft,' he said. 'That explains things. Who'd you steal it from?'

'Steal it? I found it in a skeleton's spine!'

'Ah, so you stole it from the dead. How fine.'

'Call me a thief?' Magpie blazed. 'Sure you didn't find that skin in your granny's attic!'

'Right. I didn't. I—' He bit off his words and glared at her, then asked with a tinge of bitterness, 'How did you know?'

'I know a skin when I see one,' Magpie said. 'My grandfather wears one.'

'Faeries don't wear skins!'

'Neh, they don't indeed,' she replied, looking pointedly at the shimmering sheath gathered around his shoulders. 'I never said *he* was a faerie.'

Talon looked at her hard. A lass, just a lass she was, wind-mussed and wearing feathers and gripping a blade such as that. For a moment there he'd thought he might suffocate and wake to find himself in the Moonlit Gardens! When she'd held that knife to his throat, he'd been unable to move a muscle, even to breathe. 'Who are you?' he asked her in an acid voice.

'All right in there, 'Pie?' Calypso called from outside, and both faeries started and looked to the door.

''Pie?' Talon repeated.

'Never you mind!' she said to him, then called out to the birds, 'In here, I found someone!'

Calypso and Algorab appeared like shadows in the doorway, and seeing them, Talon gave the lass another hard look. He'd seen crows arrive yestermorn, shortly before the vultures.

'You from this place?' Magpie asked the lad, seeing feed sacks leaning against the pen near him, as if he'd been feeding the pigeons.

'Well, I know you're not, if you have to ask about me,' he said. One thing about being Rathersting – folk tended to know you on sight.

'That's a Rathersting, lass,' said the raven.

Magpie looked steadily at the lad. 'I know the name,' she said. 'The guardians. Fine, ancient clan. So what are you doing flying around in a stolen skin?'

'I didn't steal it,' he said fiercely. 'I made it!'

'Aye, sure.'

Talon gritted his teeth. Reminding himself he was a prince of the realm and not one to be cowering before some strange lass, he rose to his feet and held himself tall, a full head taller than she. They faced each another, tense. 'Never mind the skin,' he said. 'I want to know what you're doing in West Mirth. You're a stranger here; don't try to deny it. So what's a strange lass doing waving a djinncraft blade round an abandoned hamlet?'

'It wasn't abandoned.'

'What?'

'Didn't you see the beds? They never got out of their beds.'

Talon felt sick. He'd known something wasn't right in the cottages, but he hadn't been able to put his finger on just what. The lass was right. The blankets hadn't been thrown back. There'd been no struggle and no sign they'd risen from their beds. It was as if they'd vanished in them. 'What do you know?' he demanded.

'Nothing,' she cried, frustrated. 'Still nothing! Except he's come here to Dreamdark, of all places! What mad devil would come to Dreamdark?'

'Devil?' Talon repeated, incredulous.

Magpie saw the disbelief in his eyes. 'Aye, devil,' she said. 'But tell me, lad, what do *you* know?'

They faced off like a couple of cats that might start hissing and spitting at any moment. 'Lad, lass,' Calypso said soothingly, coming forward. 'It's plain ye've two hard skulls between ye, but there's no need for this. Sure we're together against it, neh?'

'Against what, exactly?' Talon asked. 'And don't say devil. Every eejit knows they're long dead and gone from this world!'

'Long gone? Aye. Long dead? Neh. They were never killed. They couldn't be,' Magpie told him.

'Why? Sure Bellatrix could—'

'Ach, sure she *could*. That's not the thing. The thing is, the blighters got sparks, same as faeries. They die, they pass to the Moonlit Gardens, just like us.'

Talon looked at her, and some of the anger went out of his face, to be replaced with a dawning understanding. 'Oh,' he said softly. 'Couldn't have the Gardens swarming with devils. So then . . . what became of 'em?'

'The champions caught 'em in bottles and threw 'em in the sea, sealed with magic nothing was ever supposed to undo. Everything was fine for thousands of years, while faeries made an art of forgetting.'

'And now one's got out?'

Magpie grimaced. 'One or two.'

'And it's come here?' Talon asked. 'That's what it is? What's it done to . . . ?' His voice trailed off, and he and Magpie listened to the silence of West Mirth. 'What's it done to them?' he almost whispered.

'I don't know,' she said, softening, and finally sheathing her knife. 'I've never seen a devil like this.'

'And how many have you seen?'

'A fair few,' she answered gruffly, turning and walking out between Calypso and Algorab.

Talon followed. 'Who are you? You've got to tell me what you know. It's taken my kinsmen—'

Magpie turned to him. 'What? When?'

'Late yestermorn. At Issrin Ev. They tracked some great vultures there, and only their knives were left to find. You don't think they're . . .'

'I don't know. If it's any comfort, I've never seen a devil eat but that it left a dread mess behind. Blood everywhere, and sometimes they spit out the skeletons like owl pellets.'

'That's a great comfort, lass, sure,' he said with sarcasm. 'Thanks for your heartfelt words.'

'Ach,' Magpie muttered, realizing how crude she must sound. Her cheeks colored a little. It was long since she'd been much in the company of faeries. Snoshti was right – she *was* a barbarian. 'Come on, birds, we got to go.'

'Lass, wait!' Talon said sharply.

She turned to him, her face guarded, but when her blue eyes locked on his, she saw only anxiety and fatigue. He held his hands out to her in the manner of greeting, and after a brief hesitation she reached out and pressed her palms against his. Both faeries' eyes widened in surprise as they felt a sudden surge in the pulse of invisible force around them at the very moment of their touch. It tingled in their fingertips so that after they pulled their hands apart, both clutched their fingers surreptitiously into fists. Neither had any reason to think the other felt it, and they drew warily apart.

'You'll warn the folks hereabouts?' Magpie asked Talon.

'Aye. I'll bring them to the castle.'

'Good. That's good. And . . . be careful, neh.' She rose to her wings but hesitated a moment in the air with a thought on the tip of her mind. She said, 'Lad, that skin . . .' She gestured to the gossamer fabric that still clothed him from neck to toes. 'You really made it?'

'I finished it this dawn.'

'Well, it's . . .' She groped for a word and settled on 'Uncommon,' then turned and flickered away into the sky, flanked by birds and wickedly quick.

Uncommon. It wasn't much of a compliment, not by itself. It was the way her mouth curled up at its corners into a kind of marveling smile when she said it that made it one. Talon found he was blushing. She was gone by the time he realized he still had no idea who she was. '*Pie*?' he murmured. 'What kind of a name is that?'

15

IN THE SKY ABOVE THE MANYGREEN LANDS, MAGPIE UNFASTENED the pins Snoshti had put in her hair and let it tumble down around her shoulders. Like an arrow off a bowstring, she shot through the air with mad speed, zinging back and forth once over Poppy's workshop with her hair streaming behind her. Then she froze, folded her wings, and dropped like a stone out of the sky for one of her frightful sharp landings. A flick of her wings and she caught herself at the moment the earth loomed to meet her. She ran inside the workshop.

Poppy looked up, startled. 'Magpie!' she exclaimed. 'Where—?'

'That the batter?' Magpie asked, cutting her off.

'Aye.'

With three long sweeps of her fingers, Magpie combed the wind from her hair. It cascaded invisibly into the bowl of cake batter and settled there. 'Calypso's waiting outside with his shadow,' she said.

Poppy followed and watched as Magpie held the bowl in outstretched arms in the brightest spot in the garden. Overhead, Calypso flew in spirals, slow as he could, and Magpie chased his shadow round and round. Several times she nearly captured it, but it always seemed to slip over the lip of the bowl to freedom. At last, though, she trapped it, and after just the briefest shadowless moment another sprouted in its place, growing larger as Calypso dropped in to land. Behind him came Swig, carrying a small bird's nest in one foot, with an acorn and a blackened twig nestled inside it, and holding a porcupine quill in his beak.

Once Magpie took the quill, he said, 'Ye've Maniac to thank for that, Mags. The porcupine weren't keen to part with it.'

'Maniac?' Magpie groaned. 'It had to be him! He's already mad at me! Didn't hurt him bad, did it?'

'Neh, but he does make a fuss.'

'For true.'

'Magpie . . .' Poppy cut in hesitantly. 'Did you find out anything . . . about the devil?'

Magpie dropped the porcupine quill in her shock and turned to her friend. 'How do you know about that?'

'All the forest knows of it,' she said. 'Well, except the faeries. All they're worrying about is why Queen Vesper keeps to her chamber!'

'But what have you heard?'

'The trees say the age of unweaving has begun.'

'Unweaving? Unweaving what?' asked Magpie.

'I don't know. They're saying it's the faeries' doom to forget what ought never be forgotten and that this devil hunted in Dreamdark once before.'

'What? I never heard of a snag who . . . but that's the point, neh? That's our doom.' She said it bitterly, then asked, 'Did they at least have a name for it, Poppy?'

Poppy looked flustered as she nodded. 'Aye, they called it something, but you might not believe it . . .'

'Poppy, what?'

She let out a nervous laugh. 'It sounds so silly. It's the bogeyman, Magpie. They're saying it's the Blackbringer!'

Magpie let out a short laugh too. The Blackbringer? The name inspired no shiver. It had been dragged through too many nurseries, worn thin by the empty threats of countless faerie mothers and grannies. The Blackbringer was the thing that would get you if you were naughty, that was waiting to grab up sprouts who stayed out past dark. The Blackbringer was the dark come to life . . .

Magpie's laugh fell hollow. Perhaps it didn't sound quite so silly. 'Well, whatever it is, let's make this cake. I've got to get to the Magruwen.'

With the cake tucked into the starling's nest as the recipe directed, Magpie carried it across the whole of Dreamdark in her arms. Calypso flew at her side, wings flashing in the sun. Mile after mile they surged over the wide, wild forest, until at last they were cresting the hedge and sailing over the grounds of the human school that Father Linden had described to Poppy.

Magpie spotted the well, and they spiraled down to land on its crumbling lip. A draft of deep-buried heat rose from within the earth, cooling as it passed them and merged into the world. 'Here we are, feather,' Magpie said with a tremor in her voice. 'Onward and downward.' She spelled up a light and dropped down into the pit, Calypso following closely.

After a long, steady downward drift they reached the bottom. The stones of the shaft flared wide into a cavernous space, and Magpie could see a few ill-formed paths snaking off and twisting away where the light couldn't follow. There was a door and, carved on it, the Magruwen's sigil intertwined with the glyph for dream. The tree had told true. Magpie trembled. To think the king of Djinn was on the other side of a door . . . It was as unreal as if a statue of Bellatrix were suddenly to flick its wings and fly from its pedestal. It was legend meeting life.

Standing on the threshold of a being who had wrought the world, Magpie felt very small, very young, and utterly insignificant. Who was she to presume to awaken a Djinn? But she knew the answer to that. As with each devil she captured, she was the only one trying.

Magpie took a deep breath and walked toward the door.

In his sleep, the Magruwen sensed their coming. He smelled feathers, and an image of vultures came into his mind, planted there by the imp's riddle. He recalled the distant day his brother Djinn had made them. Some creatures had been made as art; others were pure utility. Vultures had been shaped in haste to clean a field of slaughter when a powerful elemental had first begun to toy with death in the new-made world. The notion of murder had been born that day, and the Djinn had fashioned vultures to spare themselves the sight of it. They'd made them out of shame and had done well to make them; vultures had never fallen out of use since.

But there was no scuff of death on these feathers that beat heavily down the well shaft; they smelled of rain and fires. And there was another scent: faerie.

The Magruwen came awake. His sleep had been troubled, and he had not sunk far. Flames took the shape of a horned beast rising to its feet. The scent of faerie, pure as dew, was bitter to him. His flame hands clenched with the memory of betrayal, and he waited.

Magpie leaned on the door with all her might to push it open a crack. It creaked, and a trickle of smoke began to seep out. Magpie pushed harder, cradling the cake to her chest, and stepped into the Magruwen's cave, heart pounding. 'My lord Magruwen . . . ?'

she asked tentatively. The lake of smoke before her moved with a sluggish tide, and the scuttle of salamanders up and down the stalactites sounded like a chorus of otherworldly whispers. The source of light seemed to be in the deep reaches of the cave where the ceiling sloped down like rows of teeth in a giant jaw.

'First an imp and now a faerie,' came a harsh whisper, sending ripples through the smoke and chills down Magpie's spine. 'Get you gone. I don't deal in treasure anymore.'

'My lord? I . . . I've come for wisdom, not treasure,' she said, her eyes searching wildly for her first glimpse of the Djinn.

'Wisdom? For whom?'

'For all my kind. We need your help.'

'You are past helping . . . ' the whisper said, growing louder. Magpie watched breathlessly as the glow from the deep of the cave moved closer, flickering in the rough form of legs striding. 'Past deserving,' the voice continued. 'Faeries have become a second race of butterflies, mere ornaments for the air.'

The Djinn grew brighter, and Magpie had to cast down her eyes, feeling his heat pulsing at her in waves as he drew nearer. Her mind raced. The Djinn wore skins, didn't they? In the stories they appeared clad in wondrous forms. She had expected some majestic ancient, crowned perhaps, with a beard of fire and sparks for eyes, sitting in state on a hematite throne. Not this wild open flame. She tried to look at him, but he was so white-bright she had to snap her eyes closed. Behind her shut lids an afterimage burned of a beast with curved horns of flame. She began to back blindly away.

'We are more than butterflies, Lord,' she whispered.

'Aye, you are right. You are more treacherous. More false.'

'Neh!' Magpie said. 'Not that! Careless maybe, not treacherous. Faeries aren't traitors.'

'You think you know. Faeries! You are your own undoing. Old treachery comes back to haunt you, but even now you won't learn, even when the last of you flickers out.'

'What old treachery?' Magpie cried. 'What do you mean, flicker out?'

'Don't you like surprises?' he asked. He rushed up close then, and Magpie stumbled backward against the door, feeling the intense weight of heat upon her face and smelling scorched hair. For an instant, she could find no air to breathe and sank to the floor, realizing for the first time with what simplicity the end could come.

Then, just as suddenly, the Magruwen drew away.

'What is that?' he asked in a quick sharp hiss.

Magpie remembered the cake. 'My lord,' she gasped, holding it out. 'An offering. Your favorite . . . I hope.'

'That recipe has long been gone from this world!' But even as he said it, the Magruwen's voice faltered. Into his sulfurous cavern this small faerie had carried the scent of honey, tears, and lightning, of thirsty roots in future soil, of wind through wings, a fragrance long absent, but well remembered.

'I found it,' Magpie said in a small voice. 'I hope I made it okay.' She continued to hold it out to him, her arms shaking. After a moment she felt the heavy heat again, and the weight of the cake was lifted from her arms. The twigs of the starling's nest crackled like kindling, and she waited.

The sound he made was something like a sigh. A little of the tension that held Magpie rigid eased from her limbs and she rose again to her feet. 'My lord . . . is it . . . all right?'

'Imperfect,' he said, spitting. The acorn shot from his mouth and pinged into the smoke, setting off a loud cascade of hidden treasures, and Magpie tensed, ready to spring aside should he come at her again. 'There's no thousand years in that nut,' the Magruwen said, flaring high. Then he diminished, thinned, and said quietly, 'But it was not . . . badly done.'

Relief flooded Magpie, and she found she could look at him now, if she squinted. He had made himself into a spindle of flame that still bore within it the impression of a figure rising to taper into tremendous curving horns. And there were eyes. Once Magpie found them, she felt locked onto them and couldn't look away. They were vertical windows through fire into the infinite. They were dizzying.

'Why have you woken me?' he asked, and Magpie blinked and was able to break her gaze from his.

'T-there's . . .' she stammered. 'There's a devil, escaped from its bottle. A devil you saw fit once, yourself, to imprison.'

'And how do you know this?'

'I found the bottle and your seal. I never knew you snared any devils yourself, so it . . . it flummoxed me.'

'There is but one bottle that bears my seal.'

'Not anymore, then, Lord. If there was just the one, then it's sure. He's got out.'

'I know.'

'Oh.' Magpie hesitated. 'Did you also know, Lord, that he's killed the Vritra?'

The fire wavered and a hiss issued from him. 'Aye, I felt it,' he muttered to himself. 'A rending such as this the Tapestry cannot withstand. The threads fall slack and will not sing true.'

'Tapestry?' Magpie asked.

At first the Magruwen didn't answer. Magpie felt he was staring at her, weighing her worth and finding her lacking. 'The Tapestry is unknown to you?' he asked.

Magpie nodded slowly. A dreamlike image floated in her

mind, but like the traceries of light, it flitted away when she tried to look at it.

'Get you gone, faerie.' The Magruwen's voice snapped in mirthless laughter. 'Gather up the folk that remain, and go you all to the Moonlit Gardens. Feel blessed there's such a place for you to go . . . for now. Even it won't hold forever. When the last threads snap it, too, will sink into the darkness, a soft echo of greater doom.'

'What?' Magpie asked, bewildered. 'Darkness? Doom? What do you mean, Lord, please! Sure you can't be meaning the snag! What is he?'

'Who are *you*, that you should peer behind a veil of mysteries that has been in place for years beyond counting?'

'I'm a hunter. He's come to Dreamdark! I just want to catch him, before he hurts any more faeries and before he hurts . . . *you*.'

Again the Magruwen laughed. It was a terrible sound. 'Faerie, this foe won't be caught, not by you or anyone. He is a contagion of darkness. There's poetry in his return, though a faerie wouldn't see it.'

'Poetry! *He* said there was poetry in the Vritra's death. I don't see poetry in any of it!'

'He said? How do you know what he said?'

'I touched the Vritra's last memory. The devil called him a traitor!'

'A traitor . . .' the Djinn hissed. 'Aye. We are all traitors. For what is living but a chain of impossible choices? Every choice casts a shadow, and sometimes those shadows stalk your dreams. But what do faeries know of shame? You'll be blind to your own until the end!'

'What? Lord, please. It's true faeries are less than they were. I know how much has been lost. But the end? It's just one devil. However bad he is, he can't be the end of the world!'

'The world has long been ending. Everything ends. It builds, then it is, then it slides down the far slope of nothing, back into the nothing that was before.'

'Then we have to stop it!' Magpie cried in desperation. 'Sure you can't just see all your beautiful dreams vanish like that!'

'I'll dream more dreams.'

'Oh, aye, will you, then? Feed us to the devil, then go make yourself another world to play with? Is that what you dream about? How you'll make it better next time? What about *us*?'

'What *about* you? Live with what you wrought and die from it!'

'What we've wrought? Faeries didn't make devils!'

'Nay. And yet the seals are broken.'

'Humans break the seals!'

'Aye, so they do.'

'What have humans to do with us?' Magpie demanded in a fury.

The Magruwen just looked at her, and then he did the one thing, perhaps, that could have made Magpie's fury flare beyond the power of her small body to contain it.

He yawned.

Magpie sputtered, reddened. A tingling built to bursting in her fingers, then ten whorls of light surged from them and danced in the air, spinning round the Djinn King before exploding like fireworks against his fiery essence. 'Wake up!' Magpie cried. 'This is the world! This is important!'

And to her surprise, and his, he did wake up. The sparking of fireworks around him touched off a kindred explosion within, and he was stunned by a surge of vitality. It wavered out of his control and in an instant the spindle of fire standing before Magpie bloomed into a dazzle that knocked her to the ground and blinded her. She slipped beyond her senses and lay still in a world of hot white light and knew no more.

16

THE MAGRUWEN GRADUALLY, WITH EFFORT, GATHERED HIMSELF back in. He was in shock. He felt *new*, as when he had first danced off flint to bring light to the beginning. He reared his head, felt power flow through him, and looked down at the smoke where the faerie had stood. She was gone. He waved his hand and chased back the smoke to reveal where she lay senseless on the cavern floor.

He became aware of a ruckus then: a crow, squawking a riot at him. It landed beside the faerie, and the Magruwen waved his hand once more so that the crow fell still, frozen in place with his wings arched protectively over the lass.

The Djinn needed quiet.

What he had just seen was impossible. What he now felt was inexplicable. He looked hard at the faerie. Just a lass, and yet, with his sluggishness banished – *What had she done to him?* – his senses felt cleansed, and there was something familiar in her, some hint, some wisp that sang to him.

He needed to look at the Tapestry.

For millennia he had resisted looking at it. His dreams had been haunted by its unweaving, and he couldn't bear to see it in life, its ragged runs and ruined glyphs, its faded threads. Now he wrenched opened his long-blind inner eyes and waited for his mystical vision to clear.

The Tapestry was the very fabric of existence, woven long ago by seven fire elementals spinning in an eternity of nothing. They spun the threads of living light as a net to catch their dreams and keep them from dissolving into the blackness. Fever-bright they burned, fed unwaveringly by their one ally, the Astaroth, an elemental of the air, the world-shaping wind.

And the Tapestry grew.

It was simple in the beginning, a latticework of light, but the dreamers honed their craft, and the dream grew great. When at last it was ready, they grasped its edges and shaped it into a sphere, its seams sewn tight, and within it bloomed a world. When they stitched closed the seams, they did so from within. They sealed it around themselves and they knew they could never leave, not without letting the blackness in and annihilating everything the Tapestry sheltered.

They dreamed water and earth and populated them with fanciful creatures. The Magruwen dreamed dragons first – and he doted on them, Fade most of all, the truest thing he ever fashioned. The great dragon lay curled round the Djinn while they wove and wove.

They dreamed faeries later and gave to them, as to dragons and to a lesser extent imps, something other creatures didn't have: a sensitivity to the Tapestry. They couldn't see it or alter it. Simply, they felt it. It was the pulse and vibration of their world and, like harpists plucking strings, they could make it sing.

This was magic.

What the Magruwen thought he had witnessed when the lass stung him awake – the impossible thing – was a faerie spinning a new glyph into the Tapestry. Not just playing upon it, not plucking a thread, but creating one.

Weaving.

The glowing skeins of the Tapestry began to grow clear in his vision, starting out as traceries, curls, ribbons, and streamers of light and settling into their intricate patterns, moving and living and connecting all things. For a long time, he held the crow immobile with one small finger of his mind and studied the Tapestry with the rest of it. It was much as he feared from his nightmares. There were ragged shreds and tatters held together by the thinnest of filaments. With the death of the Vritra, many threads had dissolved altogether, and the fabric was slack as old skin. Blackness peeked through the threadbare patches, taunting. The Tapestry was falling apart.

And then, among the dimming strings and patterns of the failing weave, the Magruwen's eyes detected bright points, and he looked closer. He saw new glyphs. From one to the next, skipping over the vast fabric, he followed them. Messy they were and clumsy, brilliant and shining, childlike, impatient, artless, ingenious, and *impossible.* Some small fingers had been plying new threads through the old. Short and tangled though they were, in places these new stitches were all that held great gaps from yawning open.

While he slept, someone had been reweaving the Tapestry.

Magpie awakened with a groan, still blind, seeing only white. She smelled sulfur and knew she was still in the Magruwen's cave. She smelled stale cigar smoke and knew Calypso was near. 'Feather?' she said feebly.

'I'm here, 'Pie,' came his soothing singsong voice, and she felt his feathertips caress her face.

'What did I do?' she whispered, remembering nothing but the light pouring from her fingertips.

'I don't know, 'Pie,' the crow whispered back. She heard fear in his voice and struggled to sit up, tried to blink her vision into focus.

'Faerie,' hissed the Magruwen's voice. 'Who are you?'

'Magpie Windwitch, Lord,' she said in a wisp of a voice. She began to see shapes in the whiteness.

'Windwitch? Elemental?'

'I am granddaughter of the West Wind.'

To himself the Magruwen muttered, 'That explains nothing.'

'Lord Magruwen,' Magpie said, 'I'm sorry I offended you. And I'm sorry faeries have forsaken you. But I beg you, don't forsake us back. Give us a chance to deserve the world, to become what we can still become.'

'This is not an age of becoming,' he told her. 'It is the age of unweaving.'

'Unweaving again! What does it mean?'

'It means the darkness will rush in like a tide and sweep everything back into the endless ocean.'

'But sure we can stop it! With your help.' Her vision was returning, and she squinted to look at him.

'It is already too late,' said the Djinn.

Magpie clenched her fists in frustration. 'Neh!' she said forcefully, getting to her feet and leaning heavily on Calypso.

As she did so, a gleam caught the Magruwen's gaze and drew it to her knife hilt. He hissed, 'Skuldraig . . .'

'What?' Magpie asked with a sharp intake of breath. She remembered the name. The old faerie who had guarded the Vritra had said it. Skuldraig had killed all those faeries. 'Who's Skuldraig?' she asked.

'Let me see that dagger.'

Puzzled, Magpie unsheathed it and held it out, remembering

now the runes she'd noticed on its blade while holding it to the falcon's – the lad's – throat. She hadn't had a moment to look more closely at them since.

The Magruwen studied the knife for a long moment before saying, 'This blade was lost, and well lost. Where did you find it?'

'In the Vritra's dreaming place,' she said. 'It was planted in a skeleton's—'

'Spine,' he finished for her.

'Aye. How did you know?'

'*Skuldraig* means "backbiter." That is its way.'

'But who is he?' Magpie asked. 'Sure it can't be the devil – those skeletons were long dead, and besides, this devil, he leaves nothing behind!'

'Devil? Foolish faerie, Skuldraig is the blade itself! It is cursed to slay any who wield it but the one for whom it was forged.'

'B-but . . .' Magpie stammered. '*I* have wielded it!'

The Djinn's flame eyelids drew together in a vertical blink. 'Have you indeed?' he breathed. Magpie nodded. He asked, 'And pray, what happened when you did?'

'It . . . it *sang*.'

The Magruwen guttered like a wind-licked candle. 'It sang for you?' Again he demanded, 'Who are you, faerie?'

'Magpie Wind—'

'Nay, but who *are* you? Who made you?'

'What do you mean, Lord?' Magpie asked, pushing away from him on her wings as he flared bright and hot once more.

'You weave the Tapestry, and you wield the champion's blade and it sings for you when it should slay you? Faerie, you too should be a skeleton with a knife in its back. Why do you live?'

Magpie heard all he said, Tapestry and skeleton and all, but one word caused her to gasp. 'Champion?'

'I forged this blade for Bellatrix and no other!' His voice seethed, and gusts of heat crackled around him.

Awestruck and shaking, Magpie carefully set the blade on the cavern floor and backed away, Calypso at her side. 'I'm sorry, Lord Magruwen,' she said. 'I should never have taken it—'

'You mistake me, little bird,' he said. 'Pick it up. Skuldraig has suffered you to live. It's yours, should you risk the use of it again. Many devils has it subdued in its day.'

Magpie picked the knife back up and looked at it, in awe of it and afraid. Bellatrix had held it, aye, but how many spines had known it since? She slid it warily into its sheath. 'Lord Magruwen,' she said. 'Will it subdue *this* devil?'

'I told you. He is beyond you!'

'The trees are calling him the Blackbringer—'

'Blackbringer! Call him what you choose, he will devour you just the same. Go now, faerie.'

Magpie hung her head unhappily. She wanted to ask him more questions, but he was withdrawing deeper into his cave, and she sensed she was dismissed. 'Thank you, Lord,' she said, bowing deeply before turning to Calypso to go.

She had reached the door when the Djinn said, 'Wait.'

Magpie turned back, hopeful.

'You may choose a treasure,' he said.

'Oh.' She couldn't hide her disappointment. She looked at the glittering trove scattered across the cavern floor. Maybe there was some magical thing among the jewels that could help her, but if she had days she wouldn't know how to choose! 'Thank you, Lord,' she said, taking a halting step toward the treasure. A spiral of light caught her eye then, and as she turned, it seemed to sink and disappear into the sparkling piles. Magpie felt the air pulse and urge her forward. She went where it took her and knelt over a spilled coffer of gold pieces. She dredged through them and came up with a familiar thing grasped in her hands.

She smiled, well pleased. 'My Lord?' she asked, holding it up for his approval. It was the acorn he had spit from the cake. 'You said there was no thousand years in this nut. There surely won't be unless I get it in some good ground.'

Those vertical eyes drew together like a serpent's as the Magruwen blinked. He nodded.

Magpie and Calypso backed out the door and bowed again, calling 'Thank you!' as they left.

Long did the Magruwen stare after her, watching with his inner eyes as radiant traceries unfurled in her wake, rampant as vines. The treasure had been a final test. It had always been a test, even in the long-gone days of visitors. Those through whom the Tapestry sang true chose well, much as long ago the healer Grayling had chosen her knitting needles from among the gems and flashier things. Those corrupt of spirit called down false notes from the Tapestry, and they chose ill. The sword Duplicity, for instance, doubled everything it cut, even enemies, so that where one devil stood, once slashed with Duplicity, there stood two. And sorrow to the swordsman who multiplied his foes even as he smote them!

The lass, Magpie, had chosen true. He hadn't doubted she would. But he hadn't guessed . . . she had made his test look like a sprout's game! What she had shown him, drawing that common acorn out of a spill of gold, would vibrate through the Tapestry for ages to come – if the Tapestry survived that long. Even as he watched, her traceries wove and pleached their way through the ancient threads like something living, sending out many roots, curving and coiling inextricably through the warp and weft.

He saw it plain as a picture.

There was *not* a thousand years in the acorn, because in three hundred the massive oak that was to spring from it would be struck by lightning and charged through with mystery. The Djinn squeezed shut his inner eyes, thinking sure he read wrong the new magic the faerie was even now weaving, unaware of it though she might be.

But there it was. Flutes carved of the oak's heartwood would sing directly to the Tapestry. They would sing like many pure, interlacing voices, working upon the threads in a way no faerie could when visioning glyphs. They would draw down from it such complex magicks as the Magruwen himself had never gifted to faeries, that would humble the power of those of the Dawn Days as greatly as a single sprout's voice is humbled beside a choir of seraphim.

Such power for faeries . . . the Djinn had an impulse to stop her from planting the nut, to unweave the threads before it was too late, but something stilled his fingers, some hint of familiarity, like a forgotten dream.

In all the dreams of his long slumber, coming one upon the next like waves upon a shore, had he dreamed a new golden age for faeries? Had he dreamed to life this one who would bring it? He couldn't remember. He couldn't believe it. How could he have forgiven in his dreams the faerie betrayal he had never ceased mourning in his heart?

Watching the mesmerizing dance of new threads in the Tapestry, the Magruwen was sure of only one thing: he wasn't tired. For the first time in a long, long time, he wasn't tired at all.

17

'*IF SHE HOLLERS, LET HER SING* . . .' WHISPERED BATCH, EYES AGLEAM as he peered out of the shadows. '*The lovely song of a faerie scream* . . .' A thick rope of yellowish drool dangled from his lip. Slowly he sucked it back up into his mouth and savored it, his eyes never shifting from the wings that fanned gently before him in the late golden light. He felt like an impkin at a sweet shop window with a pocketful of gold.

He'd never seen finer wings.

He wanted to taste them. He wanted to wear them.

He crept closer. The faerie was a lass, kneeling in her garden murmuring to the flowers. He didn't care a twitch for her. In the grip of his obsession, she was truly no more to him than a bit of stuff attached to his new wings, something to be rid of.

He launched himself at her and saw her start to turn just before his weight slammed her to the ground, facedown. She screamed, and Batch did nothing to stop her. There was no one near to hear. He'd made sure of it. He wound his tail round her ankles, braced his long pink feet against her back, and reached for the solid joints where her wings met her shoulders.

She screamed and screamed. Many voices joined hers, earthy voices and wispy, rough as bark and soft as moss, and their screams radiated into Dreamdark as more flowers joined in, and more trees. But it little mattered. Batch didn't hear it, and nor did anything else not rooted to the earth. The only faerie alive in the world who could hear those voices was pinned facedown with an imp on her back. His fingers curled lovingly around her wing joints, and he began to pull.

'I think he liked ye, 'Pie,' Calypso told Magpie as they flew above the forest.

Magpie snorted. 'Sure, he just adored me. Remember that part when he said I should be a skeleton? That was sweet.'

'Ach, well, count yer blessings. Ye're alive.'

'Aye, for true.' She spoke of it lightly, but Magpie was shaken and shivered by her ordeal in the Djinn's cave. She wished she had time to write a letter to her parents, but time was something she didn't have.

'What next?' asked Calypso.

'That Rathersting lad said his kinsmen disappeared at Issrin. I reckon that's our best lead. We'll go see what we see.'

'But darlin', ye heard all the Magruwen said, neh, 'bout this thing being beyond ye?'

'Aye, I heard. I'm just thinking to spy, and try to get a look at the skiving thing at last. I won't go take him on, I promise.'

Uneasily, Calypso said, 'All right, all right.'

'I want to see Poppy first, so she knows we're not scorched. And give her this acorn to plant.'

Afternoon was just beginning to fold into evening as they spiraled in toward the Manygreen lands. Just seconds before her feet set down, Magpie heard the scream. She landed in a crouch and swept the garden with a searching look. Calypso likewise went on alert. The muffled cry came again from beyond a frill of ferns, and in that instant, Magpie was airborne again, rocketing through the lacy fronds.

She saw the creature standing on Poppy for only the briefest moment before she somersaulted in the air and crashed feetfirst into it, sending it sprawling. The impact spun her aside but she landed neat as a cat on all fours, her eyes flashing at the thing that tumbled into a heap, crushing ferns beneath it. She knew it at once by its long rat's tail and its soft reek of decay. A scavenger imp.

Poppy jumped to her feet and fluttered her wings wildly. 'Magpie!' she cried.

'Poppy! Are you okay?'

The imp cowered beneath the wild wing beats and squawking descent of Calypso, and Poppy fluttered her wings again, trying to look at them over her shoulder. 'I think so . . .' she said, distraught. 'He . . . he was trying to take my wings!'

'*Take* them?' Magpie repeated.

'He was trying to rip them off!'

Magpie turned to the imp, her chin lowered and eyes glinting dangerously. 'Trying to mutilate a faerie?' she cried.

'Neh!' He was wailing in his desperate wheeze of a voice and trying to squirm away from Calypso's sharp talons. 'I just wanted to fly away! Don't take me back to master!'

'Cussed vermin!' the crow croaked, and Magpie saw the imp peer up at him with one squinting eye, then fall limp with relief.

'Blessings!' Batch whimpered. 'I thought ye was the vultures!'

'Vultures?' Magpie demanded, remembering the lad had mentioned vultures. 'And master? What master?'

The imp looked at her, snuffled, and gave her a meek, imploring smile. 'Missy faerie call off the bad birdy?'

Calypso was standing on Batch much as Batch had stood on Poppy, and Magpie knelt in front of him. She smelled scorched fur and saw how his whiskers were frizzled like burnt broom straws. In the scamper language she'd learned from Snoshti as a babe, she asked, 'What happened to you, imp? Fall in a fire?'

'Fire fell on me!'

She gave him a penetrating look, remembering how the Magruwen had accused her of being a treasure hunter. '*First an imp and now a faerie*,' he had said.

'You been to the Magruwen!'

'The who what?' Batch asked. But Magpie had seen his eyes jump open at the mention of the Djinn's name, and she knew. Vultures, master, and a trip to the Magruwen? It added up to one thing: this imp was in the middle of her mystery.

She nodded to Calypso to let him sit up. 'Bold caper, imp,' she said, musing. 'The Djinn King himself!'

'I don't know what yer talking about!'

'However did you find him?' Magpie asked with a hint of admiration. 'He's been missing for ever so long! Sure someone must've *told* you where he was. A faerie told you, I guess.'

'Faerie!' he scoffed. 'Faeries couldn't find yolk in an egg! *I* found him!'

'For true?' Magpie asked with apparent delight. 'You found the Magruwen? That's a . . . a miracle!'

'It's a gift,' Batch told her with a dignified sniff.

'Aye, I've heard tell. What's it called, the . . . *serenity*?'

'Serendipity!' he corrected.

'Aye, that's it!' Well Magpie knew what it was called: the serendipity, that gift of the scavengers that looked like eerie good luck. Batch and the scant handful of imps like him possessed the uncanny ability of finding just what they needed, just when they needed it. *Reliably*. That should have made them worthy allies in these times, but unfortunately they were also heartless, reclusive, nasty, and obsessive to the point of madness. They couldn't even stand one another, which accounted for the very small number of them in existence.

On occasion faeries had tried to bend the serendipity to their purposes. Even Magpie's parents had once enlisted a scavenger imp named Lick to help them find Amitav Ev, the lost temple of the Ashmedai. And he *had* found it. And looted it. And disappeared. To this day they had no idea where the ruins lay. They had learned the hard way that, whoever else might claim the title, a scavenger imp has but one master: itself.

But they *were* quite susceptible to flattery. Continuing in her innocent way, Magpie remarked, 'I guess your master knew you were the only one who could do it, neh?'

'The only one!' he boasted. 'There are ballads, ye know, missy, about the emperor of lost things! Sure: ye've heard 'em? That's me, Batch Hangnail, king of scavengers!'

'Well, I sure hope you got your share of the treasure!'

She wasn't sure what response she expected, but it wasn't the imp dissolving into a lump of moaning, sloppy woe. 'T-t-treasure . . .' he stuttered with trembling lips, then started to bawl, his great nose leaking syrupy streaks down his snout.

Enough of this, she thought. 'All right, you.' She shoved him with her foot. 'I want some answers, d'you hear me?'

He went on bawling.

'Who's your master? What is he? And where?'

His bawling intensified. He groped for the tip of his bejeweled tail and shoved it into his mouth, making little mewling noises as he sucked at it, like a kitten at its dam's teat. Magpie exchanged looks of disgust with Calypso and Poppy, and then she just stood there, uncertain what to do next.

'Look . . . *Batch*,' she said finally. 'Sure you had no choice. The hungry one *made* you help him.'

He cracked open one eye to peer at her, still snuffling wetly.

'And I'll do what I can to help you—'

'Ha!' He gave a high, crazed laugh. 'What could a twig like ye do? He got them warriors like a snack!'

'The Rathersting! With the tattoos? Imp, what did he do to them?' she demanded. 'What does he do to them all?'

'One by one into the dark!'

Magpie sighed. Dark. Aye, dark. Hadn't she seen plenty of dark in plenty of memories? 'But what *is* he?' she cried in frustration.

Batch just shook his head and whispered, '*Beast of night with flesh of smoke, wearing darkness like a cloak . . .*'

'Jacksmoke,' she snapped. 'Poetry. That's about as helpful as nursery tales. At least tell me what he sent you to the Magruwen for. I know you went for treasure. What did your master want?'

A glint of malice lit Batch's pathetic, slobber-slicked face. 'Nasty cheat,' he muttered. 'Cheating nasty meat . . . a turnip!'

'A turnip,' Magpie repeated flatly.

'A measly scorched nasty turnip! Waste of a treasure!' His eyes squeezed shut, and his little fists clenched and unclenched, and he was such a picture of misery that Magpie found she believed him.

To Calypso she muttered, 'What would a devil want with a turnip?'

Calypso shrugged. 'Why would the Magruwen *have* a turnip?'

'Flummox me! Look, feather, let's take the imp with us. I'm not through with him yet, sure he knows more than he's saying, but if we don't fly it'll be dark before we can reach Issrin—'

'Neh, not Issrin!' the imp cried with such terror that Magpie knew Issrin was indeed the place. 'Not there! Don't take me there!'

'Why? Is he still there?' she demanded.

'Until the dark comes and frees him from the shadows . . . but the night is like a sea to him, to swim where he will.'

'Then we'd better hurry—' Magpie suddenly tensed, listening. Calypso knew the look, so he wasn't surprised – but Poppy was – when Magpie suddenly whirled around and flicked herself fast toward the bushes. They heard a cry of 'Miminy!' in a gent's voice, and a tussle, and then a figure tumbled from the underbrush with Magpie leaping out nimbly behind. 'Spy!' she growled.

'Poppy!' gasped the gent, and they all saw who it was.

'Kex!' Poppy cried. 'What were you doing there?'

Kex Winterkill got to his feet, glared at them all, and brushed moss off his satin breeches, grimacing to see stains. 'Ahem—' he said. 'M'lady calls for you, cousin.'

Poppy let out a hiss of exasperation. 'Tell her I'm busy!'

'Indeed?' he said, eyeing Batch with undisguised contempt and flicking unloving looks at Magpie and Calypso too. 'Do you imagine she'll be pleased to learn you prefer the company of low creatures to her royal self?'

'I don't care what pleases her! Tell her I've no more potions for her!'

'Ach,' said Magpie. 'Is her hair still—?'

'Aye.' Poppy nodded. 'That spell's pulled tight. I've done all I know how. Kex, it's beyond me! Call for Orchidspike!'

Kex stiffened. 'You well know Orchidspike refuses to attend, m'lady.'

'Aye, I know. And now, so do I.'

Kex reddened. 'Think hard on your choice of friends, Poppy. After all, these . . . *actors* . . . are surely soon to grace Dreamdark with the priceless gift of their departure, and then you may find yourself quite . . . *unwelcome* . . . in polite society.'

Poppy looked him boldly in the eyes and said, 'I want nothing to do with Queen Vesper's society! I never did!'

Before Kex could reply, they were all distracted by a chortle that burst from Batch. 'Queen Vesper, did I hear you say?' he asked. '*Queen* Vesper?'

'Don't touch her name with your foul tongue, irkmeat!' cried the gent.

Batch laughed, and a vicious smile transformed his face. All traces of the woebegone sniveler were gone in an instant and he became, again, the predator that would have torn Poppy's wings from her back without a thought. 'Tell *Queen* Vesper that Batch Hangnail sends his regards.'

18

BEHIND A PAINTED SCREEN, LADY VESPER HEARD THE NAME 'Batch Hangnail,' and her lips and knuckles went white.

'Lady?' ventured Kex when she didn't respond.

'Aye, Lord Winterkill,' she said, an unaccustomed catch in her musical voice. 'An *imp* . . . is it?'

'Aye. There's no question, that lass is in league with him. What company she keeps! Imps and crows! It's shocking my cousin is consorting with—'

'Sir,' she cut in impatiently. 'What manner of imp is he?'

'Foulest I've ever beheld, Lady. Encrusted with filth! But strange – his whole tail was covered in the finest diamond rings!'

Kex couldn't see his lady. Indeed, he hadn't laid eyes on her since before the play, when she had retired to her chamber and refused to come out. If he could have seen her, he might scarcely have recognized her. The hair was the least of it – it was tight-tied in three layers of silk kerchiefs and further bound in pearl strands, with Bellatrix's circlet at its crown. She might have gone out in such a headdress and inspired a new fashion, but for the fact that it . . . *wriggled*. No, it was her face that would have shocked him.

She had drained of all color. Her lips were smashed together and her eyes wild, and all her beauty was quite lost amid the fury, disbelief, outrage, and fear that moved over it fast as storm winds.

'Do you know where they have gone?' came her voice from behind the screen, each syllable sharp as a knife.

'The lass mentioned Issrin Ev, my blossom.'

'Lord Winterkill, I thank you for this news. Kindly leave me now.' Vesper held one hand out to him from behind the screen and he kissed it hungrily.

After he left, she drew back her hand and wiped the drool from it, her lip curled in disgust, the rest of her face contorted with rage. 'The imp is *alive?*' she seethed, grabbing a gilt hand mirror off her vanity table. 'Yet *alive?*' she demanded, peering into it. Her own face was all that looked out, but she seemed to squint beyond her reflection, searching for something deeper.

She swept the tabletop with a furious glance and, not finding a sharp instrument, took the soft pad of her fingertip between her teeth and ripped it open. She didn't even flinch from the pain but only jabbed her finger at the mirror and flung her blood onto it. As soon as it hit the surface, her reflection melted away, and she saw through the glass to the hideous thing trapped inside it.

Its mottled brown skin had the texture of dried gut stretched over a skull, and so crude were its features it seemed to have been sculpted in the dark, and with one obvious omission: it had no mouth. Or rather, its mouth was a mass of scar tissue with no opening. It was pulled so tight it was clear there were teeth beneath, many teeth, and that they were well sharp enough to eat through its own puckered flesh and *make* an opening there, as it had clearly done many times in the past. Abominably, the creature's mouth was a wound that healed shut when it went too long between feedings.

'Gutsuck,' Vesper said with icy control, 'I have just had an interesting piece of news. Batch Hangnail lives.' She paused. 'Is not that odd? I find it so, since you swore to me you had finished him!'

Its eyes were deep black slits, leering back at her.

'But that's not all,' she went on. 'He's here, in Dreamdark!' A trill of laughter came from her lips, high and wild. 'So I summon you forth to do what you swore you had already done. Kill the imp!'

The surface of the mirror distorted as the thing began to push out into the world, but there was a sound like a fizz as its face emerged, and it drew back sharply, welts rising on its skin. Its slit eyes narrowed further as it glared at its mistress.

'Oh! Irksome protection spells!' cried Vesper, just now remembering them. 'Of course you can't come forth in Never Nigh!' With a groan of exasperation she stood, slid the mirror into a deep pocket of her gown, and fluttered to the window. She looked carefully around, then slid out between the curtains to be lost among the trees.

Poppy Manygreen had planted many, many things in her hundred years, and she never tired of the miracle. Each time a seed or nut or bulb awakened to its own unique life, the awe awakened in her anew. Cradling the scorched acorn in her arms now, she marveled that the dreamer king himself had touched it. It seemed to thrum with mystery, and she felt sure the pulse – as Magpie had called it – quickened around it.

By holding out a hand over the soil, a Manygreen could probe for a sweet spot, a nurturing nook of rich earth among the roots and rocks of the ancient forest where a new life could take hold. She found such a spot on a little ridge overlooking Misky Creek, and she was just tucking the nut into its bed when she felt a murmur on the move. A whisper of news flitted from fern to ivy to ash and when she heard what it was she sank quietly out of sight among the leaves.

Only a moment later, Lady Vesper landed downcreek. She drew something out of her pocket and spoke, and Poppy could just barely hear her words over the sluice of the creek. 'To Issrin Ev,' Vesper said. 'Kill Batch Hangnail!' Poppy's eyes widened. What business, she wondered, had the queen with that scavenger? Then her eyes widened further as a misshapen creature squirmed out of the mirror and unpeeled great membranous bat wings that were wrapped tightly round its body.

'Poor starved Gutsuck,' cooed Vesper to it. 'Who knows when you'll eat again. Best you finish off the feathered faerie too. And the crows, if you can stomach the taste of ashtray.'

Gutsuck hunched and went to work on his face, gobbling at his scars from within. With a horrible sound of gnashing and slurping he gnawed open a ragged, fang-filled maw and hissed with a spray of blood, 'Your wish, mistress,' and launched himself into the sky.

19

ACROSS THE FOREST, THE HUNGRY ONE WAS RESTLESS IN HIS crevice in the rock awaiting the onslaught of night. He didn't sleep and didn't dream and never had. If he had dreamed in the Dawn Days, perhaps things would have been different. It was dreams that, like threads, had embroidered the others to this world, while he had roamed and ranged, always restless, bound to nothing.

Such were the humble beginnings of the end of the world: the absence of dreams.

Later, in his prison, in the endless tossing ocean, dreams might have been a companion. Instead, every moment of every millennia had passed, waking and dreamless, in the company of two entities: his hunger and his vengeance. And, having nothing else to play with, he had nurtured them with singular devotion.

When the seal on his bottle had unexpectedly fallen open, it was his hunger that had first burst forth. But those creatures on the boat, they were like water from a wine bottle, an unsettling gulp of nothing. He knew now that they were called *humans* – a new thing, and they interested him not at all. His hunger and his vengeance had led him like a pair of leashed tigers: sometimes pulling in opposite directions, sometimes prowling for the same doomed prey. In Rome his hunger had led him to the devil ripe catacombs beneath the city to feed; his vengeance had guided him to the Vritra.

The Vritra had always been the weakest of the Djinn, but it was still a shock seeing him fallen to such a state. How simple it had been to command a wind to extinguish him for good! The wind had tried valiantly to resist, but in the end it was a slave to its secret name, and the hungry one knew all the secret names. And now he knew more secrets. For the delirious Vritra had babbled in his dreams and told him what he needed to know to unlock the world.

How wonderful.

A pomegranate! How long had he searched before the faeries had at last caught him in their bottle? He would have gone on searching too and would never have guessed that what he sought was a pomegranate. A fruit! Truly, without the fire and color of dreams of his own, he was ill-equipped to imagine the whims of Djinn. But now he didn't have to imagine. He knew.

The world hinged upon a single pomegranate.

The world, such as it was. The Tapestry was threadbare, the Djinn were guttering out, Fade and the other dragons were dead, the champions were long gone, and the faeries that remained, while not as flavorless as that pest species, humans, were a far cry from the faeries of the Dawn Days. Once, a single faerie would have sated him for days, but now he couldn't fill his bottomless hunger no matter how many of them he had.

It riled him. The gnawing hunger distracted him from vengeance. It was primal, inconvenient, an unexpected consequence of his . . . *evolution*. He had been a very different sort of creature once. The Magruwen might have imprisoned him, but this thing he had become, it was his own creation. Through sheer force of will, through vengeance, bitterness, and rage, he had warped himself into what he was now.

He was the Blackbringer.

20

MAGPIE LAY OUTSTRETCHED ON HER BELLY ON A PINE BOUGH above Issrin Ev. It chilled her to see the temple in such a state, its eight great columns leaning like old bones, its entrance obliterated. For the first time she considered the possibility that it might just be her own dark luck to live to witness the end of things. The bitter scorch in the bottom of the well was never coming out again. The old legends were gone, and there would be no new ones.

This was what remained: headless statues, their long shadows, and vultures.

Five vultures perched near the ruined temple facade. There, staring back from the stone, was the symbol for infinity that graced all the temples and that had become such a bitter irony now, four thousand years later. Infinity! Or *not*. Magpie watched the foul birds. The crows and imp were waiting near the mouth of the Deeps where she'd promised Calypso she would join them as soon as she'd gotten a glimpse of the devil. She shivered. Just a glimpse. Soon she would see it. Soon she would know what had laughed as it killed a Djinn.

The sun was all but gone.

Just as the last orange tinge of it drained away behind the hills, a fume issued from a crack in the facade of the temple below.

It neither rose to disperse like smoke nor drifted to settle like fog. It pulsed and constricted into a tight clot of shadow far deeper than the dimming night around it.

Magpie blinked. She squinted at it. She could see the vultures' every feather and even make out the veins in their bloodshot eyes, but of this thing that poured from the shadows she could see nothing but a darkness so profound it stole even the memory of light. And the way it moved . . . it didn't float but seemed to *siphon* itself through the air with a steady, hunting will.

She lay very, very still.

Its eyes . . . though Magpie made no sound, its eyes swiveled straight to her, finding her instantly across the distance and the darkness. A shiver thrilled through her blood. Its eyes were vertical slits like the Magruwen's – she'd never seen eyes like that on a devil! Its gaze burned her mind. And its hunger . . . she felt it like the tug of a tide. It was *tasting* her on the air.

When it spoke, its disembodied voice seemed to come from within her own head, invading her mind, filling it. 'What's this? Ah, a draught of the old wine,' it rasped, and came toward her.

Magpie gathered herself into a crouch on the branch, and though she was loath to invite that voice into her head again, she cried out, 'What are you?'

'I am the heavens with the stars ripped out,' came its whispered reply. 'I am the Blackbringer.' Magpie shook her head to clear the voice from it, but it went on. 'But who are you, faerie? The first taste in this pale place of the old vintage . . . a feast. Be still!'

The voice compelled her to obey it. The fume rose slowly off the ground and she found herself frozen, watching it come. Closer. Closer.

'Magpie!' a voice screamed from the sky, scouring the terrible whisper from her mind. Her head jerked up, and she saw a figure glide overhead.

'Poppy!' Magpie gasped, then looked quickly back down at the darkness sweeping toward her. Gathering herself up, she leapt skyward, twisting to see that the darkness didn't follow. She raced to Poppy. 'Come on!' She grabbed her friend's hand. 'We got to get out of here!'

'Aye,' Poppy gasped, winded and drinking in great gulps of breath. 'Devil . . . coming!'

Magpie swung around to see the thing melting back into the deep shadows below. 'I know,' she said. 'He's down there—'

'Nay! Another—' Poppy cried, just as a winged thing came wheeling over Issrin and let out a piercing cry.

It was one of the ugliest snags Magpie had ever seen. Its mouth was a bloody tatter full of teeth, and its skin was drawn so tight over its sharp skeleton that its bones seemed ready to pierce right through. 'Now *that's* a devil,' she said.

'Vesper set him on you!' Poppy told her, backing away from the thing in horror.

'Eh? That priss has a snag slave?' Magpie asked, dumbfounded.

The hideous thing whirled in the air on its jagged wings and caught sight of Magpie. It hissed, 'Feathered faerie . . .' and licked the bloody edges of its maw.

As it started forward, Poppy cried, 'Magpie! What do we do?'

Magpie shoved Poppy aside as the snag came, and on her sleek wings she darted into its path. It hurtled at her, shrieking, and reached for her. In one fluid motion, Magpie spun and grasped the hooked claw at the crook of its wing and whipped round, straining against it with all her weight. Tilting off-balance, the devil went scudding into a tree trunk.

Magpie glanced at the darkness below as the snag spun and came at her again. This was a dance she knew well, this devil waltz. Many times had she danced it, coaxing the eejits to hurl themselves at her, maneuvering easily out of their way as they thudded again and again into ground or cliff or whatever solid surface was at hand, until they grew dizzy, or tired, or crazed, and then she captured them. She had no time for that now.

She saw the vultures shake open their wings and lurch from their perches. She still felt the hunger of the dark thing lurking in the courtyard below.

She had to get away from here. To get Poppy away.

The snag pulled itself from the tangle of tree branches and leapt for her. If she dodged, it would be headed straight at Poppy. She hovered and let it come. It reached out its clawed hands. It was on her, its breath on her face, hot and reeking, spraying blood with each earsplitting screech. As it reached out with its claws, Magpie's own hands darted toward it, faster, one on each of its wrists. Then her wings swept in a powerful backbeat and she dropped, tugging the devil's arms down so that in its momentum its bony legs spun wildly over its head. She let go and it somersaulted into a pillar with a thud.

Below, the darkness was moving.

Barely fazed by his collision, the snag sprang again.

Skuldraig, Magpie thought, drawing it from its scabbard. '*Many devils has it subdued*,' the Magruwen had said. He had also said, 'It is cursed to slay any who wield it.' Her hand quavered a little and she glanced at the knife, but its weight felt right. The shine of it in the gloom gave her a bloom of strength, and she felt the pulse gather round her and urge her forward.

This time when the snag came at her, she spun aside, grabbed its wing, and jumped on its back as if she were mounting a bird mid-flight. Then she whipped Skuldraig around and pressed the flat of the blade against the snag's foul throat. The crystal keening of the knife's song rang out through the ruins at once, and the devil went limp and began to plummet from the sky. Magpie braced her feet against it, and as she jumped free, she kicked out as hard as she could, sending it spiraling toward the clot of shadow below. Wings twitching, it slid into the Blackbringer like a hand into a pocket, and disappeared.

Silence fell over Issrin. The darkness had swallowed the snag whole, and its caterwauling with it. Magpie looked frantically around for some sign of it, but all she heard was her own breath and the wing beats of the vultures. Then the squawking of crows filled the air and the birds, alerted by the snag's shrieks, came winging out of the trees, fast and loud. The vultures were there rising to meet them, and there was a hideous screech of birds in the night.

What had the Blackbringer done to that devil?

'Magpie!' cried Poppy, and Magpie turned to her, torn, wanting to go help her crows but needing to get Poppy to safety.

She flew to her friend and grabbed her hand. 'Poppy, get away from here, now!' she said when suddenly Poppy's eyes widened in shock. Then her hands were wrenched from Magpie's grasp and she was snatched away so fast Magpie went into a spin. In her surprise, she dropped Skuldraig and heard it clatter to the ground far below.

Vultures and crows wheeled and clashed, and Magpie halted her spin to find herself alone in the sky. Poppy was gone.

Magpie looked wildly around but saw no sign of her friend. 'Poppy!' she screamed.

The beast – the Blackbringer – was pooling in the courtyard below. Magpie saw a white arm reach out of the dark fume of him. A faerie's arm. The fingers grasped and clawed at nothing, then the arm disappeared back into the darkness. 'Poppy!' gasped Magpie. The devil had her. *How?* It took a split second for Magpie's body to respond to the sight of that reaching arm and then she found herself in motion, streaking toward the beast. 'Blackbringer!' she screamed.

It came at her then – the tongue – and she saw how the devil had plucked Poppy from the sky. Fury flared in her; the imp might have mentioned this! Huge and livid, the Blackbringer's tongue came at her fast as a hurled harpoon. Even in her surprise she dodged it easily, and before she could really think what she was doing, she was diving into the void of the Blackbringer, arms outstretched, hoping to find Poppy within, hoping to come out on the other side.

Thinking about it later, over and over, Magpie would know she couldn't have been inside that darkness more than a second. Her speed must have carried her through him in an instant. But that instant would always after live in her mind as a journey.

'*The darkness will rush in like a tide and sweep everything back into the endless ocean,*' the Magruwen had said.

Magpie saw the endless ocean. More than seeing it, she was plunged into it and felt it begin to devour her. There was no breathing here, and no seeing. In the darkness of the end there was no sensation except a desperate fading, the feeling of being a small shadow subsumed by the immensity of night.

Dimming and ebbing and melting.

More than death, and less.

Unmaking.

As the edges of her self began to blur, she saw – she thought she saw – lights throughout the darkness, dull as strewn embers, dim as stars in fog.

Then she was through it, tumbling to the ground. Her brow met rock, and an explosion of pain left her limp.

Vision swimming. The horrible squall of birds. Magpie struggled to revive, felt blood hot on her face, stinging her eyes. She was stunned, couldn't feel her arms and legs, and for a moment she had the strangest feeling that she'd fallen outside of her own body. Then, vaguely, she sensed tangled limbs. Poppy! Poppy was in her arms.

But where was the Blackbringer?

'Magpie?' whispered Poppy, her voice weak.

'It's okay—' Magpie started to say.

Then Poppy screamed, and her body lurched in Magpie's arms. Panicked, Magpie held on and was dragged along with her. The Blackbringer loomed. The long tongue was coiled around Poppy's ankle and he was reeling her back inside him.

With one arm still wrapped around Poppy, Magpie groped for a handhold with the other. She found one and held tight, straining. Through the haze of blood obscuring her vision, she could see Poppy's white face, and their eyes met and held. 'I've got you!' Magpie said. Her feet were braced against a broken statue, and one hand clung to a coiled tree root, but she could feel herself begin to tremble. She was weak, but more than that, she felt . . . insubstantial, like she might dissolve into the air.

And the Blackbringer kept coming. A tide of darkness swallowed Poppy's feet and then her legs. Her eyes pleaded. Magpie tried with all her strength to haul her away, but the tongue, withdrawn back into the dark now, held fast. And Magpie could only watch and hold her as Poppy began to dim.

'Poppy!' she screamed.

But Poppy no longer saw her. Though still half in the world, she was already lost in the dark. She faded. The color drained from her flesh, and, with horror, Magpie realized she could see through her to the ground beneath. Then she couldn't hold her anymore. There was nothing to hold. With a final shimmer, the faint ghost-image of Poppy opened her mouth to scream but no sound came out and she disappeared, leaving only her shadow behind where she had lain.

Magpie lay bleeding on the stone with her arm curled round Poppy's shadow. Then even that was wrenched from her as the Blackbringer dragged it too into the darkness.

There would be no diving in this time to pull Poppy out. She wasn't there. She wasn't anywhere. She had been unmade. She had ceased to be.

The sound inside Magpie's head was terrible. It was the Blackbringer's whisper. 'Aye, the old wine,' it said. 'How wonderful . . .'

And it seemed as if the clot of darkness grew.

21

ACROSS THE MOUTH OF THE DEEPS AND UP THE SLOPE OF Dreamdark Crag, the Rathersting warriors on the castle walls heard the chaos of birds and took flight. The pale moon glittered on their cool knives and bared teeth as they raced toward Issrin Ev, whooping their bloodcurdling battle cries.

Talon was not with them.

Nor was he back at the castle, cursing his wings and his weakness. If he had been, the sun would have risen the next morning on a doomed world. Because if he hadn't already been out stalking vultures, his own two blades wicked in his fists and his eyes ferocious in the gloom, Magpie would not have survived.

And without Magpie Windwitch, neither would the world, for long.

In that dreadful instant when Magpie realized she'd been clinging to a shadow and that Poppy was gone, she leapt away from the Blackbringer and flicked open her wings to flee. But as she struggled skyward, the tongue was suddenly on her, cold and clammy. It whipped round her wings and jerked her back, helpless as a bug.

Her fierce crow brother Maniac descended like a fury and seized the stretched tongue with his talons. It released Magpie at once and snapped back into the darkness quickly . . . so quickly Maniac didn't have time to release it. His feathers riffled, and there was a sound like an intake of breath as he was sucked backward and engulfed in the darkness.

Magpie plummeted fast. It wasn't one of her sharp landings, but a graceless thudding skid down the slope until a headless statue of Bellatrix finally halted her slide. Woozy, she shook her head and tried to lift her wings. Her wings. They didn't respond to the flexion of her shoulders but hung limp.

They had been crushed.

It had all happened so quickly. Maniac was gone before she even hit the ground. Her arms and legs were scraped but unbroken, but Magpie crouched motionless, as if she had no notion how to move without flying. Her breath came shallow and quick, and she had the odd sensation she was just a shadow stretched over the stones. She looked up. The wheeling birds were erratic black shapes against a black sky. And Maniac was gone.

Dizziness overcame her. Time careened off-balance, speeding and slowing as the shrieking of birds warbled from deafening to dull. Blood flowed fast from a gash at her temple. Her head felt hollow. Her vision dimmed. She struggled against it, knowing if she closed her eyes now she would never open them again.

'Lass!' a voice rang out. Dazed, Magpie looked around. ''Pie!' it came again, and to her surprise she spotted the tattooed Rathersting lad. He was perched atop a freestanding pillar in the old courtyard, poised to spring. The clarity of his eyes seemed to sear a path through her confusion, and the world stopped spinning. She wiped the blood away from her eyes and got shakily to her feet. No sooner had she risen than the lad cried out, 'Stay down!'

But it was too late. The Blackbringer had seen her.

Magpie saw the wretched tongue shoot toward her, and the sick certainty of her own doom gathered within her like held breath. She couldn't move, but only watch, mesmerized, as it came for her.

The lad sprang from his perch.

Magpie saw him leap – powerfully – and dive and stretch and reach. And his knife pierced the shooting tongue at its tip, intercepting it and pulling it along with him in his smooth trajectory. Away from her.

The momentum of his dive carried him along and the tongue – skewered on his blade – went, too. When it had swung to the end of its arc, the lad still clinging to the end of it, it began to swerve back in the direction of the Blackbringer. Magpie breathed again to gasp, seeing the lad hurtling toward the beast. But a tree loomed in the way, and the lad hung on tight to his knife as his momentum whipped him around it, again and again, around and around until the ghoulish tongue was spooled around the tree trunk like twine. Then Talon reared back, paused, gathered all his strength, and drove his second knife into the liver-colored flesh like a nail, pinning it to the wood beneath.

It twitched, and held.

Knifeless now, he looked at Magpie. 'Go!' he screamed.

The tongue struggled and the Blackbringer, the deep black core of him, swept toward the tree to free it. The sky remained a battleground of birds, and Magpie saw Calypso and Bertram side by side, beating back a giant vulture that was trying to reach its master, perchance to free him.

'I can't!' Magpie screamed back to Talon. 'I can't fly!'

He leapt, somersaulting in the air and landing at her feet. 'Neither can I,' he said impatiently.

Magpie noticed his wings and her mouth formed an *O* of surprise. He'd been wearing the skin when she met him in West Mirth, so she hadn't seen before . . . his wings. Even fully extended, they barely reached past his shoulders. They were clearly far too small to support him in flight. Magpie's eyes darted from Talon's wings back to his face. A scamperer!

Urgently he growled, 'So we run!' Then he grabbed her hand and dragged her after him, across the temple floor in long strides and down the crumbling stair into the Deeps.

22

Almost as soon as the deeps swallowed them, Talon felt the lass struggle, pulling at his hand, slowing him. He looked back and saw her face was ghostly pale beneath the blood that drenched it, and her luminous eyes were growing dim. With tremendous effort she brought her weary eyes into focus and said 'The crows!' and tried to turn back.

'Wait!' Talon said. He caught her under one arm just as she collapsed.

'I won't leave them!' she gasped. 'They're my clan!'

Uncertain what to do, he carried her into a tree with him to see what was happening back at the temple. He scampered easily up it with one arm, supporting her with the other. They reached the top of the tree just as the Rathersting war party hove into view, whooping, and began to swoop past.

'Nettle!' Talon hollered, seeing his sister. She did a double take and swerved, quickly commanding the others. They swung round and circled Talon and Magpie, hanging in the air like wasps.

'Talon!' Nettle said, staring. 'Who is that lass?'

'I don't know,' he answered. 'Listen well. The beast that got Papa and the others, it's in Issrin.'

'Let's get the creeper, then!' his uncle Orion snarled. 'To war!'

The three younger faeries began to answer with shouts but Talon halted them with a sharp, 'Nay!' and commanded, 'You'll stay well clear of it!'

His uncle, the chief's own battle-scarred brother, regarded him with astonishment.

'I've just seen what it can do. Stay well above the treetops. It has a wicked long tongue. Don't get in range of it. Your only plan' – he glanced at the lass, who was struggling valiantly to stay conscious – 'is to stay alive and save the crows. Do you hear me? Save the crows. Now! To battle!'

Talon – 'Prince Scuttle' – who was usually just the wistful shape growing small on the ramparts behind them as the war parties whooped away, spoke with such kingly command that his cousins and uncle and even his sister stared at him for a moment in blank surprise.

Nettle rallied first. 'To save the crows!' she cried, raising her knife.

The others echoed her.

'I'm taking her to Orchidspike,' Talon told Nettle quickly. 'Bring the crows there.'

Nettle nodded and whirled away. Talon didn't linger to watch the battle. He glanced at the lass just as her eyes flickered shut and didn't reopen. He gathered her against him with one arm, scampered down from the tree, and ran.

Orchidspike met him at her cottage door and gasped to see the bloodied lass in his arms. 'Bring her in, lad.'

He eased past her into the cottage and carried the lass straight to the little room where Orchidspike kept a bed for patients. He laid her on it and looked at her anxiously. She hadn't once regained consciousness during the journey through the Deeps.

She was white as a bone against the black-dried blood that painted her face.

Orchidspike came with cloths and hot water and started to fuss over her, cleaning the blood from her face and, Talon knew, visioning powerful healing glyphs that would wrap the lass like invisible bandages of magic.

'I think her name is something like Pie . . .' ventured Talon after a while.

The old healer looked up at him. '*Pie*? Not Magpie!' she exclaimed. 'Eyes like aquamarines?' she asked him, to which he blushed and nodded gruffly.

'Little Magpie Windwitch!' said the healer. 'I've been wondering when she'd come home.'

'Home?'

'Aye. Well, she was born in Dreamdark, but left as a tiny thing. Her father was a Never Nigh lad.'

'What clan?'

'Robin? None. He was a foundling, raised by Widow Candlenight in the bookshop in Never Nigh. Sure you heard the story. The babe who hatched from a robin's egg in the widow's maple?'

'Don't tell me that story's true!'

'The widow still has the eggshell. How he came there is a mystery. Such a lovely lad!' She leaned close over Magpie and began to ply a fine needle through the flesh of her brow, closing the wound so artfully it would leave no scar. 'Her mother, now,' she went on, 'she's not a mystery so much as a marvel. Daughter of the West Wind himself!'

'An elemental! She said her grandfather wore a skin.'

'Aye. He was even known to come to dances in it from time to time in Never Nigh, looking just like a blustery old codger and playing a fine whisker fiddle when called upon.' She finished her stitching and tied a final knot in the nearly invisible thread at Magpie's brow.

'Will she be okay?' Talon asked.

'I hope. What happened to her, lad?'

'It was the devil that got my folk.'

Alarmed, Orchidspike asked, 'Devil? Is it captured?'

'Nay. We barely escaped it! Never seen such a thing, like it was the dark come to life.'

Orchidspike shivered and laid her hand on Magpie's brow, conjuring stronger glyphs of healing over her.

'Lady, are we safe here?' Talon asked. 'Perhaps we should remove to the castle while this thing roams.'

'Aye, perhaps we should.'

Magpie slept for more than a day without so much as stirring. Even the jostling trip to Rathersting Castle didn't wake her. Many a curious tattooed face turned to stare as the strange lass was carried unconscious to Princess Nettle's chamber. As for the half dozen wounded and battle-scarred crows fussing after her, tracking blood and feathers up the winding stair, they were known to the warriors already. The war party had arrived, whooping, just in time to see the huge stinking vultures fleeing scared while the crows, one-tenth their size at most, even puffed with the fury of battle, chased after.

The vultures had been routed, and the crows' reputations preceded them to Rathersting Castle. Warriors saluted the bedraggled flock in the corridors and they nodded back, distracted, all their focus on Magpie.

Orchidspike assured them all she would awaken.

Fretting like biddies, they waited. Nettle's little room was so crowded with crows that every time Talon contrived to pass by the door and check on Magpie, some ragged crow part would be tufting out of it, a tail or a wing, as if all six crows could not quite fit in at once, but couldn't be persuaded to wait outside. Orchidspike just shrugged, forbade smoking, and made hearty use of her elbows when she needed to reach the bedside.

Talon slouched around the castle, restless and a wee bit peeved his home had been overrun by birds. He wouldn't consider that he might be jealous of the warrior's welcome they'd received, or because the lass whom *he* had saved belonged to *them*, and that while *they* cradled her and crooned to her, *he* couldn't so much as get a glimpse of her through all those feathers.

They'd thanked him, sure, with gusto and smothering wing hugs and jarring brotherly smacks on the back. And Nettle gave him a great proud grin. He was proud of himself, too – he'd saved her, and Orchidspike said she'd be okay. But still he was anxious. He lurked in his room next door where he'd be able to hear the crows' voices and know when she woke, but the hours passed and he ran out of reasons for lurking, and at last he had to go see to his own folk.

When she did wake, the first thing Magpie did was count crows. It was the middle of the night and the weary birds had finally fallen asleep, slumped against walls and snoring softly. 'Six,' she whispered, and Calypso heard her and opened his eyes.

'Maniac,' he murmured.

'I know. Saving me.'

'I didn't see, 'Pie.'

'Poppy, too.'

'Aye. That I saw.'

Magpie's quiet sobbing woke the other crows. They touched her lightly with their feathertips, mourning, too, and shaken to see their lass cry.

'Darlin',' said Bertram. 'Maniac wouldn't like to see you like this.'

'He's been so mad at me,' she said, her voice smaller than the crows had ever heard it. 'I . . . I made him be Bellatrix . . . and then there was the porcupine . . . and it's been ever so long since I've told him I—' She looked stricken and didn't finish her thought.

'He knew, Mags,' said Mingus in his low, gruff voice. 'He might puff up and act mad but he'd do anything for ye. Even die. We all would.'

'*Die*?' repeated Magpie. A shadow of anger crossed her face. 'That's not death,' she whispered, thinking of the leeching, sucking darkness.

'Then what . . . ?' ventured Calypso cautiously.

Magpie shook her head. 'I don't know.' She remembered the look on Poppy's face as she disappeared, her pleading eyes, her final silent scream. 'Not death,' she said, 'not proper death,' and a look of desolation swept over her features, erasing the spark of anger and leaving her blank. The crows didn't know what to do. The blankness was worse than the uncertain sleep or the crying, because her eyes were open but she was lost somewhere inside, and they didn't know what to say to make it right.

23

'It seems Windwitch lasses only come to me broken,' said Orchidspike in her matter-of-fact way. 'You know it's how I met your parents too?' she asked as she eased open Magpie's crumpled wings to examine them. 'Ach,' she muttered when she saw the extent of the damage. 'Wadded up like a bad poem.' She smoothed them carefully, humming.

Slumped at the edge of the bed with her back to the healer, Magpie said nothing.

'Your father wrote poems, you know,' Orchidspike went on. 'There was such a litter of them around him while he waited for your mother to wake up. We didn't even know her name yet, then. She'd just fallen from the sky!'

'Probably scrapping with a witch, knowing Lady Kite,' said Calypso.

'Aye, the witch Stain it was, who was not ever seen again, by the by.' Orchidspike nodded. 'These Windwitch lasses are not to be meddled with, well you know.'

The crows squawked their agreement, but Magpie's eyes were far away. Frowning at her silence, Orchidspike went on, her voice cheery. 'Robin saw her fall from the sky and land in the cattails at the edge of Lilyvein Pond. Scratched and bruised and unconscious, a strange lass with her wings torn to ribbons! So he gathered her right into his arms and carried her to me!'

The lass seemed not to be listening, but just outside the door, someone was. Talon leaned against the wall and heard every word.

Orchidspike carefully smoothed open the folds and furls of Magpie's limp wings, trying not to rip the tender membrane along the creases. She went on talking in a casual voice, though her face was somber. 'Their first glimpse of each other's eyes came as he carried her, so close their breath was on each other's lips. His eyes were blue as the robin's egg he hatched from, and when she woke again hours later, it was that blue she looked for. He was sitting right there, waiting, and when they saw each other, I swear there was a fizz of magic in the air. Even I felt it.'

Talon recalled the way the air had pulsed when his hands had touched Magpie's in West Mirth, and his face grew hot.

'They're still like that!' said one of the crows.

'I believe it. I never saw two faeries that much in love, and at first glance! She told us her name was Kite, after the little hawk with the forked tail . . .' The healer winced as Magpie's left wing tore along a particularly harsh crease. If Magpie felt it, she didn't flinch. Calypso's eyes darted anxiously between her damaged wings and her blank face.

Through a veil of shock, Magpie was dimly aware of a voice. She had a fleeting vision of her father's eyes, but it faded. Her thoughts sank back into the darkness. Surely she'd left herself there. What sat here in the world looked enough like her to fool the others, but it was an illusion – a shell echoing with the drone of the endless ocean. She was back in the darkness, where she could find Poppy and Maniac and guide them out. She hoped. Because if she wasn't there with them, they were alone. And if she wasn't there, where was she? Not here. She knew the feel of her own skin and this wasn't it, this blurred and fragile shell. It couldn't be.

Exchanging a worried look with Calypso, Orchidspike went on in her chatty tone, 'Robin asked her all about the world he'd only read of in books, and what a picture she wove of beyond! Flocks of macaws that swoop hundreds-strong through the sultry bowers of rain forests, hollow mountains that cough fire, striped cats as big as cattle, and faeries who ride to war on lizardback with fangs pushed through their earlobes. Shooting stars, hooded snakes, spiny trees, islands of ice cutting through the sea like slow ships! And sure you lot have seen all that with your own eyes, but to Robin? It was like a dream.

'I had to shoo him out so she could rest, but not feet nor wings would carry him away, and he slept outside her window and she found him there, and this time it was *he* who woke to the sight of *her* eyes, and after that there was no question of parting! Do you know they found a frog who would marry them that very night?'

'That very night?' repeated Pup.

'Aye! And they drifted off together on a lily pad down Spinney Creek. After a week, when Kite's wings had healed, Robin brought his bride back to Never Nigh.' Orchidspike's look of fond remembrance became clouded. 'She was not well received.'

'Lady Kite? Why not?' asked Pup.

Orchidspike shrugged. 'Half the lasses were in love with Robin themselves. How was Kite to make friends among them? Nay, she was never happy here. It was good you birds came along when you did!'

'And good for us,' added Bertram. 'If not for her long-life potions, we'd be dust long since.'

'And how spry you are! 'Tis a fine bit of sparkle!'

'Aye, she tricked it off a witch doctor. Wicked lot, but they have their uses,' answered Calypso.

In the corridor, Talon's head was swimming with witches and witch doctors, hooded snakes and love at first glance and long-life potions. Such a world beyond Dreamdark! He could well imagine how Robin must have felt back then – but without the love part, sure. Of course, without that.

' 'Tis a bad crush, indeed,' Orchidspike said in a low voice to Calypso, over by the window. 'But I can mend it. Don't frazzle yourself.'

'But Lady, it en't just the wings. I don't like the look in her eyes. It's like she en't inside herself.'

'She's in there, dear. She's just gone deep. She's in shock.'

'But what if . . .' Calypso hesitated. 'What if it *did* something to her, right? That devil.'

Orchidspike considered this. 'Do you know what it was?'

'It's being called . . . Blackbringer.'

Orchidspike raised her eyebrows. 'Blackbringer?'

'Aye, Lady. D'ye know of it?'

Her bright eyes drifted into memories, back and back through the centuries. She said, 'He was just a fireside story, something to frighten bad sprouts. A bogeyman, like old Rawhead.'

'Ye're saying he weren't real?'

'Nay, I don't know. If he ever was real, it was long before my time. Understand, bird, no devil has troubled Dreamdark all my long life, and much longer still. Not since the Dawn Days.'

'Ye think anyone could remember that far? Remember the old stories?'

'I can't think who.' Orchidspike shook her head wistfully.

'We could ask the trees?' suggested Calypso.

'Ah,' Orchidspike answered sadly. 'Bless us, we lost that language long ago.'

Calypso cocked his head. 'Truly? Flummox me, I had no notion how rare she was.'

'Who, bird?'

'Poppy Manygreen, Lady. Magpie's friend. She could speak with 'em.'

'What?' the healer asked abruptly, startling Calypso. 'A Manygreen? A faerie with that gift? Here, in Dreamdark?'

Calypso nodded.

'A lass?'

Again he nodded.

'But . . . where is she now?'

'Lady?' Calypso scratched his head with his foot. 'She's the one the devil got last night. She's gone.'

Orchidspike was silent, and Calypso watched, alarmed, as her expression went slack with tragedy. She lifted trembling hands and laid her face in them. A shudder went through her, and Calypso heard her whisper, 'I'd stopped looking.'

Western Dreamdark lay quiet under a heavy sky. No smoke curled from the chimney of the healer's cottage, and the hamlets on the Sills were all deserted. In Pickle's Gander and East Mirth, laundry snapped forgotten on the lines as a wind gathered and shutters began to slam. The faeries had flown.

They were tucked safe into the great hall of Rathersting Castle, where the fireplace alone was bigger than most cottages. The sprouts were whooping round the high eaves like warriors, but the older folk clustered together, tense and whispering. A summer storm was weighing down heavy as an iron lid upon Dreamdark. And out there in the blustering trees, they knew, something lurked. It had swallowed their neighbors in the night and snatched the warrior chief from the sky.

The lady of the castle and the young prince and princess had been to speak with them. Nettle had held Lyric in her arms while the lass wept over the dark fate of her betrothed. Talon had painted blackberry juice tattoos on the sprouts' faces and given them warrior names like 'Spike' and 'Slash.' But there was nothing they could say that would ease the faeries' worries. Indeed, their own faces were pale under their ink and they seemed weary, and troubled, and grim.

In Nettle's bed, Magpie hugged her feather skirt, which contained the last remnant of Maniac, and stared at the ceiling. Whether or not she had truly left herself behind in the dark, her thoughts, at least, were trapped there and wandering blind.

In the adjacent parlor, Orchidspike was slumped in a rocking chair, but she wasn't rocking. One of her precious djinncraft knitting needles had rolled off her lap and she hadn't noticed, so lost was she in her regret. She was dreaming of an apprentice, bright with curiosity and power, to whom she could at last pass her secrets. Her remorse was like an ache that rode her heartbeat out through her entire body. She'd given up too soon. She'd stopped looking, and missed her.

Messages had been dispatched to all corners of Dreamdark and Never Nigh, too, but with Magpie still silent no one had thought to tell of poor Poppy Manygreen's sad end. Out in the gathering wind, a search party of her kin was combing the woods and calling out for her, anxiety turning to anguish in their voices as the day bore on.

The worst-injured of the crows, Bertram, Pigeon, and Swig, were seeing the others off from the ramparts. Calypso looked up at the iron-gray sky just as the first raindrops fell, heavy as berries.

'Fine flying weather,' he said, his grim voice at odds with his cracked grin.

'Hurry back, blackguards, ye hear?' said Swig, who sported a new eye patch as a result of a vulture's talon gouge. 'No stopping at the tavern without me.'

'Aye, Cyclops, sure,' piped Pup. 'Calm yer pepper.'

'Cyclops?'

'Hush and no bickering,' said Calypso sharply. 'Keep 'Pie company, ye ken?' His voice softened. 'Try to get her to talk about it, if ye can.'

'Shivers me to see her like this,' said Bertram, his voice weak since being throttled by a stinking vulture foot.

'And me.'

'Ye going to bring that bossy little beetleherd back here?' asked Pigeon, whose left wing was crisscrossed with neat stitches.

'Bring her? Neh. She won't fly, that one. She has her own ways of getting place to place,' said Calypso. 'But I'll get her to come.'

'Hurry,' said Swig again.

'We'll try.'

The three tired birds heaved into the driving rain. After an hour's wet slog across the vastness of the forest, rain sheeting from their feathers with every wing beat, Calypso, Pup, and Mingus landed at last on the little green above Snoshti's underground village. One glance at their caravans had them squawking and cursing. 'We been ransacked! We been looted!' hollered Pup.

Mingus went to gather up the costumes that spilled out the open doors into the rain and hung them up carefully inside to dry. As an afterthought, he fetched Magpie's book from her bunk and tucked it under his wing to keep it dry. Then they all hopped to the door of the hedge imps' warren, rapping fast at it with their beaks.

'Get ye gone!' a snarly voice cried from inside. 'She en't here, I tell ye! And if she was, I'd have yer eyes out before I let ye to her!'

'Open up!' Calypso squawked.

'Crow?'

'Aye!'

The door swung open and Snoshti stood there, small and fearsome with her paws on her hips. 'It's about time, birds,' she said. 'What's happened?'

'I might ask ye! What happened to our caravans? And who were ye flappin' at? Someone looking for 'Pie?'

'Anyone *not* looking for her, I'd like to know?'

'Eh?'

'Birds, haven't ye heard? The Windwitch daughter is back, they say, sneaking about with imps and crows and perhaps a pet devil with a taste for faeries?'

'What? They think 'Pie—? They think we—?' Calypso stuttered, stunned.

'It must be so, neh? Ye lot show up and – spit spot! – faeries start to vanish? That queen's behind it, telling the whole city how Magpie was with Poppy Manygreen last anyone saw of her, and how they were talking devils with some crusty scavenger imp.'

'Er,' said Calypso. 'Mistress, so far that's so.'

'And where are the lasses now?'

'Well, 'Pie, she's at Rathersting Castle, with the old healer.'

'Healer?' Snoshti growled. 'Is she—?'

'Her wings . . . they'll take some mending. Lady Orchidspike says she can do it. But that's not the worst. She's . . . lost, like. Been a bad blow to her, losing Poppy . . .'

'Losing Poppy?'

'Aye,' Calypso said. ''Twas terrible. We . . . we lost a crow, too. There's a bad devil come, we never seen its like. It got the better of us, and good. Mistress . . .' He looked hard at Snoshti. 'It's time. We got nothing left but our secrets, neh? It's time ye told 'Pie the truth and let her be who she's going to be. Ready or not.'

Snoshti returned his hard look and, at length, she nodded. 'Perhaps ye're right, old feather. Time can rush up to meet ye before ye're ready. But what are ye to do? Ask it to wait?' She shook her head. 'Neh. I'll come to the castle, and we'll see.'

Calypso nodded solemnly. 'After all these years,' he said, 'it shivers me a little to think what's next. It's like turning a page, neh? And starting up at the top of a new one?'

'That's thinking small, crow. It could be a whole new book.'

24

MAGPIE WAS LYING ON THE BED WITH HER EYES CLOSED when Talon peered in. The room had cleared out considerably. One bespectacled crow sat reading at her bedside, a bandage wrapped round his neck, and he looked up when Talon hesitated in the doorway. 'Come in then, laddie,' he croaked.

Talon entered. 'Is she . . . ?'

'Asleep, I reckon, or pretending. She don't much feel like talking.'

'Ah, well, then I'll just . . .' He backed away.

'Neh, lad, stay. Here, sit with her. I'm starved for a smoke.'

The bird got up and Talon saw he was the one with the peg leg. He *thunked* heavily out of the room and down the corridor. Talon sat on the edge of the chair and looked at Magpie. Even though her eyes were closed he felt awkward staring, so he looked away.

Magpie wasn't asleep. Her weariness kept trying to pull her down into darkness, but each time she felt herself slipping away, she struggled against it. The oblivion and numbness of sleep felt too much like that sea of nothing. The terrible scenes of Issrin Ev were playing over and over in her mind, and there was no safe escape in sleep.

When Talon looked back over at her, her eyes were open and gave him a start. 'Hello,' he said.

She didn't respond.

'I thought you'd want to know, the vultures are gone,' he told her. 'After the crows ran 'em off, they seemed keen to get out of Dreamdark, back to wherever they came from. It seems the devil's cleared out of Issrin too. We don't know where he's gone. And that scavenger imp? The crows told us about him. We found him looting East Mirth. He's in the dungeon now.'

Magpie's face seemed vacant, and Talon didn't know what else to say, so he pulled out something he'd tucked into his belt. 'I found this at Issrin Ev. I recognized it from the other day in West Mirth, when you near killed me with it.' He laid Skuldraig on the bed beside her.

She stared at it for a long moment, then blinked. She looked up at him. Some expression flickered in her dulled eyes. 'You . . . you touched it?' she asked.

'Eh? Aye,' he answered. 'Just to bring it to you.'

'You shouldn't have. Never touch it! Never again.'

He stared at her, incredulity turning to anger. 'What?' He stood up. 'Sure that knock on the head is why you've forgotten the words *thank you*, so, you're welcome. And while I'm saying it, you're also welcome for your life. But by all means, I won't touch your knife again.' He spun to leave.

Magpie sat up and opened her mouth to call after him, but dizziness overcame her, and she clenched her eyes shut and clutched at the knife.

'I'd try to keep that close if I were ye, pet,' said a little growly voice, seemingly from nowhere.

'Snoshti?' said Magpie, looking around, and the imp-marm pushed open the carved door of Nettle's armoire and stepped down out of it, a cascade of Nettle's clothes spilling after her.

'Who—?' began Talon. 'What are you doing in there?'

Snoshti pushed past him.

'How did you get past the castle guard?' Talon demanded.

Hearing raised voices, Orchidspike, Bertram, Pigeon, and Swig peeked into the room. 'Ach! Where'd she come from?' croaked Swig.

'Good-imp,' the healer greeted Snoshti, a bit perplexed.

'Lady Orchidspike,' she replied with a nod.

'Did ye come all this way in the storm?' inquired Pigeon warily. 'Ye en't even wet.' Gesturing to the imp's shepherd's crook, he added, 'And yer beetles. I hope ye didn't lose 'em in the forest.'

'Don't fret, friend crow. My beetles are safe in my mistress's garden.'

'Your mistress?' Magpie repeated, puzzled. 'Who—?'

Snoshti smiled, and her black eyes glinted. 'She'd like to meet ye, in fact. She's waiting now, so we'd best hurry.'

'But—' said Magpie.

'Now, hold on—' began Bertram.

'It's out of the question,' protested Orchidspike as Snoshti came forward and took Magpie's hands in her little paws. 'She can't . . .' There was a soft sparkle in the room, and Orchidspike found herself speaking to an afterimage even as she finished her thought: '. . . leave.'

For a moment an impression of the lass and the imp hung in the air, but within seconds it had glimmered out, leaving no trace of them at all. Orchidspike, Talon, Bertram, Pigeon, and Swig stared at the empty place where they had been, and the only sound was the lick of the hearth fire and a click as Swig found his beak hanging open and snapped it shut.

The sensation was not unpleasant. Like a swirl of moths, the brief curious touch of many soft wings, then it was over and Magpie was standing beside a river, her hands still clasped in Snoshti's paws. 'What the skiffle?' she murmured, fighting her dizziness and looking around. The castle was nowhere to be seen. What manner of magic had carried her all the way to the Wendling? The river swept quietly by, shining in the day-bright radiance of a preposterous moon.

Magpie stared at the moon – she'd never seen so vast a moon – and at its dancing reflection in the river. Her wits sang a muddled warning, and it took her several moments of staring to recall that, gloomy as it was, it had been day yet at the castle. And what of the storm? No rain hung in the air here. The grass beneath her feet was dry, and silver-blue in the moonlight . . .

It came to her where she was, and she drew her hands from out of Snoshti's paws and backed away, staring at the imp with wide, startled eyes. For this silver land could be none other than the Moonlit Gardens.

'Snoshti . . .' she whispered. 'Am I dead?'

25

IN THE DUNGEON OF RATHERSTING CASTLE, BATCH HANGNAIL sat hunched in a corner with his big toes tucked into his nostrils for safekeeping. He hummed to himself and bided his time. Tattooed faces peered in at him from time to time through the little window in the door to his cell, and he pretended to take no notice of them. They brought him food and he ate it with his napkin at his neck as if he were a guest.

He seemed utterly unperturbed to find himself in a dungeon.

As soon as the guards left him alone, Batch stood, stretched, and ambled to the door. From his satchel, he took the key he'd found in the mud at the bottom of the Magruwen's well, and he slid it into the lock. It fit. It turned. The door swung open.

Such was the gift of serendipity, and a lifetime of such miracles had left Batch jaded by them. He simply closed the door behind himself and locked it again, then slunk away, singing under his breath.

Where ye going? Where ye been?
Nighttime's dark, but morning's grim.
Hurry where ye're headed,

forget all that ye've seen.
The past is inescapable, the future's just a dream . . .

He made his way through the subterranean passages, his nose and instincts leading him along the least traveled of them. He met no one. He climbed stairs, turned and turned again, and, like a rat in a maze, he found his way.

Batch always found what he was looking for.

And he always found what he wasn't looking for too. Those were the charms of a scavenger's life, the unlooked-for pretties. This time it was a little pedal vehicle with side-by-side seats and a neat red-and-white-striped awning to keep off the rain. It hadn't been driven since the chief's old mum had passed to the Moonlit Gardens decades past, and no one even remembered there was a little door hidden in the yew's roots that let it out into the world.

Humming, Batch pushed open the door and tramped down the weeds that choked and hid it. Then he climbed into the surrey and pedaled out. Once he'd gathered speed, a strange thing happened. Remnants of a floating glyph the biddy had long ago touched to her surrey awakened, and it began to rise gently into the sky.

Jaded or not, Batch's eyes gleamed with a wild joy as he threw back his head and said, 'Wheeeeee!!!'

26

'DEAD?' REPEATED SNOSHTI WITH A SNORT. 'ACH! AS IF I'D stand for that! Neh, pet, ye're not dead. Just visiting.'

'B-but . . .' stammered Magpie. 'It's a one-way journey. Everyone knows that!'

'Do they, then? Do they know I come and go as I please? And so do all my kind, and so shall you.'

'But how?'

''Twas my gift to ye at yer blessing ceremony.'

'I never knew I had a blessing ceremony.'

'Neh, for we didn't tell yer parents. We'd been looking for ye a long time, pet, since before my time, even, waiting for ye to be born. Claws crossed, hoping! We didn't know if it would work! It's a lot to trust to stories and dreams, but then along ye came. Even before ye spoke your first word, I was fair sure who ye were.'

Magpie stared at her. The imp's words were like nonsense tumbling around in her tired mind.

'Ye know what yer first word was?'

'My parents said it was *mama*.'

'Nor was it! There was another earlier only I heard, and I never told. It was *devil*.'

'Devil?'

'Aye, just as it was foretold. Then we were sure. We held the blessing after that. Floated ye down Misky Creek on a linden leaf to where the creatures waited. All the gifts we gave, yer animal senses and languages, and more ye're like to be discovering all yer life, they're just tokens and tools to help ye bear yer real gift, ye ken, that which was given even before ye were born.'

Magpie shivered. Foreboding and wonder twined together, and she wanted to know, and was afraid to know, what that gift might be. Before she had decided whether to ask, though, Snoshti said, 'But that's not for me to tell. Come along now. This way.'

She took her hand and guided her gently along the riverbank. Magpie saw a bridge ahead made all of round river rocks, and on the far bank, arrayed like picnickers on blankets, were faeries. 'Are they all . . . ?'

'Aye.'

They stepped onto the bridge, and all eyes on the riverbank turned to them. Magpie hesitated. 'What are they all waiting for?' she whispered, suddenly shy.

'It's all right, pet, they're not waiting for ye. They know no more of ye than living faeries do. They're waiting for their loved ones to come over. We're all tied to the world so long as our folk are still in it. It can take lifetimes to let all that go and become.'

'Become? Become what?'

Snoshti pointed into the sky. Magpie looked, but all she could see was a sparkle of some far thing passing before the moon, and she swayed a little on her feet, staring into the fathomless depths of the sky. She looked back down. They were nearing the end of the bridge and Magpie caught a hint in the air of that snow-sharp fragrance she'd detected in her caravan and on the recipe card. She looked sharply at the imp, only now realizing who had slipped it into her book.

She stepped off the last stone of the bridge onto the grass of the Moonlit Gardens, where no other living faerie had ever trod. The clusters of picnickers were all watching her, and she looked from face to face. She'd never really wondered what faeries would look like in the afterworld, and she saw they looked much the same as they did in life, though muted somehow, like reflections in an old mirror. Their edges were blurred, their substance soft and silvered. And in their eyes, mingled with calm, she saw pity. Snoshti nodded to them in greeting and bundled Magpie along.

'Why were they looking at me like that?' Magpie asked.

'Like what?'

'Pitying, like.'

'Ach, well, it en't often a sprout comes across that bridge. Biddies and codgers, that's who comes. They think ye're here unnatural early, and that can't mean any good for ye. They'll be thinking ye were killed.'

Magpie stopped walking and looked back over her shoulder at them, struck by a thought. 'They'll have seen Poppy and Maniac then, neh? Can't I ask them?'

'Pet . . .' Snoshti said, clasping Magpie's wrist with her paw and keeping her from turning back. 'I've already asked. They're not here.'

Magpie's insides lurched. 'They're not here?' she demanded. 'But . . . they must be! I saw them die!'

'I'm sorry, I am, but it's sure . . . and it's an older mystery than ye know.'

Magpie stared at the imp, horrified. *Not death*, she had said of the darkness. Unmaking? They couldn't have been . . . extinguished. But wasn't that what she felt her own self at the brink of? In a raw voice she whispered, 'Then where are they?'

Still clutching her wrist, Snoshti tugged her along. 'I don't know, pet, but ye're not the only one who wonders. My mistress has long been wanting to know that same thing. Come now. She's waiting.'

Magpie didn't ask who Snoshti's mistress was. A wild hope had leapt into her heart, and she didn't want to dash it.

She followed Snoshti, and it seemed they walked a long way beside the river. She didn't see another bridge. Above them meadows sloped up to a forest, and the forest rolled on from there, on and on in the moonlight until in the distance it met a line of white mountains.

Faeries waved from gardens as they passed, and Magpie waved back, seeing glints of light from cottage windows tucked among the trees. All the flowers in all the gardens were pale and the foliage was silver, and the faeries, too, were the color of moonlight, and luminous, as if lit from within. Some were paler than others and more ghostly. When Magpie asked Snoshti why this was, she answered, 'They've been here longer. They're closer to their spark,' which really didn't make things any clearer.

At length a rumbling sound resolved itself out of the placid shushing of the river and grew steadily louder. *A waterfall*, Magpie thought, and was glad the river didn't go on and on forever in sameness. It broadened as it approached the plunge, and mica-glittering rocks began to loom out of the landscape. With Snoshti, Magpie left the meadows behind and approached the edge of a cliff. She felt the vastness of space opening before her as she stepped to the brink to peer over. But as she did, her senses suddenly screamed at her – *onslaught!* – and she caught Snoshti around the shoulders and yanked her back.

They tumbled to the ground just as a shape came hurtling up right in front of them, preceded by a snort of fire and spiraling straight up into the sky. The most massive creature Magpie had ever beheld, it shone like crushed gems and left a reek of brimstone in its wake as it coursed toward the moon. Magpie pushed herself to her knees and stared after it. She heard, over the rush of the falls, great bellowing calls sounding and looked down into an immense canyon. Near and far, huge shapes hove into the sky.

'Dragons!' Magpie gasped, staring up at them. Hundreds there were, gliding and spinning, the coppery fumes of their breath seeming to inscribe fiery glyphs on the night. Magpie had dreamed of dragons. She had dreamed of a time when the heavens had glistened with them as the sea glints with sharks, but she had always woken to a world of empty skies. Seeing them now, awe bloomed within her.

'And there you are, at last,' said a voice behind her. She turned.

The faerie who stood there wasn't dressed in firedrake scales but a simple white tunic, and she wore no knives at her thighs and no gold circlet. Her dark hair hung in a single plait, and though there was a dreaminess around her edges, it was clear that however long she'd been here, life was yet bright in her.

'Lady,' said Magpie, tears coming to her eyes. 'I hoped it would be you.'

And Bellatrix took Magpie's hands and helped her to her feet.

Magpie followed Bellatrix down a narrow stair in the cliff to a cottage carved right into the rock face. From its billowing garden on a ledge of marbled rock, she could see the whole canyon spread before her, and she was torn between her fascination with Bellatrix and with the tumult of dragons in the air. Her eyes darted back and forth between them.

Snoshti bustled out the cottage door with a tray and laid tea things on a bench. She poured three cups and stirred sugar into them, and Magpie thought one was for her, but the imp set them on the ground and whistled for her beetles, who scurried over and began to lap at them like tiny dogs.

'Do you know when the first dragon came here?' Bellatrix asked her. 'It was only five thousand years ago.' She stood looking up at them, her hands clasped behind her, then turned back to Magpie. 'I'd been here already twenty thousand years and never thought to see a dragon again. The Magruwen had dreamed them immortal. They were never to come here, but there she was.

'She was screaming on the far side of the river and wouldn't cross. It was no wonder she was crazed. She'd been murdered by a human horde and arrived here with her throat full of her own blood. All the faeries, even the seraphim, gathered on the bank, keening. We didn't know what to do. There was no precedent.

'When finally I coaxed her across the bridge, it gave way under her weight, and she was plunged into the water. In panic she spat fire and set the river boiling. It was terrible . . .' Bellatrix's voice was ragged with sadness. 'Eventually she accepted what could not be changed. She was the only one of her race in all this world.'

'How lonely she must have been,' said Magpie.

Bellatrix answered bitterly, 'She wasn't alone long. Once the humans had a taste for it, the others came fast. Within a hundred years there was only one dragon left in the living world.'

'Fade?' Magpie guessed.

'Aye. Fade . . . he lasted much longer than the others, another thousand years! The Magruwen kept him at his side in Dreamdark, and he was safe. There was little in the forest to subdue a dragon's appetites, but as long as he lay dormant he had scarce need to feed. Imagine. He was the sire of his race and the last. He must have ached to join his kindred here, to fly again – for in Dreamdark he could do naught but sleep – but he wouldn't leave his master alone . . . as others had done before him . . .' Her face clouded with a look of shame, and she went on. 'And so for the Magruwen's sake, he hid there like some hunted thing and not the king of creatures he was. And he would have gone on with that living death . . .'

She gave Magpie a keen, searching look and said, 'They share dreams, the dragon and the Djinn King. They had always done and do still. Did you know that?'

Magpie shook her head.

'Nay, well, so it is. And the Magruwen saw in Fade's dreams that the dragon was withering . . . dying the death that grows from within and kills the spirit as well as the skin, and he knew . . . he knew that was worse even than murder. So he let Fade go. He sent him to fly and to feed, knowing he would never come back . . . and he never did. He was murdered like all the others.'

Magpie thought of the stories she'd heard of the dragon massacres and she had to close her eyes. Humans had a genius for devising instruments of death. Their lives were so short, and they seemed to value them so little, sending waves of men to clash in battlefields, then weighing victory by the piled corpses. And if they held their own lives so worthless, the lives of everything else were as fruit to pluck from trees.

It had been possible for faeries and imps to hide their existence, but for dragons there was no hiding, and humans had gloried in the slaying, written ballads, epics, as if they were doing great deeds! And sure the eejits believed they were. They thought dragons were predators! The dragons were the first life the Magruwen dreamed – how could they be predators, when they had existed before prey? In fact, they fed on something quite different than meat, though mannies would never guess what golden goose they'd slaughtered.

Dragons ate ore. They smelted it in their fiery bellies and excreted luminous molten metals, gold, silver, copper, that would harden into veins in the earth. This they had done since the beginning, but it was over now. There would be no new gold made, ever again. Countless humans would lose their lives clawing what was left from the ground, and they would never understand what they had done.

Magpie knew it wasn't the last thing they would erase from the earth without thought or understanding. A terrible bitterness swelled in her. 'They're worse than devils!' she said passionately. 'If there were bottles enough in the world to capture them all, I would do it!'

Bellatrix smiled sadly. 'In truth I'm glad I didn't live to see them. But Magpie, there's a strange twist to this story, and it's why I'm telling it to you. You see, the day the living world lost Fade, something was born, too. A hope.'

'Hope for what?' Magpie asked.

'For a new age. It came down to dreams. That's how everything begins. If you don't know it yet, you will. Magpie, if humans hadn't massacred the dragons, there would have been no way to reach the Magruwen, and we would all have suffered the unweaving until the very end.'

'The unweaving?' Magpie asked, puzzled. 'Lady, what is it? It seems I'm hearing that at every turn.'

Bellatrix gave her a quizzical smile and said softly, 'I *am* sorry. How strange it must be for you, not knowing. Come, child, sit with me. You look so tired. Drink some tea.'

Magpie went and sat beside her on the bench. Her eyes were huge and solemn in the moonlight, looking up at her hero. Bellatrix handed her a cup and reached out to trail her fingertips tentatively over Magpie's hair.

'I'm some mess, I fear, Lady,' said Magpie, blushing.

'Life can do that to you,' said Bellatrix. She asked hesitantly, 'May I brush your hair?'

Surprised, Magpie could only nod and be glad Snoshti had made her wash it a few days ago. She took a gulp of tea while Bellatrix unloosed the pins that held her hair in place and fanned it out over her back, taking care not to jostle her injured wings. Snoshti brought Bellatrix a brush, and she began at the ends, gently unworking the tangles.

'I couldn't help imagining you as the child I'd have liked to have,' Bellatrix said.

'Me?' asked Magpie again, shocked that the huntress would have been imagining *her*. Why, indeed, had she been brought here?

'Aye, you, Magpie. Fierce, cunning, loyal, sweet.'

'Thank you, Lady,' Magpie said, growing bashful. Then, thinking of Vesper's claims, she asked, 'You *didn't* . . . have any children?'

'Nay. My life . . . took a turn,' she replied quietly. Magpie wanted to ask her what had happened so long ago, but Bellatrix said, 'But this isn't *my* story, Magpie. It's yours.'

A shiver went through Magpie and she looked at Bellatrix over her shoulder. 'What do you mean?' she asked.

'I'm coming to it, child,' Bellatrix answered. 'For thousands of years after I came here, I had contact with the Magruwen. The hedge imps came and went between us, bearing messages. Those years were stretched so thin with longing and remorse, they passed very slowly for me. And the change was happening very slowly, too. If one wasn't a . . . captive . . . of the past, one might not notice. But I was, and did. From faeries crossing the river I saw how far our folk had fallen. Their magic was paler and paler all the time. The old folk who arrived told of young faeries with no gift for their clan's ancient ways. There was talk of a new species, humans. And the Magruwen was changing. There was a hardness and weariness in his messages. Even before the dragons began to die, it worried me. And after? After Fade was murdered there were no more messages at all. Not even a farewell. The Magruwen destroyed Issrin Ev, and my imps couldn't find him. I heard nothing more of him. It was Fade, later, who told me he slept.' She pulled the brush slowly through Magpie's hair. 'That was when the idea came, a little sparkle of an idea, wild . . . maybe impossible. But like a scavenger imp, I couldn't get it out of my mind!'

Magpie smiled at that.

'The faeries needed a new champion, and it wouldn't be me. Even if I could somehow go back – and I *had* tried – there was little I could have done. The Tapestry was falling apart, and darkness was waiting on the other side, and the Djinn were sleeping through it. The faeries – the world – needed a new kind of champion . . .' She paused. 'So I imagined you.'

Magpie started, stunned. 'What?' she gasped.

Bellatrix pulled the brush through Magpie's hair and went on, her voice rich with feeling. 'Don't you see? The dreams, the shared dreams of the dragon and the Djinn King. At last, their dreams brought new life into the Tapestry.'

'The Tapestry,' repeated Magpie. 'The Magruwen spoke of it. What is it?'

Bellatrix shook her head sadly. 'That faeries have forgotten the Tapestry; that is the greatest tragedy of all. It's the fabric of all creation, and it's woven of dreams, the dreams of the Djinn. Dreams are real, Magpie. They're seed and water and sun. They're everything.' She paused, let Magpie's hair run out of her hands.

'That is what you feel, child, what faeries have lost the power to feel, and what you've begun to see in glimpses.'

Magpie turned to look at her. 'The pulse? The light? The – the living light?' she stammered.

'Aye. Dreams spun in fire in the minds of Djinn. It's how they shaped a world out of nothing. But the nothing is still out there. You see it through the stars, the blackness of night. The world is just a tiny thing afloat in that sea of nothing, and the Tapestry is all that protects it. Now it's falling apart, and the Djinn are letting it.'

'But why?'

Bellatrix shook her head again and said, with an edge of frustration, 'I don't know. Something happened. I believe Fade knows, but he keeps his master's mysteries close. Whatever it was, the Magruwen had forsaken us. I had no choice but to trick him.'

'Trick the Djinn King? *How?*'

Bellatrix gave a short laugh. 'Bedtime stories. For the past thousand years I've been telling Fade faerie stories and hoping . . .'

It finally dawned on Magpie. 'Hoping the Magruwen would share his dreams and weave them into the Tapestry!'

Bellatrix nodded. 'It took centuries of trying, and the only way to know if it worked was for the imps and creatures to watch for you in the world.'

As Magpie's mind wrapped itself around this notion, it began to trouble her. 'So . . .' she began, her brow furrowed. 'You're saying I was one of those stories?'

'Child, you *were* those stories.'

Magpie didn't know what to think or feel. A silence stretched out between them as she waited for the words to sink in. They didn't, quite. It seemed so absurd. 'Me? Then, am I *real*?' she asked.

Bellatrix reached her arms out and drew Magpie to her. 'As real as anyone. More real! You're the first faerie in a long, long time who was *handmade* by the Djinn King! I only fed the idea of you into his mind. Left to himself, he would never have dreamed of a faerie as powerful as you.'

'Powerful?'

'Oh.' Bellatrix laughed and took Magpie by the shoulders, holding her back so she could look her in the eyes. 'Magpie . . . you have no idea. The world has never seen anything like you.'

Magpie stared at her, trying to take it in. Despite what Bellatrix said, she couldn't shake the sense of unreality that began to overwhelm her. She was someone else's dream! Well, she reminded herself, didn't everything come from the Djinns' dreams in some way or other? But this dream had been a trick. Her life was a trick.

'Magpie,' said Bellatrix. 'Listen. I know this is hard to understand. I'd thought to wait until you were grown, but the Tapestry is failing faster than I ever imagined. I just couldn't wait any longer.'

Magpie stared at her hands and turned them over slowly, thinking how her very skin and bones were spun from a dragon's bedtime story.

'Just know you're *real*, and you're *yourself*, and no one – *no one*, not me and not even the Magruwen – holds any kind of puppet strings. What you do now will be your choice, but you have more choice than anyone, because you – alone of all faeries, Magpie – you can weave the Tapestry. Like the Djinn.'

Magpie shook her head, laughing a high thin laugh. 'That's blither! How could I . . . I'm just—'

Bellatrix took one of Magpie's hands and opened it and traced her fingertips over Magpie's palm. 'There's power in you, child, and I know you feel it. I know it's begun to find its own way out. You'll see, you'll learn. And I'm sorry to say, you'll need to learn fast if you're going to stop the Blackbringer.'

That jolted Magpie out of thoughts of her own reality. 'I can stop it? The Magruwen said it couldn't be caught.'

'He thinks the strength of faeries is gone from the world. Four thousand years' worth of dreams have sifted through his long sleep, Magpie. It's likely he doesn't realize yet who you are or how he's been deceived.'

'Won't he be angry?'

'Aye, I imagine he will be. I only hope there is in him still the fiery spirit that drove him to create, that won't be able to watch a devil destroy his world!'

'Could he destroy the world? What is he, Lady? The stories of the Blackbringer are just nursery tales now. No one even thinks he was real!'

'He was real,' said Bellatrix in a hard voice. Then she gently touched Magpie's wings. 'He did this to you?'

'Aye. But my friends weren't so lucky . . . Lady Bellatrix, please, what is he? He's not like any devil I ever saw.'

'Nay, he was like no other. He was the worst of them all. He was a plague. All through the wars he eluded us, like a phantom, a shadow. How do you capture the dark? He hunted and fed, even in Dreamdark, and night became a horror. All the faeries and imps kept to Never Nigh. Even he couldn't breach it. It was like a siege town.'

'Was it you who captured him?'

'Aye, at last, with the Magruwen and the Vritra at our side. It took all the Djinns' champions, and not all survived.' Her voice dropped to a husky whisper. 'Kipay . . .'

'Kipepeo?' asked Magpie. 'The Ithuriel's champion?'

'You've heard of him?' Bellatrix's eyes lit up.

'I know his name from the ballads of the wars,' said Magpie.

'I'm glad he is not forgotten.'

'Did . . . did the Blackbringer get him?'

Bellatrix nodded and squeezed shut her eyes. When she opened them again, they were filled with such sadness and longing that Magpie asked hesitantly, 'Did you love him?'

'He was my husband.'

After a long pause Magpie said, 'I never knew you were married.'

'No one did. We had eloped. We were married only three days when we met the Blackbringer in battle. After, those of us who remained went back to our home forests with word that the devils were vanquished. I never told anyone I was a widow. They hadn't even known I was a wife! And I didn't want them to try to stop me.'

'Stop you?'

Bellatrix smiled, but her smile was bleak. 'It wasn't my time. I knew that. But all I'd done for two hundred years was hunt devils, and now they were gone, and Kipay was, too. There was nothing left for me. I just wanted to find my husband. It was wrong; it was too soon. But I went where no one would find me, and I spoke the ancient words, and . . . came here.'

'And Kipepeo wasn't here,' Magpie said, and Bellatrix shook her head.

So that was what had become of her. That was how she had slipped out of history. She had come in mourning to the Moonlit Gardens, unnaturally early. Magpie imagined what it must have been like when she realized Kipepeo wasn't waiting for her at the riverbank, wasn't anywhere here, and she couldn't change her mind and go back to find him in the world. She was trapped. 'How terrible, Lady . . .' she whispered. Her own feeling of helplessness was nothing next to that. At least she could go back and find out what had become of the Blackbringer's victims.

She looked up at Bellatrix. 'I'll find out what happened to them,' she declared.

'Aye,' Bellatrix said, and it dawned on Magpie that this was the real reason she'd been dreamed into being, so a mourning widow could learn her husband's fate at last.

She was meant to do this.

She chewed her lip and pondered it as Bellatrix silently braided her hair. She decided finally that it's not so bad to find out you have a destiny when it's something you were going to do anyway.

Bellatrix tucked night-blooming blossoms into the intricate seven-strand braid. 'There, perfect! Your foxlick, though . . .' She laughed as the tuft freed itself from the braid. 'It won't be tamed!'

'Don't I know!' said Magpie. She inhaled. 'Those flowers . . .' It was the fragrance she had already come to associate with the Moonlit Gardens. 'What are they called?'

'Nightspink. They grow everywhere here.'

'They're so delicate.'

'Aye, delicate!' agreed Bellatrix with a sigh. 'What I wouldn't give for a big brash rose now and then, a scent you can drown in! All this tranquility! Give me a thunderstorm! A stampede, an avalanche, a wild red sunset . . .'

'Sunsets would be something here,' said Magpie, going to the edge and looking out over the dragons' immense canyon.

'I miss sunrise even more. The green scent of dawn in the forest, the color blushing back into the world, different every day?'

Magpie remembered a long winter of night she'd once spent in the northern icelands and how desperately she'd craved daylight. 'Why did the Djinn make it like this? Always night?'

'Ah, well, it suits the seraphim.'

'Who?'

'Well, they're *us*, really. What we become? There are two parts to a creature, Magpie, the spark and the skin. The longer we're in the Gardens, the closer we are to our spark, and the more we relinquish our skin and all the drama and fleshly stuff of being alive. Love and anger and jealousy? Our hungers and longings. We couldn't go on like that for eternity. We'd go mad.'

'But haven't *you* been here twenty-five thousand years?'

Bellatrix smiled. 'I? But I *am* mad! The Magruwen always said I was the most obstinate faerie who ever lived. Sure he never thought he'd have such proof as this, me clinging to my skin all these thousands of years! This isn't what it's meant to be like, child. Everyone I ever knew – except Kipay, of course – they've come and become. And I've stayed just the same.'

'And the dragons?' asked Magpie, looking up at them.

'Ah, bless the Djinn for giving the dragons the temperament for immortality. They've no need to become. They're perfect just as they are. They've been good companions to me these past five thousand years, especially Fade. I visit the seraphim sometimes, too, up in the high planes. But I admit I prefer the riverbank, the faeries fresh from life in all their beautiful skins, bursting with gossip of the world! And then there's you, best of all.' She reached for Magpie's hand and squeezed it. 'Glorious with life!'

Magpie blushed. Glorious with life. Bellatrix's words chased away any fancy she still harbored about the darkness, and she felt herself, for the first time since falling through the Blackbringer, settle solidly in her own skin. She hadn't left any piece of herself behind there, and it was a lucky thing. She knew absolutely that there would have been no hope of defeating the devil if she had.

'You've a world to go home to now, and much to do. I wish I could come with you.'

'I wish you could too,' Magpie admitted, feeling a thrill of fear. Where was she to begin? She snuck a look at her hands, wiggling her fingers, thinking of what Bellatrix had said about the magic that was finding its own way out. Indeed. It was like rescuing a stolen artifact from a plunder monkey's stash and not knowing what magic lay dormant in it. But it was stranger by far when the mysterious power lurked inside her own skin! 'I'm not ready yet,' she said. 'I don't understand what I'm to do—'

A riffle played suddenly through the air, and the hairs on Magpie's arms stood on end. She had just time to look aside at Bellatrix before that urgent feeling of onslaught invaded her senses. Again, something was hurtling toward her fast, and the air crackled like a storm surge.

Dragon.

Her first instinct was to take to her wings.

Her wings hung crushed from her shoulders.

A single heartbeat passed between her sense's warning scream and the shuddering of the cliff as a dragon cannoned into it, hooking hold with his great claws. If Magpie's wings had been whole, that heartbeat would have been enough time to leap clear. As it was, her instinct to leap into the air simply plunged her right over the edge of the cliff, and she fell.

27

AGAIN THE MAGRUWEN WONDERED: WHO IS SHE? SINCE THE faerie left, he'd been going over the Tapestry, thread by thread and glyph by glyph, finding every moment more of her handiwork. Who was this lass who'd made such tangles in the Tapestry?

He focused on a new glyph and turned it around in his mind. He winced. Graceless! Fused threads, clumsy stitches, no symmetry, no pattern! When he had first become aware of Magpie's inexplicable ability to alter the Tapestry, he kept expecting to find devils born of her twisted threads. For so it was in ancient days that the monsters had first been brought into being, by another creature's artless meddling. Instead, in the faerie's glyphs, again and again he found new magic. *Strange* new magic.

Between the great warp threads of the Tapestry stretched the sheen of countless weft threads, and each one, each fire-bright fiber, represented a dream made real on earth. One for granite and one for salt, one for the tiny biting bugs in the swamp, one for mildew, one for pollen, one for the bees that carried it flower to flower. One for everything, some long, some short, and all connected into a living, shimmering whole. And all across that whole the threads intermingled in patterns. It was in the patterns – the glyphs – that dwelled such of the Djinns' dreams as love, flight, memory, laughter, invisibility, luck, music, and many, many more. These were the mysteries and complexities of the world and the magicks too, and the faerie, without even knowing it, had been making her own.

The Magruwen traced the threads of one of her glyphs to their origins and saw what she had done this time. He scowled, and then from deep within him welled up . . . laughter. It was absurd. Henceforth, because of this unlikely clump of threads, a cake with the footprints of a gecko in its frosting would enable any who ate it to walk on the ceiling!

Surely she had no idea what she had done. What she had was an unconscious intuition about the unweaving, a sensitivity to weakness in the Tapestry. These whimsical glyphs, they didn't exist for their own sake; they were simply the by-product of something much more profound. Once a thread or glyph failed in the Tapestry, the dream failed, too, and the world was changed. And each messy, tangled glyph the lass wove caught the end of some unraveling thread before it could dissolve forever and take a Djinn's dream out of the world with it. Here: she had tied a jumbled knot in the glyph for invisibility as it unraveled. She had tethered it hastily to other threads, those for the crocus flower and the cinnamon tree, and all were bound tight to the massive warp thread for fire. Now one had only to drop powdered crocus petals into the ashes of a cinnamon wood fire and a new dust spell for invisibility would be born. Just like that.

The dust spell was new magic in and of itself, but more important, the knot had stopped an ancient art from slipping out of the world, and, even more important, it had kept the Tapestry from weakening further. Most of Magpie's knots were like that. She had saved such glyphs as footprint magic, scrying, fire husbandry, and hypnosis, to name but a handful. She had even rescued the sixth glyph for flight from oblivion, which had resulted in a funny little spell involving eggshells and rain.

Most of the spells born of the knots relied upon confluences so unlikely they would never be discovered by accident, such as this one: playing a harpsichord while wearing emerald rings on every finger would make plants grow at twice their natural speed. What harpsichordist had emeralds enough to stumble innocently upon this spell?

But the important fact remained: the knots were strong. They would hold. Indeed, they were holding the world together.

The Magruwen could wish them to be less unlovely, though.

And so, while he muttered much and sighed long and shook and reshook his great blazing head, he found himself consumed with something he had long forgotten the flavor of: curiosity. He had thought the world empty of surprises and himself past caring. Things had been done that could never be undone, that could never be forgiven, and what had changed? Not much. It was the same world he had turned away from, filled with pettiness and wasted gifts. One intriguing sprout and a few new glyphs didn't heal all that had passed.

The Magruwen roared, and a trembling was felt in the fields and dwellings near his well. He paced. He sought the peace of sleep, but it had been stripped from him in that cunning explosion. He was not only curious now; he was alert. He was confounded. And he was impatient. Impatient for the faerie to return. She needed to learn what the clever fingers of her mind were up to.

In the bottom of the well, his flame undimmed by the cover of a skin, the Djinn King paced and waited, and his cave seemed to grow smaller around him with every turn.

28

JACKSMOKE! MAGPIE THOUGHT TO HERSELF AS SHE FELL, WINGS fluttering after her as useless as scarves.

One moment she was plummeting through empty air, and the next she was caught in the grip of a massive paw, and she saw the knife edge of a claw twice as long as her entire body arcing toward her from above. She froze as its tip hooked the back of her shift.

The dragon lifted her with one claw out of the paw it had caught her in and flicked her – ungently – back onto the ledge. She skidded into a billow of nightspink in Bellatrix's garden and, head spinning, looked up into a tremendous face. Broad charred nostrils emitting a slow fume of sulfur. Orange eyes with vertical pupils drawn tight. A hide like beaten copper, with a dull patina of verdigris and bronze muting its metallic sheen.

He stared at Magpie and she stared back, speechless.

'I know you . . .' he hissed at her in Old Tongue.

Bellatrix interposed herself between them, a tiny bold figure before his huge head, but his eyes never wavered from Magpie. As a thin lick of flame issued from his nostrils, Magpie had no illusions that the lady could protect her from him.

'Good even‘ to you, Fade,' Bellatrix said mildly.

'You never told me she was born,' breathed the dragon. It sounded to Magpie like an accusation.

'She's still very young. I wasn't certain.'

'And now?'

'Now I *am* certain. Here she is, Fade.' Bellatrix stepped aside and swept her hand toward Magpie. 'Hope.'

'*Hope*,' spat the dragon. 'This is what all your scheming has wrought, Bellatrix, wearing your voice away year after year with your fancies, for one small sprout?'

'Aye, one sprout who can do what the Djinn will not. The Tapestry is failing, Fade, and he does nothing!'

'It is not for you to decide,' said the dragon in a dangerous tone.

'Nay? Why not? It was his will that made the world so it's his whim to let it die?'

Magpie was keenly aware of how helpless she was at this moment, flightless and in the path of dragon nostrils larger than her entire body. And as he stared at where she lay tumbled in the nightspink, she had a feeling that even the intensity of those orange eyes could set her on fire.

'You meddle in the mysteries of the Djinn!' His voice rose from a rumble to a low roar.

'*Mysteries*?' Bellatrix roared back. Like the champion of legend she was, she stood fearless before the dragon. 'Aye. Perhaps you'll shed some light on those mysteries, dragon. I know you know! Why did he forsake us?'

Fade said nothing.

'Nay. Faithful Fade. I know you'll never tell. Secrets! All the years I've been in this place, I've watched the faeries come, each generation weaker than the last. What's happened to them? I've guided screaming dragons over the bridge! How did that come to pass? How did humans creep into being to slaughter all your kind? Who was watching the affairs of the Djinn then? And now? Devils are roaming free with but this one small sprout against them, and if it weren't for her, and for your part in this and mine, there would be no hope at all!'

Magpie watched wide-eyed as the two legends argued about her.

'Fade,' Bellatrix went on, her eyes flashing in the moonlight, 'the Blackbringer is free.'

A burst of flame shot from Fade's nostrils, sending twin fireballs straight at Magpie. She had to fling herself aside and roll to a crouch as the flowers sizzled and blackened where she had been. He turned his great head to the canyon and snorted great jets of flames out into it, seeming to cleanse his head of fire before risking turning back to the two faeries.

'The Blackbringer, free?' he hissed.

'Aye.'

'Then it's already too late. What can one sprout hope to do against such a foe?'

'Without the Magruwen's help? Perhaps nothing. Fade, he must be persuaded. You could—'

'I will not defy him.'

'Not even to save faeries? Imps? Dryads, hobs, finfolk, and every other creature?'

'Nay, not if it's his will.'

Magpie rose from her crouch. 'How about to save *him*, then?' she asked.

Fade turned back to her. 'What did you say?'

'The Blackbringer already killed one Djinn.'

Fade stared at Magpie, and she thought his eyes grew brighter, like a stoked fire. 'Killed a Djinn?' he repeated.

'The Vritra,' said Magpie. 'And now he's killing in Dreamdark and sending his spies down the Magruwen's well!'

Fade's head moved closer to Magpie, and the smell of brimstone grew strong. 'Spies?' he asked.

'Aye, he sent a scavenger imp down hunting for something.'

'Did he get it?' he demanded sharply, his eyes blazing.

'Get what?' asked Magpie, squinting up at him. Seeing the intensity in Fade's eyes, she was filled with curiosity as to what Batch had been after. What had he said, a turnip? She thought not.

But the dragon just blinked his huge, inscrutable eyes and said, 'It is not for me to say.'

'More secrets!' exclaimed Bellatrix. 'Fade, something must be done! The devils were his own mistake, and he must unmake them!'

Fade turned to her with a snarl. 'He never made such mistakes! He *never* made a devil.'

Bellatrix and Magpie fell silent and looked at each other. Everyone knew the devils were the Djinns' mistakes. Where else could they have come from? Where else would *anything* have come from?

Still snarling, Fade went on. 'Creatures with no dreams of their own can do naught but destroy the dreams of others. So it has been since the beginning. So were the devil armies forged, by one who did not dream.'

Bellatrix said irritably, 'Dragon! This is no time for riddles. Please speak plain. If the Djinn didn't make the devils, where did they come from?'

Indeed. If not from the Djinn, then where? Magpie was silent. A thought was skimming the surface of her mind, and she felt as if she were looking up at it from underwater. Then, suddenly, she realized what it was: eight. The eight sacred columns of the temples. Why eight and not seven? Traceries of light spun in Magpie's sight and she saw painted there the symbol for infinity that graced all the temples. It twisted then and she saw it, too, suddenly, as an eight. Why eight . . . ?

'Fade,' she said in a rush. 'Was there another once? An eighth Djinn?'

He snorted. 'There have only ever been seven Djinn!'

Magpie chewed her lip, ashamed to have voiced such blither. The idea had seemed to simply spin into her mind on a curl of light.

Fade spoke again, more quietly. He said, 'The eighth was not a Djinn.'

And Magpie and Bellatrix stared at him, dumbstruck.

'In the time before time there were seven sparks . . . and one wind.'

'A wind . . .' breathed Magpie.

'The Astaroth, the world-shaping wind. He was the bellows to the Djinns' fire, tirelessly feeding their flames so they could burn bright as suns and pour their dreams forth in unbroken threads. He was their ally and equal. Pure power, an unfathomable force, and without him the Tapestry could not have been woven.

'He had no dreams of his own, but he shared theirs. When the time came to shape the Tapestry into a sphere and bind closed its seams, he chose to remain and witness the burgeoning of the world he had helped forge. This was the mistake that has shaped everything.'

'How?' Magpie asked, her head spinning.

'He was a creature of infinite space. He had never yet known boundary. The Tapestry had seemed vast, laid open in the emptiness, but once sewn closed, it was . . . small. The work of world-making went on, the Djinn gathered dreaming, the Astaroth fed them, and the world bloomed, but a time came when he was no longer needed, and it became a cage to him.'

'The Djinn couldn't . . . let him out?' asked Bellatrix, as confounded as Magpie.

'Not without letting the nothingness *in* and obliterating everything. He had made his choice, but he couldn't live with it. The confines of the world warped him. He tried to free himself, even at the expense of all else. He gathered his full force and tried to blast his way through the Tapestry to freedom, but it was strong – he'd helped make it so – and he couldn't breach it. Again and again he tried, hurling himself against it, but all he succeeded in doing was mangling it, twisting its perfect threads. Making devils.'

'Ah . . .' Magpie whispered, understanding at last.

'Abominations,' continued the dragon. 'What the Djinn dreamed pure, he turned monstrous. And when he saw what he had done he went to work at it even harder, believing he was at last creating something of his own. Hundreds upon hundreds of creatures were thus warped. The Djinn knew something had to be done. He'd been their ally, but they had to choose between the Astaroth and the world . . .'

'What did they do?' the faeries both asked, breathless.

'They chose the world,' said Fade simply, and heaved a deep sulfurous sigh. 'It was a terrible choice, and it diminished them. They erased all memory of him—'

'But for the eighth column in all the temples,' said Magpie.

He looked at her closely. 'Aye, faerie. Those they left as symbols of their shame. They never again burned so bright as they had in the harmony of eight, with the Astaroth's strength on their side. Faeries never knew the Djinns' full glory. By the time you came to be, that was all memory.'

'This all happened before the days of faeries?' Bellatrix asked.

'Aye,' said Fade, with the grim ghost of a smile on his reptilian face. 'Of course. The Djinn had to create a race to rid the world of devils. That race was faeries.'

Magpie stood very still. She felt a sickness in the pit of her stomach. She saw the same feelings written on Bellatrix's face. They just looked at each other and felt the force of the dragon's words. Faeries had been dreamed into being to rid the world of devils. Faeries, who had always believed themselves to be the light and color and soul of the world, they were just the solution to a wretched problem, like vultures who had been dreamed to devour the dead.

'Now you know,' said Fade.

Magpie blinked, and the stunned look on her face was replaced slowly by ferocity. 'Well, then,' she said. 'If he dreamed us up as hunters, he'd best let us do our job, neh? This Blackbringer. What the skive is he, dragon?'

'The Astaroth's final plague,' said Fade. 'And his worst.'

29

AGAIN CAME A SOFT TOUCH LIKE THE FLUTTER OF WINGS AS Magpie visioned the glyphs Snoshti taught her, holding Rathersting Castle clear in her mind. When she opened her eyes, she found herself in Nettle's room, and released her held breath with relief.

It was quiet under the drum of rain. Bertram was asleep in the rocking chair with his peg leg propped up on the bed. She thought at first he was the only one in the room, but then she saw the Rathersting lad in the window. He was sitting looking out and hadn't heard her arrive. She remembered their last meeting, how she hadn't had time to explain to him about Skuldraig, and a flush of shame rose on her cheeks. How ungrateful he must think her! She held still, knowing as soon as she was noticed the questions would begin, and she couldn't begin to imagine how she would answer them.

Then Snoshti glimmered in beside her and silence was no longer an issue. 'Well done, pet!' cried the imp. Instantly Bertram leapt awake and Talon swung round in the window. His eyes were full of suspicion.

'What happened?' he demanded. 'Where did you go?'

Calypso hopped in. 'My 'Pie!' he cried, sweeping her up in his wings. 'Heard ye had a bit of a vanish!' He held her face with his feathertips and looked into her eyes. 'How are ye, pet?'

Though his voice was jovial, Magpie knew what he was asking. 'I'm fine now, feather,' she said, meeting his searching stare.

'Does me good to see a gleam in yer eye. But ye look awful tired.'

'Aye, exhausted, since you mention it. Feel like I haven't slept in ten years.'

'Bet ye're hungry, too, Mags,' said Pup from the doorway as the rest of the crows crowded in.

She put her hands over her belly and realized she was. 'About to start gawping like a baby bird!'

'There's biscuits and pumpkin soup left from lunch, full of ginger to bring your strength up,' offered Orchidspike, elbowing her way through the throng of black feathers. 'Back in bed and rest, lass, from . . . wherever you've been. I'll fetch you some.'

'Nay, Lady,' said Talon. 'Let me.' As he passed Magpie, his hard eyes seemed to ask, *Who are you?*

Magpie allowed herself to be fussed back into bed. Orchidspike bent to examine her wings, and Magpie's elaborate braid caught her eye. 'Whose handiwork is this, now?' she asked.

'Er,' said Magpie, 'Snoshti did it, neh, Snosh?'

But Snoshti seemed to have vanished. The crows set to clamoring about it. 'Another sneaking imp vanishes!' groused Swig.

'Another?' asked Magpie.

'Aye, that scavenger was in the dungeon, but he disappeared from his locked cell.'

'They left him *alone*?' Magpie cried. 'Jacksmoke! I need to talk to him! I need to know what' – she glanced furtively at Orchidspike – 'what his master sent him down the well for *really*.'

But Orchidspike wasn't listening to Magpie. The scent of the nightspink in her braid had caught the healer's notice, and as the crows complained of imps, she quietly removed a blossom and held it to her nose. A curious look came into her old eyes. She sniffed it again, then tucked it into her apron. She stood. 'It's time we get on with the healing, lass. 'Twill be no quick job of work. I'll see how Talon's coming on with that food.' She bustled out.

In the corridor she took the silver-white flower out of her pocket and held it to her nose again.

'What's that?' Talon asked, coming back with a tray.

''Twas braided into the lass's hair,' she said in a peculiar voice and held it out to him.

He sniffed it. 'Sure I never smelled that before,' he said.

'Nor I,' Orchidspike replied, and Talon frowned. Orchidspike was the finest herbalist in Dreamdark. She knew everything that grew, and where, and what it could be used for. There simply wasn't a flower in the forest she hadn't smelled. 'Wherever it was she went with that imp, it wasn't in Dreamdark, that I know. Nor anywhere near.'

'Then where—?'

'I don't know, my lad, but I'd like to. Come. We'll begin soon.'

As Magpie ate, Orchidspike and Talon made ready for the healing. A wheel was set up by the fire and loaded with a wide bobbin of spidersilk, while a balm of angelica, hyssop, and clove was set out to simmer in a copper basin.

'The silk is a binding for the spells,' Orchidspike explained as she purified her knitting needles in the balm. 'I vision a glyph into every stitch, and the silk knits them together into a whole. It takes a few days for the glyphs to bond and transmute to living tissue. Then the silk threads melt away, leaving behind only wings, real as they ever were.'

'Does that mean I won't be able to fly for a few days?'

'Maybe longer, lass. This is quite severe.'

Magpie frowned and grumbled. Then Orchidspike's knitting needles caught her eye. 'Those must be djinncraft,' she said.

'Aye, my foremother Grayling chose them long ago from among the Magruwen's treasures.'

'Did your apprentice use them to make that skin of his?'

'My what?' asked Orchidspike, startled, for the word *apprentice* had been much on her mind. 'Ah, Talon? Nay, lass, the prince isn't my apprentice.'

'Prince?' Magpie repeated.

'Aye, Talon will be chief one day, after his father . . .' Her voice wavered. 'Indeed, that day may be at hand.'

'Would the Rathersting have a clan chief who's a scamperer?' she asked, and at that moment Talon came back into the room. He stiffened. Magpie had simply been curious – she'd scarcely ever known a scamperer: they were exceedingly rare – but she saw his face color with shame, and she cursed herself. He avoided meeting her eyes, and she could think of nothing to say that wouldn't make it worse, so she just frowned and resolved to speak no more.

When Orchidspike was ready to begin, Calypso tried to talk Magpie into lying down to sleep through the healing. 'Ye can't just go and go, 'Pie, after what ye been through. Ye're pale as biscuit flour, and yer folks would have my feathers for it. Ye need sleep.'

But she resisted, seating herself on a low stool in front of Orchidspike's rocker. 'My mind's buzzing too much. I wish I had my book to write in.'

'Here, Mags,' said Mingus, holding it out to her. 'I got it from the caravan for ye.'

'Ach, Mingus, thank you,' Magpie said, taking it and giving him a kiss on his beak while he shuffled his feet and examined the floor.

She held her book in her lap and unspelled it so it fell open to the page she'd last written. She'd been en route to Dreamdark then, and knew the devil only as 'the hungry one.' So much had happened since! She had found the Djinn King in the bottom of a well. She had fallen through the darkness of the Blackbringer and lost two dear friends in it. She had journeyed to the afterworld and had her hair braided by Bellatrix! She had fallen off a cliff and been caught in a dragon's fist. And she had learned of a gaping hole in the legends she had always cherished. An eighth ancient!

She wished she could talk to her parents. They were so far away, probably shape-shifting themselves into fish with the elders of Anang Paranga right this moment. She would tell her book instead, and maybe in the writing things would come clear. She tapped her quill against her lip and began to write.

Behind her, holding Magpie's right wing taut while Orchidspike worked on it, Talon could just see the page over her shoulder. The crows were all around, though, so he couldn't stare, and he caught only a word or two now and then when the birds nodded off for little naps. Magpie didn't nap. Head bent over her book, she wrote. Orchidspike's needles clicked steadily, and the spidersilk reeled off the bobbin. Rows of spells danced off the knitting needles, rows of words filled Magpie's page, and time passed.

She had been writing, pausing, frowning, remembering, and writing again for several hours when she finally gave voice to what was frustrating her. 'Is he a snag, or isn't he?' she blurted suddenly.

'Eh?' muttered Calypso sleepily.

'It's just not right somehow. I can't get past it. He leaves no rooster tracks, he's got no smell, he's not stupid like a snag . . . That snag the so-called queen set on me, now that was a devil, horrid and sure. To compare them—'

'What snag, 'Pie?' asked the crow.

'Ach! I never told you!' she cried. 'Aye, it was why Poppy came to Issrin Ev, to warn me that Vesper had a snag slave she'd set after us, and it came, sure, and it was some nasty meat, I tell you.'

Talon cut in incredulously, 'Lady Vesper set a devil after you?'

Magpie glanced over her shoulder at him. 'Aye,' she said defensively. 'Your fine queen's got some dark dabblings.'

'She's not *our* queen!' he returned hotly. 'Lady Orchidspike and my father were the only elders in Dreamdark who wouldn't recognize her claim and the others ignored them. Only time those Never Nigh fops care what a Rathersting thinks is when they nick their wings dancing or spot Black Annis too near their hamlets!'

'Ach, well . . . Lady Orchidspike, you were right. Vesper's a fake and worse. That snag was grim, and it's because of him Poppy's . . .' She choked on the word *dead* and finished instead with a bleak '. . . *gone*.'

'Is it still out there?' asked Mingus, puffing himself up.

'Neh. The Blackbringer got it, just like that. Like it just vanished or melted. That's the thing, feathers, I can't get past it. That was a devil, and we seen plenty and that's what they're like, stringing drool and snaggle teeth and suckers and stink? But the Blackbringer, he's not like them at all . . .' She paused. 'The Magruwen called him a contagion of darkness—'

At the mention of the Magruwen Orchidspike's fingers fumbled but she caught her stitch and kept knitting, eyes alert, and Talon's jaw dropped open. 'The Magruwen?' he gaped. 'You've seen the Magruwen?'

'Aye.'

Talon stammered, 'B-but how . . . ? Where? What . . . what was he like?'

'Mean! Sure he couldn't care a twitch what happens to faeries or anything else. Calypso was right: he's through with the world.'

Silence fell, broken only by the clicking of knitting needles.

After a moment, Magpie said with a sigh, 'Well, he might be through with it, but I'm not. I'm going to catch the Blackbringer with or without his help.'

'That's right, Mags!' chirped Pup. 'Ye can do anything!'

'How . . . ?' asked Talon. 'How do you catch a shadow? It sounds impossible—'

'So ready to cry impossible?' Magpie snapped. 'And leave that beast to eat the rest of your kin?' As soon as she said the words she wanted to bite them back. She squeezed her eyes shut.

Talon's face grew hot.

'Lass, lad . . .' said Orchidspike in a soothing voice.

'Nay, she's right, what do I know of impossible?' Talon said in a wretched voice.

Magpie slouched and said miserably. 'Neh, I'm sorry. I'm a brute. I just can't seem to hold it all in my head, what I know of him, what I don't know . . . what he is, and how to catch him . . .'

'Now 'Pie,' Calypso said encouragingly, 'ye'll catch him, sure. Come now, what do we know of the beast?'

She took a deep, shuddering breath and tried to calm herself. 'He's the Blackbringer,' she said slowly, 'and sure faeries only remember him as a nursery story. But that's our own doom, to forget. He was the worst devil there ever was. He was the dark come to life. A contagion of darkness, the hungry one . . . beast of night with flesh of smoke, wearing darkness like a cloak . . .'

Talon had a sudden clear and piercing thought. His eyes flew open.

'He called himself . . .' Magpie thought back. '*The heavens with the stars ripped out* . . . but ach, that's just poetry, neh?'

Talon spoke up. 'What if he's wearing a skin?'

Magpie looked skeptical. 'A skin?' she repeated.

'What you said about wearing darkness like a cloak, it made me think of a skin,' he said.

'Usually I can spot a skin.'

'Don't I know!'

'And made of what? The dark?'

Talon shrugged. 'The legends say the Djinn wove light, nay? Why not dark?'

'A skin . . . I don't know. When I was inside it,' Magpie said, 'it wasn't just a little patch of shadow. It was . . . I don't know, endless, empty . . . *infinite*.' The word leapt like a spark in her mind, and she felt the rush of an idea forming. It danced just out of reach.

Calypso asked, 'But why would the Djinn make something so nasty?'

'Could something else have made it?' Talon asked. 'If it's a skin, anything could be inside it.'

Magpie stared. Anything, she thought. Infinite. And she was reminded of the glyph for infinity, that eight laid on its side, and her pulse quickened.

'Lad . . .' Orchidspike said in a frightened whisper, and Talon turned to her. He saw a look of puzzlement on the healer's face and followed her gaze to Magpie's wings. At first he didn't know what was amiss. The knitting needles fairly flew along, unfurling neat rows of silk and spells behind them. He looked back at Orchidspike, then hastily back at the knitting needles.

They were moving very, very fast.

Spidersilk was flying off the bobbin.

'Every choice casts a shadow,' Magpie said low to herself, repeating the Magruwen's words, 'and sometimes those shadows stalk your dreams . . .'

Orchidspike's old fingers couldn't keep up with the furious pace of the spells. She lost her hold on the needles, and they clattered to the floor at her feet. Magpie didn't notice and neither, apparently, did the spells. Needles or not, the silk kept right on, zipping off the bobbin into the weave of Magpie's wings. Orchidspike drew back, astonished.

'He meant the choice between the world and the Astaroth,' Magpie said, speaking faster now, trying to keep pace with her thoughts. 'But what does that mean? Fade said the Djinn chose the world, but he never said what they did to the Astaroth. He never said they *killed* him.'

'Fade?' Talon repeated weakly. He glanced at the bobbin and saw it had almost run out. *That would put an end to it*, he thought, but when the tail end of the thread disappeared into the weave . . . with no spidersilk binding them, no physical substance at all . . . the spells kept right on going. Magpie's wings were knitting themselves, and perfectly. As fast as her thoughts moved, the spells moved, caught in the flow of some strong magic like leaves in a river, pulled inexorably along.

And that wasn't all.

Talon suddenly felt himself lose contact with the floor. He was lifted gently so his feet hung just above it, and he grabbed at the mantel in surprise. He saw Orchidspike clutching the arms of her rocker and the crows treading air with their wing tips as they all floated, helpless and wide-eyed. Magpie too was hovering above her chair, but she didn't seem to notice.

'And its eyes,' she said excitedly. 'No snag has eyes like that, like the Djinns' eyes!'

All around the castle, from the biddies to the stable sprouts to the ink-faced warriors on the ramparts, feet floated off the floor and a collective gasp went up every corridor and down every winding stair.

Magpie had forgotten the healing entirely now, and even as the last spells shimmied along the crisp new edge of her dragonfly wings, she rose into the air on them. 'The fire that burns its bellows can only turn to ash, he said to the Vritra . . . and . . . *he* was the bellows! The Blackbringer's no snag! He might be the Astaroth's final plague, but the Astaroth didn't *make* the Blackbringer . . . the Astaroth *is* the Blackbringer!'

Still hanging in the air bewildered, Talon asked, 'What's the Astaroth?'

Magpie whirled to face him. Her eyes were alight with revelation. 'He's the worst thing that ever was.' So enthralled had she been in her thoughts, Magpie didn't feel the impact of them until she heard herself speak those words. Suddenly she paled. Talon's feet dropped back onto the floor, and Orchidspike's rocker settled with a thud. 'The Astaroth . . .' Magpie whispered. A look of slow horror spread over her face. 'Jacksmoke, the skiving Astaroth . . .'

It all made so much sense now, so much dreadful sense. The Djinn hadn't killed him. They had translated him, somehow, into that thing of darkness. They had robbed him of his element. And he had returned for vengeance. *He* was the shadow that stalked the Magruwen's dreams. 'I got to go see the Magruwen again,' she whispered.

She turned to Orchidspike and said a distracted, *Thank you, Lady*, but the healer was too flabbergasted to respond. 'And Talon . . . thank you for the idea.' Even in her daze, their eyes caught for a moment, and both felt the air pulse faster around them. Magpie turned to the window, stepped up onto the ledge, and launched herself out. Talon saw her begin to fall in a graceful arc, and he felt his heart catch in his throat, thinking sure her wings weren't ready, weren't healed yet – they couldn't be, after all, it was impossible – but then she flicked them sharply and was propelled forward like a loosed arrow, and he remembered, *What do I know of impossible?*

'Come on, feathers!' she called back, and the crows roused themselves from their own stunned stupor and squeezed one by one out the window after her.

Talon and Orchidspike turned to each other. Their looks said, *How? What?* but before they could speak, Nettle and Orion charged through the doorway.

'Talon!' Nettle cried. 'Did you feel that magic? The devil—'

'Nay,' Talon said hastily. 'It wasn't. It was the lass.'

'What? How?' Nettle looked around the room. 'Where've they all gone?'

'To the Magruwen . . .'

'The Magruwen?' Orion gaped.

Talon went to the window. He had a strange look on his face when he turned to them and said, 'And I'm going to follow them.'

Nettle and Orion looked at him like he was crazy. 'Talon . . .' his sister began, 'how? Sure they're flying . . .'

He reached deep into his pocket, pulled out a wadded bit of stuff, and shook it. It fell open shining and much larger than it had seemed at first glance, and Nettle and Orion watched perplexed as Talon stepped into it, one foot at a time. 'Prince, is that a . . . *stocking*?' Orion asked with a look of dismay.

Talon didn't answer. He pulled the gauzy stuff over his head, and was Talon no more.

Nettle gasped. Orion stared.

A falcon hopped onto the window ledge and glided off into the forest.

30

'YE GOING TO TELL THE MAGRUWEN WHO YE ARE?' CALYPSO asked Magpie as they flew above the treetops.

Magpie snorted. 'Who I am? I'm flummoxed if I know that myself! Some skinful of secrets is what. But you were in on it all along, neh?' She fixed him with a glare. 'For shame, blackbird! You owe me a hundred years of secrets!'

'The imp made me swear!' he protested. 'Just doing my part, trying to grow ye up right. Besides, I only know what Snoshti told me.'

'Which was what?'

'Not the half of it, I reckon. I know my old dad, Dizzy, blessed ye himself here in Dreamdark when ye were wee. He gave ye a thief's iron nerves and fast fingers! And all those creatures who came to see ye were sure ye'd grow up some kind of special. I tell ye, the creatures might've had no magic to lose, but they had to watch the faeries dither theirs away, and we all suffer for it, neh? When the imps started telling how there'd be a faerie born to take things back to how they used to be, the creatures were mad keen on it and kept their eyes peeled for ye.'

'Take things back . . . ?' Magpie repeated. 'How am I supposed to do that? There's no turning back time! The world's different now. There's humans . . .'

'Ach,' Calypso croaked. 'Don't get in a frazzle. Just think on the next thing to do. The Magruwen, now, what're ye going to tell him? He weren't quite itching to help, as I recall.'

A flush came to Magpie's cheeks as she imagined actually speaking any of the words that might tell the Djinn King the truth of her. *You didn't mean to, but you dreamed me up to save the world, Lord.* Ha!

'Hoy there,' called Mingus from the rear of the flock. 'Looks like we're being followed!'

'Followed?' called Magpie, turning to look back.

'He dipped into the canopy just now, but he's on us, I ken. 'Tis a small falcon.'

'Falcon, indeed!' Magpie declared. 'It's that lad. Let him come.' With a twinkle in her eye, she added, 'Let's give that skin a good test. Come on!' She doubled her speed, zinging so fast forward the wind unworked her braid in no time and had her hair streaming loose behind her.

The crows sighed and groused. 'Don't she know we're no spring chicks?' Bertram grumbled, but the birds picked up their pace behind her.

And farther back, so did Talon. When Magpie sped up, he followed suit and found with a thrill that the faster he flew, the smoother he glided and the easier it was to stay aloft. He hadn't soared like this since early sprouthood when his father, keen to accustom his small son to the rush of flight, had carried him in his arms.

Those times were like little jewels he kept wrapped in velvet in his memory. Sprouthood had veered after that into darker times, when the other sprouts had lined up on the ramparts, gathered their courage, spread their wings, and leapt. Some had soared on the first try. Others had faltered and fallen into the waiting arms of uncles and aunts, to be carried up and encouraged to try again. He alone had never stood there and leapt. Not until today, leaving Nettle and Orion behind with their mouths hanging open.

He smiled and flew on.

It wasn't how it had been in those young days in his father's arms, though. He could still remember the feeling of swimming in sky, the way the air swirled and eddied around you, tangling itself in your hair, filling your mouth. The weavework of his falcon skin was like a glove, muting that sensation, so when a cool whisper of pure air hit his neck, he knew something was wrong. He remembered the lass's djinncraft knife pressed to his throat, and he swore.

'Bilge!' he cursed, trying to see the hole. 'Skive!' But he had no more luck seeing his own throat than was to be expected, and he couldn't pause to feel it with his fingers without dashing himself out of the sky. 'Skiving blast!' he muttered, and he began to slow.

The crows and the lass were growing smaller in the distance, and the air hitting Talon's throat was more than a whisper now; it was a steady flow. His perfect falcon skin was unraveling.

He knew he should turn aside and head back home before it gave out altogether and dropped him from the sky like a piece of windfall fruit. Where was the lass going, anyway? There was nothing down in southeastern Dreamdark but some recent Black Annis sightings and a whole lot of hedge imp warrens. It would be a long walk from here back to Rathersting Castle, long enough to catch him out after dark, and there were far worse things than the Black Annis abroad in the night these days.

He knew he should turn aside.

But he didn't.

Talon Rathersting whooped, and all the years of longing, all the nights of standing on the ramparts wishing, poured into his arms and uncommon wings, and he surged forward and began to bridge the distance between himself and the crows. Within moments, he knew they weren't headed for southeast Dreamdark at all, but beyond. Beyond. He caught a glimpse of the southern hedge, and on the far side of it an immense roof, a tower, and land rolling away to the south in a vast patchwork.

The human world.

The crows had scattered and disappeared into the forest just short of the hedge. Talon approached with caution, landing on an oak branch from which he could peer over and up the tidy lawn and gardens to the human place. For a moment, he forgot Magpie and the crows and stared at the gargantuan brick structure, its dozen chimneys, and the massive cattle grazing in the distance.

'Slap the slowpoke!' Magpie cried, suddenly dropping down from overhead and giving him a light cuff to the back of the neck. Talon nearly jumped out of his skin. Her hair was loose and wild over her shoulders, her eyes sparkled, and she was smiling. 'A game we play,' she told him as a couple of crows fluttered round on the branch. 'I'd smack you harder, but you didn't know the rules. So you get one pass.'

'Nice flying,' one of the birds said jovially. 'But hoy, have a care for your skin, neh?'

'Aye,' agreed Magpie. 'You're undone.'

Talon parted the skin and it slid aside, revealing his face, neck, and shoulders. He examined the hole and found it to be as big now as his fist. 'A djinncraft knife will do that,' he muttered.

'Ach! Did I do that?' Magpie cried, dismayed. 'I'm sorry! I'd never want to wreck a thing like that.'

'I can mend it later,' he said, stepping the rest of the way out of the skin and folding it away into his pocket. He looked back out through the hedge. 'The Magruwen's here?'

'Aye, down a well over in the garden.'

'What is this place?' Talon asked.

'Just a school for human lasses to learn their books.'

'Humans can read?'

Magpie nodded. 'Sure. They even write their own books. It's funny about mannies. They're no eejits. The things they can build, like bridges and ships? And they carve statues you'd swear could start breathing. But . . . they *are* eejits! All the killing! They'd as soon kill as look at one another half the time. But then I've seen 'em sleeping all scooched on one side of the bed so not to wake a little kitty. I can't figure 'em. Ach, there's one now.'

Talon spun to see, and he stared, transfixed. 'That?' he asked, surprised.

'What, you've never seen one?' Magpie asked.

'Nay,' he answered, craning his neck for a clear view of the human lass. She had yellow hair braided back and wore a white frock and shiny shoes. 'Doesn't look like a killer,' he observed, 'and she's not so big as I thought.'

'She's a real small one. Pretty too. They're not all, you know. Mannies can be devious ugly. And the smell? Devils got nothing on an unwashed human!' They watched the lass for a moment in silence. She sat herself daintily on a patch of grass and began spinning the wheels of a little toy she'd brought with her.

'First one I ever saw wasn't pretty at all,' Magpie said. 'He was a great, gnarled, evil-eyed brute with a matted black beard and all reeking of brew . . .' She realized Talon wasn't listening. He was still staring at the human lass, but he'd squinted his eyes and now he stood and leapt nimbly to a higher branch for a clearer view.

She followed him on wing. 'What is it?'

He was still squinting. 'That thing she's got,' he said, not breaking his gaze from the lass.

'The toy?'

'It's no toy. I know it well.'

'What do you mean?' Magpie squinted at it too.

'It's my granny's surrey, from the castle. I haven't seen it since I was wee. How the skiffle did that come here?'

'I can guess *how*,' Magpie said, her voice hard, 'but not why. That meat wouldn't dare go back down the well!'

'Who?' Talon asked.

'Crows!' Magpie called, and they all fluttered round. 'It seems that gobslotch of a scavenger is in the neighborhood.'

'Ach!' Pup puffed up. 'That irkmeat?'

'The one who escaped the dungeon?' Talon asked.

Magpie nodded. 'Talon, he's vermin, but he's cunning vermin. He was in service to the Blackbringer, though sure not of his own free will. His master sent him to the Magruwen for something; he said it was a turnip—'

'A turnip?'

'Aye, of all the blither! We need to find out what the Blackbringer was really after. Let's find that scavenger, crows.'

'Now?' asked Pigeon, scratching his head. 'What about the Magruwen?'

Magpie chewed her lip and said slowly, 'He's not going to just offer to help us. I got to convince him, and I want to know as much as I can know first. I got a feeling this thing the Blackbringer's after is important.'

'All right, 'Pie.' Calypso sighed. 'But I want ye to wait here and have a rest whilst we search.'

Magpie rolled her eyes. 'Feather—'

'Feather, nothing,' he said sternly. 'Rest.' He turned to Talon. 'Lad, ye'll see to it?'

Talon looked back and forth between the stubborn faerie and stern crow. He shrugged helplessly.

'Good lad,' said Calypso, spreading open his wings. 'We'll have a look around. Come on, blackbirds!' The crows burst squawking from the trees.

As soon as they were gone, Magpie said to Talon, 'Let's go.'

'Go? Calypso said—'

'Ach, you think I'm going to sit here? There's something else you should know. This imp? He was there when your folk met his master!'

Talon was still, his face frozen, staring back at Magpie. 'Indeed,' he said quietly. Suddenly he stood. 'What's he look like, this creature?'

'Like a scorched rat with a great big nose, wears diamonds on his tail.'

'Think I'll join in the search,' Talon replied, and dived from the branch. He caught another with one hand and whipped himself around, jackknifing and shooting out past the bramble, where he dropped from Magpie's sight.

Talon had never set foot beyond the hedge. He'd peered through it on the northern border of Dreamdark, where the land without was as wild as the forest within, and no humans ever wandered. A few days ago, he'd never have dreamed of venturing out into the world, even with a gang of cousins, and now he was leaping into it alone. *What a change a few days could make*, he thought, stalking through the grass.

But he wasn't alone. 'This way,' Magpie hissed, skimming up beside him. Together they darted into the shadow of the hulking school, Magpie flying low to the ground and Talon running, leaping. When he grabbed hold of a trellis post and swung himself wildly airborne, stretching headfirst and landing in a somersault to keep right on going, Magpie found herself grinning. She'd never known scamperers could move like that. She couldn't help watching him and had to remind herself to keep her eyes peeled for imps and roaming mannies.

'There's a kitchen garden past that fence,' Magpie said. 'Let's try there.'

Talon reached the fence first, and when Magpie landed at his side, he slapped the back of her neck and said, 'Slap the slowpoke!'

'Eh!'

'I'd smack you harder, but you're a lass,' he said with a wicked twinkle in his blue eyes.

'Ach.' She gave him a surly look and rubbed the back of her neck. 'Don't let that hold you back. The crows don't. But you won't have to worry – sure that's the last time you'll ever win.'

'Oh, aye?'

'Aye, now hush your spathering. See anything?'

They peered through the slats of the fence at the rampant mess of herbs within. Eyebright and lavender, sweet basil and lemon balm, a great jumble of shivering leaf and flower. A gnarled apple tree hung heavy boughs over a bench where a human lass sat shelling peas, and a dozen hens scratched in a sunny dooryard where another lass tossed out handfuls of grain.

Just then, another human came out the door. A mountain of manny she was, cradling in her arms a cat as gaunt as she was huge. She tossed it and it twisted in air, landing among the scattering hens with its ears flattened back and tail lashing. The human barked at it in her unlovely language and it skulked away, low as a weasel.

'That meat looks mean starved,' Magpie said, eyeing the cat warily. 'Don't let him see you. I don't like his looks one bit. Come on.' They prowled through the fence into the garden, taking care to keep well hidden as they scouted for any signs the imp had been there.

When Talon came across a human's abandoned shoe, it really sank into his mind where he was. He experienced a moment of wonder. He was in a manny garden! He felt as if he'd slipped into someone else's life, the way he'd slipped into his falcon skin. And watching Magpie prowl forth with the stealth of a fox, he realized that he *had* slipped into someone else's life: hers. Or at least, he was tagging along with it. Spying, hunting down devils, vanishing into thin air, visiting the Djinn King, racing with crows, all in a day? What must her life be like out in the wide world?

She suddenly drew back even with him. 'Bless me if that's not a shindy,' she said, pointing at the cluster of hens.

'A what?'

'A shindy. Look, see the featherless one?'

He saw it, a naked chicken scratching among the rest. 'Poor meat,' he said.

'Neh, that's how they are,' she told him. 'Wizards hatch 'em from rooster eggs they incubate in their armpits.'

'*Rooster* eggs?'

'Aye, shindies are mad rare. Wizards use 'em for servants. I'd guess his wizard's passed on, and he's made himself at home here.'

Talon laughed and cocked his head. 'You sure it's not just a bald chicken?'

'Aye, and we'll want to talk to him. Maybe he's seen Batch. But skive, that cat's keeping a cool eye over the place.'

They crouched side by side, scanning the garden with calculating eyes. There was half an open yard between the shindy and themselves, with two mannies and a starved cat standing by. Magpie clasped her fingers into fists, remembering Bellatrix telling her there was magic in her, and she smiled ruefully to herself. If there was, she had no notion how to summon it, not even to scare a cat, much less a monster like the Blackbringer!

Talon interrupted her thoughts. 'I'll go around the side and distract the cat, and you can get that shindy's attention.'

'Eh? What will you do?'

'I'll just make him a phantasm to chase,' Talon said. 'It's a clan spell. We use it to trick the spiders on raids, get 'em going the wrong way. Well . . .' He colored slightly. 'The others use it, anyway . . . on raids.'

Magpie was on the verge of telling him she'd handle it herself when she realized that was probably the story of his life. He didn't get to go with the other warriors because of his wings; he probably didn't get to do much but get left behind. 'Okay, then,' she said. 'But be careful.'

He nodded and disappeared into a thatch of dill. Magpie crept as close as she could get to the shindy while remaining hidden. She hoped the lad knew what he was doing. A picture came into her mind then of him skewering the Blackbringer's tongue on his blade, and she recalled he had saved her life. Surely he could trick a cat. She relaxed among some strawberry runners to see what he would do.

She didn't see him climb the apple tree, so she was as surprised as the cat when he – or rather, his phantasm – suddenly dropped from its branches to land right before the cat's nose. It was very lifelike for an illusion, Magpie thought, seeing no hint of the telltale traceries she'd detected around his falcon skin. She wouldn't have been able to tell the phantasm from the real lad. The cat's green eyes snapped open, but before it could move, the phantasm had flipped over its head and sprinted the length of its back, diving off its tail to land rolling and spring through the fence. With a yowl, the cat gave chase. Magpie wanted to watch, but she had her own part to play. She turned back to the shindy and lobbed a small strawberry at it, hitting its bare rump.

It turned and she waved and, after pausing to peck at the strawberry, it shuffled toward her. 'Bless me,' it said. 'A faerie? Never seen one of ye lot here.'

'Blessings, master shindy,' Magpie started to say.

'Strag,' he cut in. 'No masters among the clucks and mannies! Just Strag.'

'Strag, then. And I'm Magpie Windwitch—'

He cut in again with a low whistle. 'Well, feather my britches,' he said. 'If it en't little Foxlick, come back home!'

'Foxlick?' Magpie's hand flew to her hair. 'How do you—?'

'Oh, I know ye, I do indeed! How's the blessing coming on?'

'Eh?' puzzled Magpie. Just then Talon came up behind her, and Strag jumped at the sight of him. 'Skaw!' he exclaimed. 'Who scribbled on ye, faerie?'

'My great-uncle,' replied Talon, nonplussed. 'Who plucked you, chicken?'

Magpie nudged him with her elbow and made introductions. 'Strag, we're looking for someone.'

'Not so hasty, little missy. After all these years? Here I didn't think to see ye till ye were grown, but there ye are, in my own little yard! Let's see the blessing, eh? Please?'

Magpie glanced at Talon, who looked bewildered, and she said hesitantly, 'Er, the blessing? See, Strag, I didn't know about all that till yesterday.'

'Ach, imps and their secrets! Me, I'd've spilled the beans years ago. It was my finest bit of sparkle. I learnt it off my wizard. I gave ye a glamour, missy, a disguise for slipping amongst the mannies. Know what it is? Know what they never look twice at? A little brown bird! If it en't got color to catch their eye, it's nigh invisible to 'em. Ye'll see.'

'You mean . . . I can turn into a little brown bird?' Magpie asked.

'Aye, nothing simpler! Just picture it, like it's standing there in front of ye, ye ken, a wren or a nuthatch or what, then sort of step into it like boots.'

Magpie glanced at Talon again. He had his suspicious look back and he arched his eyebrow at her like a question. She chewed her lip and turned back to Strag and did as he described. She knew from Talon's gasp that it had worked. She fluttered her wings and caught sight of dull feathers out of the corner of her eye. Strag crowed with delight. 'Perfect! If a manny even noticed ye he'd just shoo ye out the window and forget all about ye!'

She stepped backward out of it and returned to normal. 'Sharp!' she said. She could feel Talon giving her a hard look, but she ignored it and hugged Strag. 'That'll be mad handy for spying. Thank you!'

His puckered chicken skin blushed all over. 'My pleasure. Now, what ye doing lurking in a hen yard if ye didn't come special to see me?'

'We're looking for someone,' Magpie replied. 'Big haunchy imp been sizzled bald. You seen him?'

'Hoy, aye, I saw the scoundrel! Never thought he'd haul his rump up the drainpipe but he did, and quick. Sure it helped, the cat being on his heels! Slink nearly made a meal of him!'

'Where did he go?'

'Right in that window.'

Magpie looked where he pointed, a drainpipe up to an open second-story window. 'Talon, you up for a shimmy?' she asked him.

He just gave her an icy look and nodded sharply, and Magpie frowned uncomfortably.

'Ye'll come back and see me, missy?' asked Strag.

'Aye, we'll be back, and soon. We got to go and see the Magruwen.'

'Skaw!' cried Strag. 'The Magruwen?'

'Aye, he's down the well there. Didn't you ever know?'

'The well?' The shindy looked stupefied. 'Neh! Sure but the mannies think it's cursed and won't go near it cause of the smoke and the smell of sulfur! Ye're saying it's the Djinn King . . . ?'

'Aye, and he's woken up from his long sleep.'

'The old scorch himself! Explains why carrots and turnips been coming out of the ground already cooked!'

'Turnips?' Magpie repeated, flicking a glance to the window Batch had climbed in. She muttered, 'That explains where the turnip came from, anywhich.'

'Hoy,' said Strag. 'Better hurry on. Slink's back.' The cat was perched on a fence post staring right at them.

'I'll distract him,' Magpie announced. Seeing the two human lasses so near, she added, 'I'm going to try on my glamour!', and she took a step and blinked herself into a little brown bird. 'Talon, run for the pipe. Thanks, Strag. Blessings!'

'My pleasure, Foxlick!' he called.

Magpie made straight for the cat, and she might have looked like a dull garden bird but she flew like a faerie. She zinged spirals round his head as he batted at her, and she scolded, 'For shame, you suck-toe, gawping after manny scraps! The Djinn dreamed you finer than that!'

'Djinn?' scoffed the cat. 'It's the humans' world now, bird, and we cats'll be snug in their laps while they pick the bones of every last creature! They'll clean their teeth with yours, if I don't first!'

Magpie gave the cat's whiskers a good tweak and darted out of reach so it keeled over backward swinging for her and toppled off the post with a yowl. Then she spun round and saw Talon had made it to the drainpipe and was well up it, so she sped to the windowsill, stepped out of her glamour, and sat herself down to wait for him.

When his head came into view, she said, 'Slap the—' But he knocked her hand away and scowled at her. 'Ach, what the skiffle, lad?' she asked, surprised.

'I didn't come all this way to play eejit sports,' he growled, climbing up onto the windowsill. 'Or to maraud manny schools with some lass who'll tell her secrets to some plucked chicken but not me—'

Magpie stared at him.

'I saved your life,' he went on, 'and I got you that skiving knife back that you near slit my throat with, and you just scolded me for it like I'm some sprout, and I helped knit your wings and I haven't asked you who you really are, even though I've seen you do things no faerie can do and for all I know you're in with that devil yourself!'

Magpie flushed. 'I didn't ask you along, if you'll recall,' she replied hotly, 'and I'll be happy to "maraud" without you! But I am sorry if I insulted you by including you in "eejit" games I've been playing with the crows since I was wee. You want to get back to Dreamdark and sit around fretting with all the others, you go. Better still, go on to Never Nigh, where they're saying I'm in with the devil. You'd fit right in! But about the knife . . .' Her hand went to Skuldraig. 'The only reason I didn't want you touching it is 'cause it's cursed, and if you'd tried to use it, it would have murdered you!'

There was a thick silence between them until Talon said with an awkward frown, 'Oh. Well, maybe you shouldn't leave it lying around, then.'

Magpie's mouth dropped open, and she chuffed indignantly. 'I'm sorry if nearly dying, I didn't keep better *inventory* of my things!' Then a flicker of shame came into her expression, and she chewed her lip and said roughly, 'But about saving my life . . . of course, thank you. Of course! I'm sorry I didn't say so sooner. I could barely even think; I just lost my friends . . .'

Now Talon looked ashamed, and his blush deepened. 'I know,' he said quickly. 'It's okay; I'm not grubbing for thanks. Just, all the secrets . . . I thought maybe you'd tell me, but you told that shindy—'

'I didn't! Strag knew it all before I did! I only just found out myself—'

'Found out what?'

'Er,' Magpie said, coloring crimson as she tried to imagine telling him what she'd learned. Even in her own head it sounded preposterous, so after a long pause she blurted, 'The imps and creatures gave me a blessing ceremony. I don't even remember it. They gave me gifts, like that glamour and seeing in the dark and all. First I knew of it was when Snoshti . . . er, took me, yesterday!'

Puzzled, Talon asked, 'Why? Why'd they bless you?'

Magpie shrugged. 'Look, you want to maraud or neh?' she asked in a surly voice. 'Or you can leave. Whichever.'

Scowling, Talon said, 'Okay then, let's go,' and they turned their attention to the window.

31

INSIDE WAS AN EMPTY SCHOOLROOM WITH TWO NEAT ROWS OF desks facing a world map and a globe, and shelves of books on the far wall. 'It looks like the schoolroom at the castle,' Talon said, 'only huge.'

They leapt to the floor and crossed on foot to the door. Peering out, they saw they were at the end of a corridor, with two more doors facing them. The first room was cluttered with painting easels and lumps of clay in sad replicas of manny heads, and it stank of turpentine. The second room stank too, but the odor wasn't turpentine. Magpie fluttered up to the top of a cabinet, and Talon climbed up beside her. Grimly they surveyed the room.

On shelves high and low creatures stood and crouched, frozen still, their eyes peeled open but lusterless. There were varmints with their tiny claws outstretched, tails curled, whiskers eerily still. Mice, voles, raccoons. A long row of dull-eyed birds stood upon the highest shelf; and below them, a sad little collection of their nests and eggs. Nothing moved. For a moment, Magpie thought the creatures were under some enchantment, but then she saw the jars.

They were jars not unlike those in a manny's pantry, from which she'd once or twice pilfered jelly. But in these were no apricots or honey, only creatures afloat in stinking liquid. Skinks, snakes, tiny frogs. Nothing moved. Nothing breathed. So many eyes in the room, and nothing blinked.

'All dead . . .' murmured Talon, stunned. Ill from the stink and the horror of it, he quietly took Magpie's hand. She held it tight.

'It's a collection,' she whispered, seeing how each dead thing was labeled in neat letters.

'It's murder,' Talon answered.

They heard muttering at the same moment their eyes fell on the butterflies. Case after case hung on the wall, of butterflies and moths pinned open dead and arranged like art.

And there in their midst was Batch Hangnail.

He stood poised at the edge of a tall cabinet. He seemed to be wearing wings. As Magpie and Talon watched, he brought his hands together, bent his legs, and sprang. It was the imp version of a swan dive, and for a moment he seemed to float, his luna moth wings catching the air, and a pure and nearly beatific look of hope came into his face. The next moment he dropped like a stone and hit the ground cursing.

'Come on,' Magpie said, dropping Talon's hand and taking to her wings. Talon followed, leaping easily from cabinet to cabinet. They reached the corner the imp had plunged from and found there a sickening sight. The luna moth wings had not been Batch's first attempt, clearly. One of the framed displays had been smashed open and plundered, and the cabinet was littered with butterfly carcasses bereft of their wings. One glance over the edge at the floor showed what had become of them. A litter of wings had gathered below in a drift, like leaves beneath an autumn tree, and Batch lay on his side in them, half buried and moaning.

With an icy look, Magpie stepped off the edge and dropped to land sharply in front of him. He peeled open one eye and saw her, snapped it shut again, and redoubled his moaning. 'Oh, woe . . .' he whimpered in scamper. 'Woe to poor Batch . . .'

'Get up,' Magpie said impatiently, nudging him with her foot, then harder when he didn't respond. 'I said get up!'

Snuffling, he sat upright. A pretty blue morpho wing was plastered to the dribbling mucus on the side of his face.

'You're lucky those butterflies were already dead, imp, or you'd have a bitter time of it!'

'Already dead . . .' He nodded and moaned. 'Mannies killed 'em, not me! I just want to fly away . . .'

'You didn't really think dead wings would fly you, now, did you?'

The great slubbering imp sat in the sad debris of spent wings and sobbed. Talon came headfirst down the edge of the cabinet like a lizard and stood next to Magpie, and they both listened as the imp moaned about how the magic had worn off his flying surrey as he made his great escape.

'Can't really blame a wretch for wishing to fly,' Talon said under his breath.

'Neh, perhaps, so long as he's given up on maiming faeries. But you know what I *can* blame him for?' She knelt down in front of Batch and forced him to look her straight in the eyes as she said, 'For not telling me about his master's tongue.'

The life seemed to drain from Batch, so that he drooped into a miserable, quivering mass. 'The tongue . . .' He fumbled for the tip of his tail with shaking hands and shoved it into his mouth, commencing to suckle it with loud, wet sounds, and his eyes squeezed tight shut.

'Imp, listen up!' Magpie said harshly, in no mood for pity. 'You left out some details before, neh? And because of it I lost some friends to your master! Now you'll tell me something else.

You said your master sent you to the Magruwen for a turnip. Well, that's blither! What's he really after?'

With a long snuffling sigh Batch answered her. Speaking around the tail in his mouth, he said something sounding like 'Mommamammid.'

'Eh?'

'*Mommamammid!*' He repeated the slobbering mumble until Magpie reached out and yanked his tail. 'Pomegranate!' Batch said as it whipped out of his mouth, flinging a spray of warm spittle.

Wiping her hands and grimacing, Magpie repeated, '*Pomegranate?*'

Batch nodded.

'Well, that doesn't make much more sense than a turnip! What's he want it for?'

'Flotched if I know!' retorted the imp. His tail groped for a large and particularly lovely monarch wing, and he held it to his face and honked his nose into it repeatedly before crumpling it and tossing it back onto the heap. Particles of orange wing clung to his quivering nostrils.

'A pomegranate,' Magpie said to Talon. 'What the skiffle?'

Batch caught sight of Talon's face then and did a double take. 'Munch! Ye're one of them shouty faeries,' he declared, drawing back.

'Aye,' said Talon. 'You want to tell me what happened to the others you saw?'

The imp sniffed and snuffed, wiped at his eyes and nose with the backs of his hands, pulling himself together. 'Master happened,' he told him with a shiver that worked itself all the way down his tail and set his rings to rattling.

Talon noticed the brass handles on the cabinets were rattling, too, and realized it wasn't Batch's shiver that was doing it. He nudged Magpie and said 'mannies.' They both turned to the door.

'Quick,' Magpie said. 'Put on your skin. And you, imp, you're coming with us.'

As Talon pulled his falcon skin out of his pocket, Magpie visioned the glyph for floating, and Batch rose right up out of his mound of butterfly wings with a squeal. Magpie stepped hastily into her bird glamour and grabbed his tail.

By the time the crowd of white-frocked lasses thundered into the room for class, all they glimpsed were the shadows of a falcon and a small brown bird darting out the open window, dragging a squealing rodent through the air behind them.

'Hoy! There's the lad in his skin!' Magpie heard Swig's voice. 'Jacksmoke, Ming, there's the imp!'

Still in their disguises, Magpie and Talon flew up to the roof of the school as Swig and Mingus came sweeping toward them, cawing out the squawk that would alert the others to come. 'Ye seen Mags, lad?' demanded Swig. He gave the little brown bird a curious look as it deposited the imp on the broad stone ledge of the roof, and just then it shivered and turned into Magpie.

Swig and Mingus gasped.

A hint of dizziness came over Magpie, and she teetered slightly on the edge of the roof before Talon reached out fast and grabbed her wrist. 'Steady!' he said.

'Eh, Mags, y'all right, pet?' the birds fussed, but their voices were cut off by the noisy arrival of Pup and Pigeon, followed shortly by Calypso and Bertram.

'Ye don't go off without telling us, ye hear?'

'Gave us a fright!'

'No more disappearing!'

Magpie let them carry on for a moment, but when their scolds showed no sign of slowing, she cut in loudly, 'Ach, birds! Stop spathering! We found the imp, neh? And I found out what the Blackbringer was after.'

'Eh, what?'

'A pomegranate!'

'For true?' They all cast skeptical glances at Batch. Pigeon asked, 'Ye sure he en't lying?'

'I don't know,' said Magpie. 'You lying, imp?'

But Batch wasn't paying attention. He was watching with a queer gleam in his eye as Talon folded up his falcon skin and put it in his pocket.

'Where'd that bird come from before, Mags?' Mingus asked.

'You mean this bird?' she said dramatically, conjuring the glamour and stepping into it. All the birds exclaimed and puffed up their feathers.

'How'd ye do that?' demanded Pup.

Magpie told them about Strag and they made her show them the bird again and again, and though she was smiling and laughing, the dizziness suddenly overcame her once more. This time it was Calypso who steadied her.

'What's that, 'Pie?' he demanded.

'Nothing.' She tried to shake it off. 'Look, it's time we get down the well, neh? I'm keen to know what this pomegranate is all about.'

Calypso was studying her closely. 'Ye're in no shape for it, little missy. Look at ye, swaying on yer feet. Sure ye're not fit to match wits with the Djinn King! Ye need to rest, pet, like I been saying.'

'There's no time for that, Calypso!' she protested, but even she could hear the feebleness in her voice as she said it. Her arms and legs felt leaden and slow, and her eyelids heavy. Stubbornly she claimed, 'You don't just sleep at times like this. Anywhich, it's nightfall, and the Blackbringer will be going on the hunt anytime now.'

'And what do ye think ye'll do if ye see him? Fight him, in this state? That'd serve the world poorly, I ken, getting yerself killed!'

'I'll be fine!'

'I'm sure ye will be, after some food and some sleep.'

Magpie tried to argue, but Calypso just looked back at her through eyes narrowed to slits, and she knew this was one she wouldn't win, because she knew he was right. She wasn't fit to meet either the Djinn or the Blackbringer right now. But she did hate to lose an argument, so she kept on, hands on hips. 'What if the Blackbringer goes back for the Magruwen tonight, eh? And we just sleep through it?'

'Is that the well?' Talon asked, pointing across the school gardens that lay blue in the twilight below.

'Aye, that's it.'

'Can't we just keep a lookout while you rest?'

Magpie chewed her lip.

'Aye, Mags. Sure there's someplace cozy to camp in the attic,' said Bertram. 'It's just under our feet. We can fix ye up a nice little bed.'

And so it was decided, they would take a few hours of rest while the crows kept a close eye on the Djinn's well.

The sprawling attic of the great manor was one long, dark, low-ceilinged room full of cobwebs and sheet-draped shapes that loomed like phantoms in the crimson light of evening. Mingus and Swig flew off together to steal food while the rest went in through a broken window. The faeries prowled among the stacks of old steamer trunks, dressmaker's mannequins, and crates of mysterious junk, looking for a place to make camp. They peered through the cracked door of a giant armoire and found it already occupied by bats. They lifted the visor of a suit of rusted armor to a pungent wilkie nest. In one corner a fort had been built of musty books, but a hobgoblin was curled up inside reading a romance by candlelight, and he waved them angrily away.

Finally they found a trunk with its lid flipped open, filled with a pile of old silk slips. Dust lay over it thick as snow, but Magpie and Talon climbed in and pushed the top layer of slips carefully into one corner, rolling the dust up with it, and the layer beneath made as soft a nest as they could have hoped for. Magpie called out quietly to the crows, and they winged their way through the dim forest of broken hat racks to perch on the trunk's edge, depositing Batch inside with a grunt and a squeal.

The faeries watched as the scavenger rubbed at his backside and dug through the silks to come up with a diamond ring. His eyes lit up. Magpie just shook her head, the serendipity never ceasing to amaze her. Why, she wondered, had no scavenger imp happened to be present at *her* blessing? Here was a gift she could have used. Not for diamonds, sure, but useful things, like where the Blackbringer was lurking now. Batch mumbled, 'I sat on it, it's mine!', and Magpie and Talon shrugged as he strung the ring on to his tail with all the others.

Finally giving in to her fatigue, Magpie collapsed into the deep cushion of silks and groaned, 'I can't decide if I'm more hungry or more tired.'

'Ach, Mags, ye don't need to decide. I know ye can eat in yer sleep,' teased Bertram.

'Aye, that I can. I'll just lie here with my mouth open and when the food comes, drop some in.'

That sounded good to Talon too, who flung himself down on the silks and lay there, sunk in the luxurious fabric, while a bone-deep exhaustion settled over his limbs and eyelids. The exhaustion was strangely satisfying. It brought to his mind the warriors returned from a web raid, lounging in front of the great fireplace, laughing and chewing lazily at whatever was put into their hands before falling asleep one by one to the glissando of their aunts' harps.

Swig and Mingus returned, carrying between them a linen napkin that they unfolded in the trunk to reveal an instant picnic of white cake, walnuts, sugared plums, and damp, dirty radishes just plucked from the garden. Pup and Pigeon took some away with them to keep the first watch, while Mingus tossed Magpie a little square wrapped in paper. 'Here, Mags,' he said.

'What's this . . . chocolate? *Chocolate?*' She swooned. 'Ach, Mingus, you always were my favorite!'

The other crows squawked in protest, and Talon watched with curiosity as Magpie unwrapped the paper to reveal a simple brown square. She sniffed it and swooned again with rapture, and to Talon it all seemed a bit of a fuss over a little brown square. He could tell Mingus was pleased, but the crow didn't say much until Magpie insisted he take the first bite.

'Not on yer feathers. I stole it special for ye. Eat, lass, eat.'

'I'll save it for dessert,' she decided. 'I like that, cake for dinner and chocolate for dessert!'

Talon found that hunger did in fact win out over exhaustion, and he dragged himself within reach of a walnut, a plum, and a bit of cake. Between six crows, two faeries, and an imp, the feast didn't last long, and soon they were listening to Batch lick and suck every last dribble of plum syrup from his fingers and toes.

Magpie caught a glimpse of his pink tongue gently probing between his toes, and she grimaced and turned toward Talon, producing again the little brown square. 'Ever tried chocolate?' she asked.

He shook his head, and she grinned. 'You won't believe this,' she told him, breaking him off a corner.

Skeptically he took it, and he saw she was waiting to watch him eat it, and he squinted at her. 'This some prank?' he asked.

'Neh! It's why humans aren't all bad. The Djinn might've dreamed up the cacao tree, but humans made this from it! Go on.'

So he tasted it. His eyes went wide, then closed, and he sank back into the silk and let the flavor overtake him. He could hear Magpie and the crows laughing at him, but it wasn't nasty laughter and it didn't bother him at all. When he'd finished eating his bit, he asked shyly, 'Do you think I might take a taste to my sister?'

Magpie smiled. 'Aye, sure! It can be my thanks for the use of her room!' She ate her own corner of the sweet and insisted on all the crows having a nibble. Then, catching a longing look from Batch, she flicked him a little piece, too. The remainder she wrapped back up in the paper to save for Nettle, then sank back with a groan. 'Thanks for the food, birds and mannies,' she said sleepily, then, as if remembering something, turned to Talon. 'That was a fine phantasm you made before.'

'You saw it?' he asked. 'What, can you see through fences, too?'

'Neh, but when it jumped out of the tree and near landed on the cat's head.'

Talon laughed. 'That? No doubt it looked a fine phantasm – that was me.'

'*You*, you?' She lifted her head. 'I thought you were doing a spell.'

'Sure, but first I had to get him to follow me. Once he came through the fence, he caught sight of the phantasm and chased it off.'

Magpie shook her head at him. 'You tetched?' she asked. 'Pouncing on that meat? I wouldn't have let you.'

'And who are you to let or not let me?' he asked, amused.

She shrugged. 'It's your first journey beyond, neh? I feel responsible for you.'

'Well, you're not.'

Calypso cut in. 'We're all responsible for one another, and that's how it is, lad. When ye're with us that goes for ye too, be ye a prince or neh.'

Talon flushed at the scolding. 'I didn't mean—' he started to say, but Magpie cut in.

'Piff! You should've seen him jump on that cat, birds, Like a lunatic!' It sounded like a criticism, but Talon saw the same wondering smile at the corners of her lips as when she'd called his skin 'uncommon,' and he found himself blushing just the same too. 'I want to see a phantasm, though,' she went on. 'You too tired to make one?'

'I can muster one up,' he said, pushing himself up on his elbows. He squinted a little in concentration, and while Magpie and the crows looked on, a ghost of himself seemed to stand up and step out of his body. It flickered a little, looked around, and suddenly leapt up onto the edge of the trunk between Calypso and Bertram, where it performed a silly dance before backflipping off the side and blinking out in mid-air.

The crows squawked and laughed, and Talon collapsed onto his back, grinning. 'Sharp!' Magpie cried, clapping.

Within his fort of books, the hobgoblin had come to a smooching scene and shouted for them to pipe down.

'How'd you do it?' Magpie asked Talon.

'It's the fifth glyph for phantom,' he told her, 'joined with what you want your phantasm to be – I used "self" there, but you don't have to. Then you just picture what you want it to do.'

Magpie's brow furrowed in thought. 'I only know four glyphs for phantom,' she said.

'Oh, aye?' he asked casually, adding, 'I know six.'

'*Six?*' she demanded. 'Flummox me! Can you show me that one you just did?'

'*Show* you?'

'Aye, look, just vision it, and I'll use memory touch to see it.'

'Memory touch? I read about that in one of Orchidspike's books . . . you're a memory mage?'

'A what? I don't know. I just learned the spell from some Sayash faeries. I'll teach you, if you teach me the phantasm.'

So Talon visioned the glyph, and Magpie touched her finger to his brow, and the glyph burned to life brightly in her own mind, too. Within a few moments she had a phantasm of her own doing a silly dance, and it was soon joined by another of Talon's, which mimed kicking Magpie's in the backside. 'Eh!' cried Magpie, and they dueled with their phantasms until they were laughing too hard to hold the glyphs clear, and the images faded away.

Once they'd stopped laughing, Magpie used the mirror image of the memory touch spell to touch the glyph into Talon's mind, and he carefully committed it to memory before opening his eyes.

Bertram had begun to snore on his perch, and Calypso gave Magpie a stern look and said, ''Pie, for the love of all that's blessed, *sleep*.'

'Ach. Bossy bird,' she grumbled, lying down and nestling herself into the silk. 'Good night, Talon,' she said, adding, 'and once we get back to the castle, you have to teach me the sixth glyph for phantom.'

'Sure,' he said softly. He closed his eyes. *The castle*, he thought, and a strange reluctance overcame him at the reminder of his real life. Not that the day had been all magic – nay, he felt sick just remembering the dead things floating in jars – but the thought of returning to the castle ramparts to stand watch, after all he'd seen today, all he'd done, made him feel dull and weary.

'It was a lot to take in all at once today, neh?' Magpie whispered, as if reading his mind.

'Aye,' he whispered back. 'This what it's like for you every day?'

'Neh, we keep clear of mannies as much as we can. But there's a wide lot to see in the world, sure, and a lot to do. And not just catching devils either. There's spells to save, and things to steal back from plunder monkeys, and temples to find, and the Djinns' old libraries to explore.'

'So that's what you do?' he asked. 'You go around hunting down spells and things?'

'Aye. My parents figured out a long time ago that magic is slipping out of the world, but it turns out it's worse than they know,' she said, thinking of the Tapestry, the unweaving, the Astaroth. 'Far worse.'

'What do you mean?'

'I been finding out some things lately,' she said. 'Some real dire things. But the one to worry on first is the Blackbringer.'

'What was all that you were saying back at the castle? About it being the . . . what was it? Asterisk?'

'Astaroth,' she corrected. 'He was a wind elemental, as ancient as the Djinn, who helped them make the world.'

'Eh? I never heard of that.'

'Neh, no one did. Things went bad betwixt 'em. The Astaroth made the devils, so the Djinn did away with him. I thought Fade meant they killed him, but now I think maybe they just changed him somehow, into the Blackbringer.'

'What's this about Fade?' Talon asked, arching an eyebrow at her.

'Er . . .' Magpie said, and nimble lies filled her mouth, ready to tumble out. But she bit them back. 'Well,' she said slowly, her eyes holding his gaze steady. 'When Snoshti took me away before . . . I met him.'

'What?' he asked with a laugh, thinking she was joking. 'Where?'

'In the canyon where he lives.'

He stopped laughing. 'I thought he was dead.'

'He is.'

'Don't tell me you've been to the Moonlit Gardens.'

She just looked at him.

'Impossible!' he exclaimed, remembering only as he said it: *What do I know of impossible? Less and less every minute, sure*, he thought, and paused before asking, 'Okay, but . . . *how*?'

'That blessing ceremony I told you about . . .' she said, and took a deep breath, blushing. 'Talon, listen, this is all going to sound mad, but here it is.'

She told him everything in one swift rush. By the end of it, he was just staring at her, and she said peevishly, 'You wanted to know, now you know. Say something.'

'So it's . . . the Tapestry? The . . . energy . . . that's all around us? Like a river?'

Magpie cocked her head and looked at him keenly. 'You feel it too?'

He nodded. 'When I'm knitting, it's like my mind falls into a river full of glyphs that just takes me . . .'

Magpie was nodding, too, and that wondering smile was playing at the corners of her lips. 'Flummox me,' she said. 'And Poppy felt it too. I guess I'm not alone like I always thought.'

'Do you think all faeries feel it?' Talon asked.

'I know they used to, before the Djinn forsook us.'

'Maybe when the Magruwen dreamed you his dreams sort of spilled over and touched other sprouts who were being born, too.'

'We are all the same age,' she mused. 'And we were all born in Dreamdark. I wonder if it's just us or if there are others too.'

'I wonder.'

'So you . . . believe me?' Magpie asked timidly.

He shrugged. 'Sure I never knew anyone like you before,' he said easily. 'But Magpie . . . if you were in the Gardens, did you happen to see . . . my folk?'

'Neh. The Blackbringer's victims aren't there.'

'What? Then where are they?'

'I don't know,' she said in a bleak voice.

Batch rolled over then and farted in his sleep, and Magpie and Talon both had to suppress snorts of laughter. 'It's good to know,' said Talon, 'that nothing's ever so serious that a squelch can't make you laugh.'

'Words to live by,' Magpie agreed.

Calypso said in an exasperated voice, 'Jacksmoke, faeries! Do I have to knock ye on the heads to make ye rest?'

They tried to stifle their laughter. As she rolled over onto her side, Magpie felt something dig into her hip, and she sat up suddenly. 'Oh!'

'What is it?' Talon asked.

Magpie was holding a little metal flask that was hooked onto her belt. 'I forgot about this,' she said sadly. 'Poppy gave it to me the day she . . .' Her mind rejected the word *died,* and she just trailed off. 'It's a potion she made. It's supposed to help you remember your dreams.' She unscrewed the little cap and took a deep breath before drinking a swig of it. 'Hmm,' she said. 'It tastes nice. Want some? Dreams, you know, Bellatrix said that dreams are everything.'

Talon shook his head and murmured, 'Bellatrix' with wonder as he reached for the flask. He took a sip and handed it back.

They flopped down back-to-back and nestled snug in the deep silks. 'Good night, Talon,' said Magpie.

'Good night, Magpie.'

They were fast asleep within a minute. On the edge of the trunk Calypso muttered, 'About time!'

32

THAT NIGHT TALON DREAMED OF FLYING, AS HE DID MOST nights. But when Calypso woke him a few hours later, he was filled not with longing or disappointment as he often was on waking to his real wings, but with an idea. His eyes snapped open, and he stared unseeing at the dust drifting overhead as an image spun slowly in his mind. An image of all twelve glyphs for flight joined into one exquisite pattern, a pattern he was certain had never existed before in all of time. A new spell for flight, which he would use to knit his next skin.

Magpie dreamed she was pursued by darkness, and in the dream she stood and let it steal over her like a numbing tide. She tossed in her sleep, murmuring. All around her the emptiness spread like a devastated sky, its dead and dying stars all but extinguished. But then in her dream she held aloft a light, a pure and piercing light, and those sparks flared in answer, one by one, and began to shine. She turned in a circle, and they were everywhere. She walked on with her light, and they began to fall into step behind her, and all night long in her sleep she walked through the darkness, until at last she found the edge of it and stepped back into the world. They filed out of the emptiness behind her, one by one: Poppy, Maniac, the tattooed warriors, even the fishermen, their turbans fallen sadly askew on their huge human heads as they came blinking back into the light.

She woke with a gasp and sat straight up, expecting to see them all around her, but she saw only Talon lying on his back, staring at the ceiling with a look of awe. He turned slowly to her, and when their eyes met, they were shining, bright with dreaming, filled with new magic, new ideas, and new hope.

'I think I know what happened to them,' Magpie said. 'The Blackbringer's victims, I think I know how to save 'em!'

33

THE HUGE HUMAN COOK AWOKE BEFORE DAWN WITH HER mouth watering from a dream of strawberries, but when she went yawning into the dooryard to gather some, she found the runners plucked clean of every last fruit. She didn't know who to blame, the kitchen maids or the cat, so she woke them all by banging two pots together and set them to work early without any breakfast. Some hedge imps took advantage of the noise to knock over a jar of nutmeg and stuff their pockets full before vanishing in a blink.

Not far away, two faeries and a crow stood on the lip of the old well with their bellies uncomfortably full of berries. 'You shouldn't have eaten that last one,' Magpie whispered to Talon.

'Couldn't leave *one*,' Talon replied with a groan. 'Got to finish what you start.'

'I don't know if my floating spell will hold you up now!'

Talon snorted, remembering the floating spell that had swept every soul in Rathersting Castle off their feet. 'You'll manage,' he whispered back.

'Ready, love?' asked Calypso. The other five crows had positioned themselves in the trees to keep watch from every direction.

'Aye. Here we go.' Magpie touched the spell to Talon's shoulder and when he stepped into the darkness, he drifted slowly downward. His moth wings fanned the air, guiding his drift, while Magpie hovered beside him and Calypso heaved overhead. They descended. A small ring of spelled light clung to them, but it made the darkness below all the blacker. The plumes of magic wafting up the well shaft were stronger than they had been the first time Magpie had come, and the air was hot and acrid as bad breath.

Magpie glanced at Talon and saw his face was white. 'You sure you want to come?' she whispered, at which he looked irritated, and some color came back into his cheeks.

'Aye,' he said. 'Why? You scared?'

'Sure. Only a fool doesn't fear. But it'll be okay . . .' she said, and mumbled as an afterthought, 'I'm almost sure of it.'

Down below, the Magruwen could hear their whispers as clearly as he could smell their bouquet of scents. Crow and cheroot, a breath of berries just eaten, and a curious whisper of nightspink that reminded him of the imps who used to bring Bellatrix's messages from the next world. He also detected the faint musk of that other imp, the Blackbringer's stooge, and wondered what business the lass had with such a dismal creature.

His pacing had worn a track through the treasure, and the smoke had taken on the motion of a tide, surging with him as he strode. He stopped now, an inferno contained by nothing but will, and faced the door.

'He wasn't wearing a skin before,' Magpie whispered to Talon when their feet touched down. So be careful for your eyes.' She pushed the door open and called out 'Lord Magruwen?' as she stepped into the cave. 'It's Magpie Windwitch, Lord. I hope it's okay—'

The Magruwen swept toward her. She felt his great restless

energy and saw he had grown still brighter than when she had sparked him awake. His flames whipped in a frenzy within his rough shape and she could scarcely look at him. He was pulsing, frenetic, thinly contained. Here was the Djinn King at full strength, and he was terrifying.

'You should have come years ago,' he hissed. 'You must learn to see before you wreak more havoc.'

'Havoc?' Magpie blinked in surprise, but before she could say any more, the Magruwen sucked her toward him in a funnel of heat and then flared wide, whipping himself into a vortex around her and sealing her from sight.

''Pie!' Calypso squawked, charging forward. The ends of his feathers sizzled against the wall of fire, and he had to hop back. He couldn't see through it. He tried to fly around it. There was no opening. Magpie had been enveloped. Frantic, Calypso called out to her.

Talon gaped at the cyclone of fire that had swallowed Magpie. He looked quickly around, crouched, and leapt, catching a stalactite and swinging himself up to a crevice in the cave ceiling where he wedged his feet and squinted down into the eye of the fiery tornado. He saw Magpie suspended within, apparently unconscious with her head thrown back, eyes closed, feet drifting above the smoke as she spun, limp, inside the wide whorl of flames.

'Calypso!' he called, and the crow beat his way over the flames, the stench of singed feathers strong on him. He spotted Magpie and exchanged a look with Talon. They both nodded, then the lad leapt and the crow dived, down into the center of the flames roaring round Magpie's floating figure. They perched upon the arched lid of a coffer that rose like a small island from the sea of smoke, one on either side of her, to guard her.

*

Magpie's eyes were closed, but other eyes had opened. Whether within her or beyond her, she knew not. A door had been flung open in her mind to reveal the thing she had always sensed waiting there, that coiled and patient power, the unseen pulse. The Tapestry.

Here the living lights didn't shimmy off the edges of her vision. They were all she saw. She lost track of her body and just stared at them, dazzled. Streamers of light shimmered and undulated in a pattern as intricate as the whole history of dreams poured tirelessly into its weave. It was vast, curving over every horizon of this mystical space where Magpie's mind now joined the Magruwen's.

He guided her eyes across the mesh of harmonious traceries and came to rest on a bright clot of light where they didn't interweave so much as snarl and snag. A flaw. Twisted threads, tangles. This was how devils were made. The Djinn was showing what the Astaroth had done, Magpie thought. Did that mean he was going to help her? But his next words stunned her. 'Behold your handiwork, little meddler,' he said.

She gasped. 'My—? Neh, I've never . . .' Her voice trailed off. But, of course, she had. Hadn't Bellatrix told her she could weave it? All these years of feeling the pulse all around her, was this what she'd been doing? She'd been desecrating the Tapestry! She was flooded with horror. 'I made snags?' she asked in a tiny, desperate voice.

He said, 'Nay, little bird. I don't know why these hideous knots of yours have wrought no devils, but they haven't.'

'I haven't . . . ruined it?' she asked.

'Nay,' he said. 'These knots of yours, you could consider them . . . *scabs*.'

'Scabs?'

'Ugly things, but without which a wound would never heal. They were a dream of the Vritra's, in fact, back in the time of the devil wars when wounds were many. Healers know the glyph for them and use it in their magic. It was one of those you saved when the Vritra was killed.'

'*I* saved . . .'

'Aye. Your knots have healed the Tapestry, little bird. Without them, the nothingness would have bled through its wounds and overtaken the world.'

Magpie was too stunned to respond.

'And we would not be here now,' the Magruwen's voice continued. 'I don't know where you came from or whether the world deserved to be spared, but it seems that choices were made whilst I slept, and I will accept them, for I had forsaken my place. But I am awake now, and I can't allow the fabric of creation to become an eyesore.'

Magpie braced herself. He was going to tell her not to meddle in the affairs of the Djinn. To close these new mystical eyes he'd just opened for her. Was he also going to tell her to let the Tapestry fall apart?

'You must control your wild magicks, child. If you knew the things you'd done! Gecko footprints in frosting! Is this the stuff of magic? You must learn to see and to weave. We must begin at once!'

'What? Lord, do you mean you'll *teach* me?'

'It's that or spell you into a bottle for safekeeping. The choice is yours.'

'But – *teach*, of course, Lord. Thank you!' Magpie cried. She could scarcely believe it. He didn't want to stop her! The Djinn King was going to teach her! 'I know just where to start,' she said eagerly. 'Stopping the Blackbringer – I haven't figured out how to go about that yet, you can help me with that, but there's something else—'

The Magruwen interrupted her. 'We will begin at the beginning. Hush.'

She closed her mouth.

The Tapestry began to roll before her then, and she had the sensation she was flying over a luminous landscape. The rolling slowed and stopped, and before her gleamed a thread, straight and true and much brighter than the smaller ones that anchored on to it. 'A warp thread,' the Magruwen told her. 'These are the bones of the Tapestry, and all other threads hang on them. The greatest are earth, air, water, and fire, and the lesser are the component elements of everything in this world, carbon, gold, manganese, and on . . .'

Magpie had never been to school. She'd learned at campfires while fanning cheroot smoke out of her face, or in selkies' caves or dungeons, or wherever the caravans set down for a season. With her parents and grandmother, she'd excavated the ruins of the Djinns' forsaken temples in four far-flung lands – those of the Ithuriel, the Sidi Haroun, the Iblis, and the Azazel – and she had helped her father bind and translate the ancient manuscripts they unearthed there. She had learned her glyphs from dozens of faeries in as many forests, from books she stole back from monkeys, even from the eyeless imps who swam the unfathomable springs of the water elementals.

Now here she was at the fount of all mystery, the Tapestry, with the Djinn King himself for a teacher. She knew her parents would pay toes for this chance, and so, ordinarily, would she. But her mind kept turning to the shadow that hunted in Dreamdark, and the look in Poppy's eyes as she dissolved right out of life.

'It will take you years to learn to read it,' the Magruwen went on, plucking each thread and glyph as he named it so it glowed brighter. 'Diamond, flamingo, rust, snow . . .'

'But I don't have years!' she said. 'The Blackbringer—!'

'Be still. The Tapestry will be no use to you unless you can understand it.'

Unhappily, Magpie listened. 'Fig, lava, zinc, spider, teeth . . .' She wouldn't have thought that here, beyond her body, she would be in danger of getting the wiggles, but she couldn't help herself. The Djinn's rasping voice began to wear away like a file at Magpie's patience. She fidgeted.

He came to a glyph she recognized, and she called out its meaning. 'Threshold!' It was part of the spell Snoshti had taught her for traveling to and from the Moonlit Gardens. It hit her how when she'd held that glyph in her mind, this was what she'd called upon, this bright symbol – it was something real – and she began to understand how it all worked. In her excitement, she felt a tingling in her fingertips. She gasped, and froze. Three curls of light were winding away from her like water snakes.

'Stop!' the Magruwen commanded, but it was too late. The threads hurtled into the Tapestry and sent a ripple through its weave. They burrowed into the fabric and cinched tight, making one more ugly knot.

'I'm sorry!' Magpie said. 'I didn't mean to!'

The Magruwen's voice seethed through her mind, filling it like the Blackbringer's had. 'You have no control. It's stronger than you, this gift. It will crush you.'

'Neh, Lord. Please! I can learn.'

'Look what you've done!' He guided her eyes closer to the new knot. 'Wild faerie feelings set loose? Is that the way to weave the world? There was not even a tear in the fabric here. Do you see what you have done?'

Her new threads had bound the thread for teeth to the glyph for threshold. The Djinn plucked at them and fell suddenly silent.

Then, while Magpie watched, the whole of the Tapestry spun with a dazzle of traceries as if the Magruwen were shifting it to see it from below. 'Nay . . .' he hissed. 'Devils?'

'Devils? I made devils?' Magpie cried.

He shifted the Tapestry again, fast. Threads glowed bright as he plucked and tested them. In agony, Magpie waited while he hissed and muttered to himself. Just a few days ago, she'd been fretting about turning a queen's hair into worms, and already she'd moved on to devils? Unable to contain herself, she asked, 'Lord? What did I do? Did I make a devil?'

'Nay . . .' he said at last. 'I thought – but, nay. It is a protection spell . . . it seems that now, a devil's tooth embedded in a doorway – threshold, you see? – will prevent other devils from entering.'

'But that's—'

'Rather fine, aye,' he interrupted. He was still muttering, but his tone had changed. 'You'll want to remember that,' he said. 'It may prove useful to you.'

Magpie was already itching to write it down in her book. She thought that if she learned to read the Tapestry, her pages were going to fill up fast. Her parents wouldn't believe it! She'd need a new book – or ten! 'Aye, mad useful!' she agreed. 'Of course, it probably won't work against the Blackbringer, since he's not a devil.'

'What?' asked the Magruwen sharply.

'Neh, for is he not the Astaroth dressed in shadow?'

No sooner had the words left her lips than the Tapestry disappeared and Magpie found herself shunted back into the sleeve of her body, falling. Some arms caught and held her. She peeled open her eyes, her real eyes, and blinked them back into focus to see a ring of fire racing around her.

''Pie!' Calypso squawked.

The Magruwen's voice cut in. 'What do you know of the Astaroth?' he demanded, abruptly coming to a halt and sucking all his swirling flames together into one blazing beast.

Talon's arms steadied Magpie on her feet, and she stood as brave as she could on the little island in the smoke. 'I know he's in Dreamdark right now, masquerading as the Blackbringer!' she said.

'How could you know that?' he demanded, flaring close to her face so she had to close her eyes against the searing heat. 'You stink of scavenger imp. And you, crow, of vulture! Who are you? More minions, come for it? No other could have told you. Are you his work after all?'

'Neh!' cried Magpie. 'I'm *your* work!'

'*My* work?'

A blush came to her cheeks and she cast sidelong looks at Calypso and Talon. She had a sudden thought and pulled the flask of Moonlight Mist off her belt. 'If you drink this, Lord, it can tell you better than I could.'

'Tell me what?'

'How . . . how you dreamed me . . .'

'I? I went to sleep to forget your deceitful race. I would never dream a faerie such as you.'

'I know. That's just what Bellatrix said.'

He wavered. '*Bellatrix?*'

'Aye.' Magpie held out the cordial.

'That scent of nightspink . . .' he began.

'Please just drink it,' she pleaded. 'It helps you remember your dreams. Then you can tell me I haven't dreamed it all myself!'

The Magruwen was still so close. Magpie, Talon, and Calypso were breathing raggedly, choking the hot air down in gasps and the flavor of their own scorched hair with it. Then the Djinn reached out his arms, took the flask, and tipped it into himself. A hiss of black steam issued forth where liquid met fire. He dropped the flask into the tidal smoke and said, 'Moonlight' heavily, before drawing closed his vertical eyes with a sigh.

34

THE MAGRUWEN HADN'T SEEN MOONLIGHT IN THE FOUR thousand years since he'd buried himself under the earth. The taste of it from the bottle flooded through him, and he experienced an intense craving for light, any light – sunset, starlight – and for horizons and wind and a feast of open sky. The cave seemed to be closing in around him.

Then the potion took effect. The first he knew of it was the remembered touch of Fade's mind curled against his own.

Fade's was the first life he had ever dreamed, when the world was yet a bare young orb, unpeopled and ungreen. And until the dragon's terrible death their minds had touched, like two countries with a shared border. After the dragon was ripped away from him – screaming hot wind and hot blood – one edge of the Djinn's mind lay ravaged and bereft, a cliff that fell away to nothingness. But in dreams the Magruwen became whole again, for there Fade's mind met his as it always had, even across the worlds.

So in his fury with this world and its treacheries, he had chosen sleep.

He had dreamed and dreamed, century after decade after day. Now those dreams washed over him anew. Memory opened, and all that had passed lay plain before him. And much had passed.

The lass spoke true. He had indeed dreamed her, but the dream, he saw, had come from across that border, somewhere in the deep realms of Fade's mind. Or rather, he thought, from deeper still. He knew Fade's dreams. These wild fancies of faeries – a faerie who could weave the Tapestry! – had not been born in a dragon's mind. In that far moon-washed world there was another mind he knew well, one obstinate soul who wouldn't shrink from such a trick. He had gone where her imps couldn't find him, so she had found another way of reaching him.

'Bellatrix,' he said, opening his eyes and blinking down at the lass.

'Aye, and Fade, too, Lord,' Magpie said.

'You've seen him?'

'Aye.' She twisted around and waggled a finger through the hole in the back of her shift. 'This is from his claw. He caught me falling off a cliff when my wings were crushed. Of course, he made me fall in the first place. He gave me a mad shiver. He—' She squinted up into the Djinn's bright face. 'He frets for you, Lord. He about roasted me when he heard the Blackbringer was back.' To the relief of the faeries and the crow, the Magruwen ebbed down to a thin column of flame. Breath came easier, and they were able to relax their squinting eyes.

'It was he who told you about the Astaroth,' he said.

'Aye,' she admitted. 'But he made me think you killed him. But you didn't, did you? Somehow, he's the Blackbringer.'

'What makes you think this, faerie?' he asked, sounding more intrigued than angry now.

'He has eyes like yours,' she said. 'And he's not like a snag. And' – she gestured to Talon at her side – 'Talon guessed the darkness was a skin, or I don't reckon I'd have thought of it at all.'

The Magruwen turned to Talon. 'What do you know of skins, Rathersting?'

'Er—' he stammered. 'Next to nothing—'

'He made one, Lord,' Magpie piped up.

'Indeed.'

'Aye, he's got it right here. Would you like to see it?'

Talon blushed around his tattoos, and the Djinn nodded.

Talon fumbled the skin out of his pocket and held it up with trembling hands. Its threads took on the orange glow of the Djinn, but the subtle sparkle of many other colors gleamed in its folds. The Magruwen's eyes moved over it quickly from top to bottom, then bottom to top, and then, after a glance at Talon, top to bottom again. 'Who taught you this?' he asked.

'Orchidspike the healer taught me to knit with the needles her foremother had from you, Lord. But I taught myself to spell a skin together.'

'Do other faeries now craft skins?'

Magpie answered, 'None I ever heard of.'

He reached out his hand but stopped and curled his fume fingers into a fist, knowing his touch would burn it. 'Won't you put it on?' he asked.

'Oh – aye, sure!' Talon answered, flustered. He shook out the skin and stepped into it, and Magpie had to reach out to steady him as he caught his foot in his haste. He shrugged it on, visioned it awake, and turned falcon in an instant.

The Magruwen exhaled curls of smoke and stared at him. 'Remarkable . . .' he breathed. 'Does it fly?'

Talon spread his wings and lifted himself into the air, where he wheeled among the stalactites for a moment before landing and peeling the head back from his skin. He was grinning. 'It's not as good as flying on real wings,' he said. 'But it beats staying on the ground.'

The Magruwen moved in close, his eyes reading Talon's skin like a page in a book and pausing only briefly at the flaw in the throat. 'Barbules from falcon feathers interknit with glyphs for flight and phantom . . .' he said. 'Very cleverly done. Did you think of using the glyph for floating as well, so you need expend no energy in staying aloft?'

'I thought of that *after* I started flying in it,' Talon admitted. 'It is some work. But I have another idea, Lord Magruwen . . . I thought of a way of joining the twelve glyphs for flight into one. I thought I'd try that in my next skin.'

At his side, Magpie's eyes popped wide open, and she turned to look at him in surprise.

'Join all twelve?' asked the Djinn.

'Aye. Do you think that would work?'

'Can you show it to me? Hold it clear in your mind.'

'Oh, aye.' The new pattern was still turning in Talon's mind, clear as when he'd dreamed it.

The Magruwen closed his eyes, and Talon held very still, hoping the Djinn wouldn't have to touch his forehead as Magpie had, but he felt only a slight prickle on the back of his neck, and then the Djinn blinked his eyes open again. 'Lad,' he said. 'Have you tried this yet?'

'Neh, I only dreamed it last night.'

'It is a very complex spell.'

Magpie cut in, 'I never even heard of a spell that fuses *twelve* glyphs! The most I ever saw was seven, and even that was only the one time.'

'Truly?' asked Talon, shamefaced. 'I didn't know . . . I reckon it won't work.'

'It will work,' said the Magruwen. 'It is extraordinary. You dreamed it, did you?'

'Aye, after I tasted that cordial.'

'Indeed.'

'The cordial was made by a faerie too, Lord Magruwen,' said Magpie. 'You see, we are more than butterflies.'

'I begin to see.'

'And the faerie who made it fell to the Blackbringer just days ago, as did Talon's father, who's the chief of the Rathersting, and his cousins, and many other faeries and creatures, too.'

'I warned you about this foe.'

'What good is a warning? I want help catching him! Can't you see now that there might be something in the world worth saving? Even Fade thinks so, even after what happened to him!'

The Magruwen sighed heavily, and long plumes of black smoke curled from his fiery horns. 'Perhaps,' he admitted at last. 'But it may be too late.'

'It can't be, Lord, it just can't be!' Magpie cried. 'Isn't there some way to make peace with him?'

'Peace? Nay, he is a force of hate. Even at his best he was fickle and tempestuous. Now? He is wrath. He is fury.'

'What did you do to him?'

'We were divided. Three of the Djinn were for ending him. The other three wanted mercy, something that could be undone one day if ever . . . if ever this world failed. The Vritra was for mercy, and it has been his own undoing. Mine was the deciding vote. I chose . . . mercy. Though now it's clear death would have been more merciful by far, to him and to the world.

'We met in secret. I reached up into the sky and cut down a swath of night, and we plucked out all the stars one by one until absolute blackness was all that remained.'

'The heavens with the stars ripped out!' said Magpie. 'That was what he called himself!'

The Magruwen nodded. 'Out of the fabric of night we fashioned a skin. We let him discover where we were hiding, and we lay in wait for him, and when he came sweeping down to earth we closed it around him and sealed it shut and there he was trapped, within a skin of darkness, his terrible power contained.'

'But—' began Magpie. 'He has other powers now. And that tongue—'

'Aye. He wasn't always so. He was only a shadow without voice or strength. But rage is a colossal force, and what the Astaroth lacked in dreams he made up in sheer, wicked will. He disappeared for centuries and then, when the whole world was the battlefield of the devil wars and the race of faeries was young and strong and the tide of the war seemed to have turned at last, he returned. He hunted the battlefields, devouring the wounded, faerie and devil both, and he grew stronger. That hideous tongue he cleaved from a dying devil and kept for himself. He gave himself a new name. He was the Blackbringer, and every living thing he touched turned to shadow.'

'Until the champions caught him and you sealed him in his bottle.'

'Aye. And now, again, he is returned.'

'What does he want?'

'To free himself and destroy the Tapestry.'

'Could he?'

'The Astaroth is the greatest force that ever was. The Tapestry is weak now. Even without him it has nearly fallen apart, and without you, little bird, it would have.'

Talon's head turned sharply in Magpie's direction, his eyebrows arching high in surprise.

Magpie asked, 'But what about the skin? Could he get out of it?'

'He will never get out of it.'

'Neh? How can you be certain?'

'Of this I can be certain. Only I can release him. And I never will.'

'Oh . . . so that's why he's come here, then. Not to kill you, at least not until he gets you to release him.' She paused, thinking. 'And the pomegranate, neh? That must have something to do with it.'

The Magruwen flared for a wild instant, then caught himself and sank back into a low burn. 'Pomegranate?' he repeated.

Magpie squinted at him. 'Aye, the one he sent the imp to you for. I can't figure what he'd want with a pomegranate.'

'Nor I,' said the Djinn.

Again Magpie squinted at him. It was clear from the way he had flared up that she had caught him off guard. Well, now he wanted to lie to her. What could she do about that? Chewing her lip, she said carefully, 'That's mad strange, neh? He came all this way for it. And you know nothing of it?'

The Magruwen was silent.

Magpie crossed her arms and frowned. 'Okay, then. But supposing we can put the Blackbringer back into his bottle, will you make a new seal for it?'

'If you capture him, little bird, I will seal the vessel.'

'Good. Thank you. This seal, though, it will have to hold out humans too.'

'I'll need something from them to work that magic.'

'Will hair do?'

'Aye.'

Magpie turned to Calypso. 'Would you mind, my feather, fetching us back a pigtail or two from above?'

He fluffed up his feathers, looking more ragged than ever after his brushes with the Djinn, and grumbled, 'I don't like leavin' ye, 'Pie.' He gave the Djinn King a hard look and asked Magpie, 'Ye'll be careful, neh?'

She hugged him around his neck and whispered, 'Aye, feather,' and he flew off. She turned back to the Magruwen. 'Will it take you long to make it?'

'Will it take you long to catch him?'

Magpie scowled. 'Go quicker if you'd help. But there's something else first, anywhich.'

'Oh, aye?'

'Aye . . .' She took a deep breath and blurted, 'I'm going to get them back! His victims.'

'Get them back? From where?'

'Well, I don't know! They never turned up in the Moonlit Gardens, Lord, and . . . I had this dream last night—'

'Quite a night for dreams it was.'

'Aye, and maybe we dream such things each night and don't remember them. Think of what's lost! Bellatrix said dreams are how everything begins, and I dreamed I let the darkness overtake me and then, inside, I held up a light—'

'No light can withstand that darkness. It will fade like everything else.'

'There *are* lights there, though,' she said. 'I've been there. I was inside him for an instant—'

The Magruwen flickered, surprised.

'And I saw dying lights everywhere. Sure you could fashion something. Stars – stars burn bright in the emptiness each night, neh?' A thought struck Magpie then. 'Wait. When you made the Blackbringer's skin, you said you plucked out all the stars?'

The Magruwen said nothing.

'Well, what did you do with them?' Magpie asked.

But even as she asked, she knew. Traceries spiraled across her vision, gleaming and glorious, as she caught a glimpse of the Tapestry with her inner eyes, without the Djinn's help. In that instant she saw the threads the Djinn had spun in secret so very long ago, gathered in hiding while the Astaroth raged against the Tapestry. Here it was, not just the skin of night, but also the receptacle for the stars the Djinn had plucked from it like berries.

'The pomegranate!' she cried. 'That's what it is! That's where you hid the stars!'

Before Magpie's eyes and Talon's, the Djinn suddenly flared again, as he had when Magpie had first mentioned the pomegranate, but now he didn't catch himself, and the deep blue fire of his core surged and overtook him, and the heat, like a woodstove door blowing open, knocked the faeries backward from their perch and into the deep smoke.

Lying on their backs with treasure poking into them while the smoke swirled madly just over their heads, Talon whispered to Magpie, 'I wish you'd quit surprising him like that. He's going to torch us one of these times.'

'Don't I know. First Fade almost snorted me into ash and now him. I wish he'd put on a skin.'

They rolled over onto their bellies and crawled through a spill of jewels. 'Look,' said Talon, holding up the edge of a piece of tattered fabric. It was much heavier than his own skin, but he knew it for what it was. 'There's why he isn't wearing a skin.'

'Ach, that thing must be mad ancient.'

'Aye, I reckon. Bet it has dragon scale woven in it, by the weight of it, to make it fireproof.'

'Come on.'

They crept and scampered under the smoke to a place where a

stack of helmets rose like a tower with its peak lost in clouds. They climbed it cautiously, holding their breath through the choking layer of smoke, and peered out to see that the Magruwen had gathered himself back in. He was waiting for them. 'There are . . . *lights* . . . within him?' he asked.

Magpie and Talon clambered onto the uppermost helmet and stood. 'I saw them,' Magpie answered. 'And in my dream, I held up a light and they all flared to life!'

'It was a dream.'

'Aye, a dream. And don't you think it could be true, that those could be their sparks still burning? Poppy, who made that cordial, could be trapped there, and Maniac, my crow brother, and Talon's kin . . . Lord, I have to try. I can't capture the Blackbringer without knowing – I could be trapping all those sparks in the darkness with him forever!'

'What you speak of, going willingly into him, it is suicide. He will do to you what he did to your friends and kin. He will unmake you. You will never enter that empty place, do you hear me?'

'But Lord Magruwen, if you give me the pomegranate, I—'

'In this you will be ruled by me! I would no sooner give you the pomegranate than unfasten the skin of night and loose the Astaroth on the world. It would amount to the same thing. Don't you see? That's what he wants. It's all he wants.'

'Oh,' said Magpie, understanding. 'The stars . . .'

'Restored to the skin, they would unlock it.'

Talon said, 'And he'd be free . . .'

'To destroy the Tapestry,' concluded the Magruwen.

'But *one* star—' continued Magpie stubbornly.

'Beyond question!' the Djinn King roared with such scorching finality that Magpie's mouth, opening out of habit to argue and cajole, found itself empty of words and snapped right shut.

'You will capture the Blackbringer,' the Djinn went on. 'And I will seal the bottle. You will attempt nothing else, do you understand?'

Magpie's mouth had pinched itself into a straight line, and her eyes flashed as she stared up at the Djinn, unblinking, and said nothing. He flared brighter, and still she didn't blink. Talon looked back and forth between them, the towering figure of living fire with his terrible horns and the twig of a lass perched on a teetering stack of helmets. The stare they held in common was like a fuse running between their eyes that any moment could ignite an explosion.

Finally Magpie said in a tight voice, 'I will make no promise to forsake my friends and brothers, if there is any possible chance I might save them.'

When the Magruwen let out an exasperated hiss, Talon had to duck under the spray of sparks.

'Pigtail delivery!' squawked Calypso from the doorway. They all turned to him unsmiling, and he caught sight of Magpie's face. 'Ach,' he said, flying over. 'Ye got on yer ornery mouth.' He whispered hoarsely in her ear, 'Sure ye're not defying the Djinn King, pet. I was *that* sure ye were no eejit.'

She turned her stern face on him then, and the line of her mouth softened into a frown. 'Ach, well, you may yet be surprised,' she said, then looked back up at the Magruwen. 'Lord,' she implored. 'Please . . . how better to start a new age than to right old wrongs? All those sparks the Blackbringer stole leave a lot of cold places behind in the world, empty shoes and torn lives, and why not start fresh by stealing them back and making things whole? Whatever it was faeries did in the past, whatever treachery, it's done, and sure the past can't be undone, but it can be forgiven. I swear I'll do everything I can to make you proud of faeries again, and how much finer will it be to build a new age on forgiveness than on anguish?'

'There will always be anguish.'

Magpie heard what he said, but paid closer heed to what he didn't say. He didn't say there would be no new age; he didn't say he could never forgive. With a stir of hope, she tried one last thing. 'And Lord, what of this? I saw all those lights in him! What if he keeps their sparks burning inside him? What if he *needs* them? What if they give him strength, and we can take them away?'

The Magruwen's vertical eyes looked hard at her. After a moment he said, 'Put the hair there, crow, and leave me. All of you.' He turned away. 'I'll have the seal for you tomorrow.'

Magpie waited, holding her breath. At length the Djinn muttered, almost inaudibly, 'And one star. One. Only one.'

The faeries had rejoined the crows and were well into Dreamdark when, behind them at the school grounds, the earth began to tremble.

The quaking was rhythmic as the approaching footsteps of some slow giant. In the manor, windowpanes rattled and fell still, rattled and fell still, again and again. White-faced, the humans listened in silence until the headmistress looked out the window to see smoke roiling out from the old well. Its plumes were *braiding* themselves in patterns as they rose to disperse on the wind. She gasped, and her gasp unlocked the moment. Schoolgirls shrieked. White frocks fluttered.

'To the chapel!' cried the headmistress, grabbing lasses and shoving them in the right direction.

In the dooryard the chickens ate on, merely jumping a little with each tremor. Strag the shindy perked up and looked around.

With unchickenlike agility he hopped up onto a fence post and gazed at the column of smoke. He had not yet been hatched the last time the world shook from the force of a Djinn's hammer on anvil, but he knew the sound for what it was, and his heartbeat quickened. Long had he dreamed that he would live to see the Djinn reclaim the world, and if the old scorch was back at work under the earth, that meant that times, well, they were most certainly going to change.

He threw back his bald head and crowed.

35

SEVERAL TIMES DURING THE FLIGHT OVER DREAMDARK, TALON switched crows midair, perfecting a daredevil leap between Bertram and Mingus whenever one or the other began to flag from his extra weight. As they swooped in toward the castle, he spotted his sister on the ramparts and dived off Bertram, flipping once to land in a crouch at Nettle's feet.

'Talon Rathersting!' she breathed in a deadly voice, grabbing his tunic with both fists and drawing his face close to hers. 'Where you been? Flying off like that—'

He answered, 'Beyond. I've been beyond,' and watched her mouth fall open. Magpie dropped down abruptly beside him and the crows began to land noisily on the ramparts. 'You won't believe it, Nettle,' said Talon. 'We saw the Magruwen!'

'Stubborn old scorch,' added Magpie.

'*Him* stubborn? I thought I was watching a stubborn match, and I'm still not sure who won!' Talon teased her. 'Oh, and by the way,' he added, reaching out to smack her neck, 'slap the slowpoke.'

'Skive!' She twisted away, smiling, and said, 'I thought you didn't play eejit sports, eh?'

Nettle, looking back and forth between them with her mouth still hanging open, managed to say, 'What?'

'Oh!' Magpie reached into her pocket and produced her last bit of chocolate.

Talon gave it to Nettle. 'It's manny food, Nettle. Try it!'

'Manny food?' she repeated, but before they could attempt an answer, Pup and Pigeon barged forward, tugging at Batch's tail while the imp still floated above their heads like a balloon.

He had a look of glee on his face and was crying, 'Wheeee!!!' and flapping his little arms, until Magpie unspelled him and he plopped back down onto the stones with a howl.

'Back to the dungeon with him,' Magpie said. 'But he's got to have a guard full-time.'

'Neh, not the dungeon!' protested Batch. 'Mudsucking munchmeats!'

'All right, come on,' Talon said, leading the way down a flight of stone steps. He glanced back at Nettle and said sternly, 'Eat that!'

Nettle watched the whole procession go by – faeries, crows, and one cursing imp – as her eyes narrowed with suspicion. But when they were gone, she unwrapped the little paper and hesitantly put the sweet in her mouth, and she felt considerably more forgiving after that.

After a quick encounter with some hot water and soap and a misguided attempt to drag a comb through her hair, Magpie straightened her tunic and headed down the labyrinthine corridors and stairs toward the great hall. There she found Talon in front of the massive fireplace with Orchidspike, Nettle, and two older faeries whom he introduced as his mother, Lady Bright, and his uncle Orion, the chief's brother. Like most of the ladies Magpie had seen about the castle, Talon's mother – Rathersting by marriage, not birth – had no tattoos. Orion was gruff and grizzled, with a broad scar marring half the black designs on his face.

Magpie curtsied to the lady, and Orion nodded to her and she nodded back, but her attention was claimed by the food on the long tables, platters and platters of food. As she greeted the others, her eyes kept returning to it. Chestnut pudding, corn bread, ripe red tomatoes, custard in fig syrup, soft blue beetlemilk cheeses wrapped in leaves, steaming stew, crispy fried squash blossoms . . . Her stomach rumbled loudly and a mere instant later Talon's stomach cut in even louder.

'Eat, then,' said Lady Bright, laughing, as a biddy set down an enormous tray of hot loaves.

They grabbed plates and heaped them high, then hauled them to a table where they began to eat as if it were a competition. If it *was* a competition, Magpie lost, for she slumped back in her chair and groaned while there was yet food on her plate. She said, 'If I had food like that waiting for me at the end of each day, I'd be fat as a tick on a manny's backside!'

Talon laughed into his second custard, and the faeries sipped cider until Orion called the council to begin.

Brandy was served and pipes were lit. Everyone but the warriors left the Hall, though Orchidspike and Magpie stayed in their places and the crows hunched in a cluster smoking the chief's tobacco. Chairs were scraped nearer the fire and elbows slung across knees as the warriors leaned forward to listen.

Orion stood. 'Gents,' he declaimed, then gave a nod to Orchidspike, Magpie, and Nettle. 'Lady and lasses. 'Tis a terrible time! Never in memory have the Rathersting failed in our duty to protect Dreamdark, but now we fail every night. Since the battle at Issrin Ev, we been chasing shadows whilst the fiend hunts free! Word's come that last eve, the whole Followtide clan down river way was took and only Codger Spindrift left behind, who'd fallen asleep in his canoe.'

A murmur went round.

'And that's not all. This very morning, as well you know, our raiding party came back smaller than it left. We lost Spiro and Bruxis in the Spiderdowns, but not to spiders, nay, and so we know now where the devil lurks. He's there in the worst of all places, and the spiders do his bidding like those vultures did, so it seems.'

Magpie and Talon stared at each other, alarmed.

'Dark's falling fast,' said a bearded older warrior, rising to his feet. 'And more will vanish tonight, nay? It's intolerable. We must end this devil now!'

'But you haven't seen it, Hornet,' said Orion. 'How do you stab a shadow? How can you kill a cloud?'

'You can't,' said Magpie. All eyes turned to her when she spoke, three dozen fierce pairs of eyes, framed in tattoos and mirroring the firelight back at her in their stares. She continued, 'You can only hope to capture it, and I've got its bottle.'

'And who are *you*?' asked a younger warrior, his voice hostile.

Talon's chair scraped back suddenly as he stood. 'Hiss, well you know the name of our guest, so mind your manners. She's Magpie Windwitch and she knows more about devils than any of us, and she's our best hope for catching this foe.'

There was a stir among the gents, of surprise and, Magpie thought, derision.

Talon went on. 'These two days' past, we've been beyond.' The murmuring grew louder. 'And we've had council with the Magruwen.' Gasps burst out. 'And we'll tell you what we've learned and what must be done.'

Talon and Magpie related all they knew of the Blackbringer,

and a dark silence settled over the Rathersting with the revelation that there was an eighth ancient stalking their wood on a rampage of vengeance.

'But can he be captured?' someone asked.

'The Djinns' champions did it once,' said Magpie, 'and we'll do it again.'

'Then we should do it tonight!' someone yelled, and a roar went round, and the stamping of feet. 'To war!' they bellowed, and some rose up on their wings.

'Neh—' said Magpie, but her voice was overpowered by the roaring, so she called out in her loudest crow squawk, 'Wait!'

They all swung to look at her. 'Wait,' she said again. 'The Magruwen's making a new seal, and we'll need that first. And there's something else. The chief and all the others? Once the devil's been caught there'll be no hope for 'em. If we're to bring 'em back, we got to do it first.'

They stared at her. 'Bring 'em back?' said Orion. 'Lass, what are you on about? Much may we mourn our fallen, but there's no coming back from the Moonlit Gardens!'

'They're not in the Moonlit Gardens,' she said.

'Now how could you know that?' demanded the one called Hiss with scorn thick in his voice.

'Indeed,' said Orchidspike, speaking for the first time. 'Magpie, what is it that you know?' she asked.

Magpie glanced around at the ferocious faces and wondered how to answer. Sure they wouldn't believe what she had to say. 'They're just not there,' she told them. 'I saw my friend Poppy turn into a shadow even as I held her. I was inside the Blackbringer for an instant myself and I felt my skin begin to melt away. I reckon I'd've become a shadow, too. So I think that's where they are.' She paused. '*In* him.'

There was silence, until Hiss broke it with a short laugh. '*In* him? You *think*?' He looked around at his fellows. 'What is she even doing here? This is a warriors' council! I say we go a-hunting, tonight!' he cried, and was joined by others.

Magpie gave Talon an anxious look, and he nodded and cried sharply, 'Hiss! Viper! The lot of you, have a thought. This is no spider or marsh hag, cousins, but the king of all the devils! You'll need a spell that's equal to him or you'll just be flying out to make yourselves his meal! Has any of you got such a spell up his sleeve? If you do, I'd very much like to hear it!'

No one answered.

Hiss shifted uneasily on his feet and looked surly. 'Then what, Prince?' he asked. 'Has *she* got a spell like that?'

'Aye!' said Talon. 'She has!'

This was a revelation to Magpie herself, and she cast Talon a sidelong glance.

'Let's have it then, and go!' Hiss went on.

Talon looked at Magpie and all the others did too. She lifted her chin, took a deep breath, and said, 'I won't be doing any capturing until I've brought back my friends and your kin and all the others, and that must wait till tomorrow, with the Magruwen's good grace.'

'That's madness! Whilst you play at raising the dead, the devil will be making more dead all the night long, and none are ever coming back again! Best to stop him before he gets anyone else!'

'Magpie's mouth drew into its most stubborn straight line, and she said, 'I know they're not dead, not proper dead, and they're nowhere in the Moonlit Gardens, and I'm going to get them back!'

'How?' asked Nettle simply.

'Magpie turned to her and said, 'I know what to do. I dreamed it—'

'*Dreamed* it?' interrupted a grizzled older faerie with a scoff that was met with laughter from the others. 'Lass, dreams are stuff and air, not battle plans!'

'You're wrong,' she said fiercely, meeting his eyes. 'Dreams are everything! I can't stop you trying to capture the Blackbringer yourselves, but nor will I help till I've brought out all those folk and creatures he made to shadows. I won't see them go in the bottle with him for the rest of forever. I won't!' Her voice had been steadily rising and with it the color in her cheeks, so that when she finished speaking her face was flushed and her eyes were flashing. She felt a tingling in her fingertips and clasped her hands together, but a soft shimmer had already flowed from them, though no one seemed to see it. They did, however, feel the air suddenly shift and sharpen round them and squeeze. It was so subtle they weren't certain what was happening, if anything at all, but the feeling silenced them. Talon looked sharply at Magpie, and the hairs on his arms stood up. The warriors weren't laughing now, but were eyeing Magpie warily.

'Orchidspike broke the silence. 'My lads,' she said. 'I know 'tis a sore and hollow thing for a warrior to sit idle, but there's magic in this lass that makes me hope. We don't know that she's not right. This Blackbringer, maybe he's wrapped his terrible cloak round our kinsmen and kept them. And maybe we can yet do something great. Aye, there's great risk, too, that more will be lost and none saved. But then, mayhap *all* will be saved.'

'But Lady, to balance lives on a sprout's dream . . .'

'You'll decide what you must, Orion, but I've felt a tide of mystery wash over us such as I've never felt in all my life, and it's my belief these are no ordinary dreams and this is no ordinary sprout.'

Orion frowned and looked at Magpie, small and ornery, and at his nephew by her side. He sighed, then told his men, 'No hunting tonight, then. I don't know about dreams and that, but

Talon's right. We're just not ready for this foe. There's naught I know to do against him.'

Not all the warriors were happy about this. Grumbles of 'another night' and 'strange lass' and 'Prince Scuttle' could be heard in deep muttering voices.

'We've warned all the hamlets and clans. We've done what we can. Tomorrow we'll hunt the Blackbringer in the Spiderdowns and be ready when he comes out again. But he'll hunt tonight, of that we can be sure, and I want to double the watch,' Orion continued. 'Hiss, Viper, Howl, Lash, Prowl, Thorn, Hornet, and Mars, with me. The rest of you, sleep.'

And so ended the council. Magpie felt some tension go out of her as the fierce tattooed faces found other things to scowl at besides herself. She left the hall with Talon and the crows. 'Tough crowd,' she told Talon with a shiver.

'They're feeling feeble and not much liking it.'

'Aye, bless their scowls. Sure I never met a warrior yet who didn't sneer at me as a wee useless lass . . . except you, anyway.'

'Well, I'm no warrior.'

'What? Course you are! Prince of 'em!'

'Nay,' he told her, flushing. 'I've never even been on a raid, because of . . .' He fluttered his wings.

'Well, maybe you haven't. But do you think you'd have ever made a skin if you could fly?'

He shrugged.

'I bet not,' she went on. 'You'd be just one of them in there, saying "neh" and never dreaming up a single new thing.'

They had come to a fork in the corridor, where Talon would turn toward the chief's tower and Magpie and the crows to the castle's guest cells. He asked her, 'Lass, do you really mean to go inside the Blackbringer again?'

‘Aye.’

From behind them, Bertram cut in. ‘I don’t like it, Mags. Sure I want Maniac back, but not if ye got to risk yerself.’

‘He’s right, ’Pie,’ said Calypso. ‘I en’t spent this life raising ye up ever so careful, and Lady Bellatrix didn’t talk Fade’s ear off all them years just so ye can go like that.’

‘And if he gets ye,’ added Pigeon, ‘who’ll get him? Sure nobody could, and that would mean the end of everything, forever!’

‘And wouldn’t yer mum skin us then!’ squawked Pup. ‘*And* good-imp Snoshti! She shivers me fierce.’

‘Ach, birds! You’re supposed to be on my side!’

‘We are,’ answered Bertram. ‘On the side of yer skin, love. How can ye keep from turning shadow like the others?’

‘There’s got to be a way.’

‘Maybe you’ll dream it tonight,’ Talon suggested.

‘I hope,’ she said. She hugged all the crows good night and went her way, calling back, ‘Good night, Talon.’

‘Good night, Magpie. Dream of magic,’ he called back.

‘You too.’

But the kind of dreams they meant, the ones that come tumbling like springs from unmapped deeps, full of hints and secrets, wouldn’t visit them this night, because both faeries were too anxious to sleep.

36

MAGPIE CLOSED HERSELF INTO HER WINDOWLESS CHAMBER deep within the castle and slouched on the edge of the bed, chewing her lip. Magic didn't come to you only in your sleep, sure. The Djinns' dreams – the luminous threads – those were open-eyed dreams, things of intention and will. But they were art, and hadn't the Djinn shown her just how artless she was? The magic she'd made – turning Vesper's hair to worms, sparking the Magruwen awake – had she ever done a bit of it on purpose? It just blurted from her like curse words when she was in temper and made chaos in the Tapestry. That was no way to take on the greatest foe her folk had ever known!

She opened her book and leafed through it. So the Magruwen would give her a star to light her way. That was something. But did she know any protection spells strong enough to withstand that sucking dark? Unlikely. Nothing in these pages would help her. She slammed the book closed. Things were different now. Bigger. And the same went with capturing him when that time came. Her usual tricks would be useless.

She stared at her hands, remembering the tingling that had come into them when the warriors in the hall had laughed at her. She'd had to bite her lip to quell the magic she'd felt surging up in her. How could she summon it when she needed it? How could she bend it to her will? The Magruwen had said the Tapestry would be no use to her unless she understood it. Well, she didn't, but there sure wasn't time just now to learn!

She sighed, wondering how the champions had captured the Blackbringer before. Suddenly she sat up straight with a grin. *Why not ask?* she thought. She closed her eyes and did as Snoshti had taught her, imagining herself fading while she visioned three glyphs in her mind, for threshold, for moonlight, and for garden, linked in just the right way. She held her breath, waiting to feel the winged touch, and when she did she sighed with relief, opening her eyes to the moon-washed riverscape.

Crossing the bridge to the Moonlit Gardens, Magpie caught the startled looks of faeries who'd witnessed her first crossing and who were stunned to see her come again. They whispered amongst one another and pointed, and she gave them a shy wave before taking to her wings and setting off toward the cottage carved into the cliff. Flying beside the whispering river, she felt a pang of loneliness. To be here, the only living soul in this quiet land, made her wish for the stuffiness and dust of that trunk in the mannies' attic, for the crows gathered round on all sides, the stolen picnic, the farting imp, and Talon.

Talon. She realized she'd memorized his tattoos as if they were a glyph and wondered what would happen if she visioned them like one. Would it summon him? She smiled at the thought. That would be sharp. He wasn't so bad to have around.

She reached the cliff's edge and descended on her wings down the rock-cut stairs, but as they curved and Bellatrix's garden came into view, she slowed and stopped. The lady was sitting there on the same stone bench where she'd braided Magpie's hair. She seemed to be looking out into the canyon, but one glance at her face made it clear that whatever she was seeing, it wasn't the familiar landscape.

Her beautiful face was a portrait of longing, of loneliness, and need. She had the eyes of one who knows exactly where the border lies between hope and despair and who has stood before it many times and looked across. Magpie had never seen such a look and a wave of sympathetic misery washed over her to see Bellatrix in such a state. She who was so brave . . . but it was more than bravery that bound Bellatrix here and kept her from joining the seraphim in the high planes.

What was it? She'd called it obstinacy, but even Magpie, who had but a sprout's understanding of it, could see that it was love, and it shivered her.

Love. She'd always thought of love as . . . affection, the look that passed often between her parents, or the feel of their arms around her. But wasn't it this too, the core of iron in someone's soul that made them capable of impossible things? It seemed a terrifying force.

If Kipepeo had never fallen to the Blackbringer, Magpie wondered, where would the world be now? If Bellatrix had followed the path laid out for her, had lived her life in the world, crossed the river as a biddy, and joined the seraphim when it was her time, there would have been no one here to notice when things began to go wrong. There would have been no one to trick the Magruwen, and Magpie might never have been. It was the lady's tragedy as well as Fade's that gave a flicker of hope to the rest of the world.

Magpie longed to give her hope in return. She thought of telling her of her dream, of the sparks trapped inside the Blackbringer, but she was afraid. What if it was all a fancy? Or would it be worse if it wasn't? Even if she could rescue some souls, surely Kipepeo had long ago subsided to darkness. Surely his spark couldn't be among those dull embers after so many thousands of years. She resolved to say nothing of it.

Bellatrix sensed her presence then and turned to Magpie, and her face lit up. She stood and held out her arms. 'Magpie, blessings, I needed a breath of life just now.' Magpie went the rest of the way down the stairs and stepped into Bellatrix's arms, and the lady clung to her and whispered, 'Child of my heart.'

A little later, when Bellatrix had poured some cordial for them into crystal glasses and they were sitting on the cliff's edge with their feet dangling over, watching the dragons, Bellatrix asked her, 'What brings you to visit, child?'

'I was wondering, Lady, how you . . .' She hesitated, knowing the question would bring memories of Kipepeo, but she went on. 'How did you capture the Blackbringer before?'

Bellatrix nodded. 'Ah, aye, I thought it might be that.' Her eyes went far away into memory. 'We tried many things,' she said. 'But it was one glyph that worked in the end, though there were six of us visioning it together. Magpie, do you know what a vortex is?'

Magpie answered hesitantly. 'It's . . . a whirlpool?'

'That's one kind of vortex,' said Bellatrix. 'A vortex can also form in the air, a whirling that draws all things to its center. Let me show you . . .'

And the two faeries bent their heads together and talked of magic. Bellatrix visioned a glyph, and Magpie touched it from her mind with her fingertip, and for a time they practiced conjuring the spell together. Magpie watched with fascination as the empty air below their dangling feet stirred, then spun – lazily at first, then whipping steadily faster until it began to tug blossoms off the tufts of nightspink overhanging the cliff and suck them in. She could feel the tug on her feet and hooked her toes to keep her slippers from flying off. 'Sharp!' she said.

But the spell faltered when a voice distracted them. 'Mistress! Mistress!' Magpie and Bellatrix both spun to see Snoshti hurrying down the stairs. The imp paused when she saw Magpie, then rushed down, crying, 'Blessings! My lady, my lass, it's bad, it's awful bad!'

The faeries both lifted themselves with their wings and rushed to meet the imp. 'What is it, Snoshti?' asked Bellatrix.

'It's—' she gasped, struggling for breath. 'It's the Magruwen! Strag . . . the shindy—' She gasped again. 'He saw . . . the Blackbringer . . . go down the well!'

37

IN DREAMDARK THE BLACKBRINGER SEEPED THROUGH THE TREES, seeming like a shadow cut loose from its moorings. Other nighthunters – foxes, bog hags, bats – fled before him as his hunger reached long fingers into the night. He was moving away from the school and the Djinn's well, headed back to the Spiderdowns, where he would sink out of reach of the coming light.

Throughout the great wood, creatures and faeries crouched hidden in cellars and burrows, tense and sleepless, knowing the darkness could come for them at any moment. Only in Never Nigh did the faeries sleep soundly within their wreath of ancient spells. But one bed, at least, was empty, for the Blackbringer was not the only one hunting this night. Queen Vesper sailed among the treetops, clutching her mirror in her hand and whispering a steady chant, 'Whatever your will, whatever your whim, come back to my mirror, your place is within,' as she searched furiously for her wayward slave.

At Rathersting Castle, Talon too was awake. All through the night he had hunched by his fire, clicking his needles together and knitting glyphs into spidersilk. All night his mind had flowed with the river of energy he now knew was the Tapestry, and it had guided his fingers and his mind as he made this new thing, rushing to finish it before the break of day.

Beyond the hedge, Magpie glimmered in silently beside the Magruwen's well. She lifted her head and sniffed the breeze like a creature. She prowled up the side of the well, cocked her head to listen, and sniffed again. Then she descended into the sulfurous dark. When she reached the bottom, she saw the Djinn's door stood open. Within was . . . darkness. Neither flame flickered nor ember glowed. Sick with memories of the Vritra's dreaming place, Magpie sagged against the doorframe.

The Magruwen was gone.

Despair filled her like a cup. She could scarcely find breath as panic overtook her, and she leaned there, gasping and dizzy. The Magruwen had only just awakened, and the world had trembled on the brink of a new age, but now . . . he was gone. She hadn't even gotten the seal or the pomegranate seed. It was too late. The Blackbringer would have the pomegranate. Even now, he could be peeling back its withered skin. The light of all those stars could be flooding back into the fabric of night, unlocking the ancient being imprisoned within.

At any moment, the Astaroth could burst free to destroy the world. Millions and millions of lives would subside into the endless ocean, just as the Magruwen had predicted. And then there would be nothing. Ever again.

Magpie fought to steady her breathing, and as she did she became aware of the pulse of the Tapestry all around her, aswirl and urgent, tugging at her like a tide, lifting her like a wind. She stood. She rose up on her wings, following it. So strong was its compulsion she felt she had scarcely to beat her wings but simply let it carry her, and as it did, a small hope flickered within her.

In the grip of the current of magic, she flew swiftly westward across the vast expanse of Dreamdark as the sun rose.

At the castle, Pup straggled bleary-eyed down the corridor to wake Magpie and opened her door to an empty room. Thinking she had already gone to the great hall for breakfast, he went to find her there. Within moments the crows were in a panic. They raced along the corridors, down to the dungeon where Batch lay muttering in his sleep, up to the ramparts where the warriors nodded grim good mornings to them. Magpie was nowhere to be found.

Hearing a ruckus, Talon laid his work aside and hurried from his room. Visions of the knives scattered at Issrin filled his mind, and for a terrible moment he was certain he would find that the guards had been swallowed in the night. But as he rounded the corner of the uppermost stair with a bound, he saw the guards all gathered with the crows and his panic eased . . . until he got a look at Calypso.

The bird's eyes were wild. 'Magpie's missing, lad,' he said.

Magpie hovered uncertainly above Issrin Ev. The ruin was as forlorn by dawn as it had been by dusk, more so now that grim memories of Poppy and Maniac haunted the place. She shuddered and wondered why she was here. The pulse had simply ebbed away and left her. She hung in the air and looked down, and then, through shadow and pine bough, suddenly she saw eyes peering up at her. A jolt went through her, and her first reflex carried her backward and away, but an instant later she realized whose eyes they were and who it was lurking down in Issrin Ev.

It was Vesper.

With a steely look, Magpie dived like a hawk, swooping low to the ground and coming in for a sharp landing in front of the lady, who drew back a step and looked at her with hate-filled eyes. 'Alive?' she hissed.

'Aye, and why should I be otherwise?' Magpie hissed back. 'If you're hunting your devil, you'll have no luck.'

'My devil?' repeated Vesper with a forced laugh.

'Aye, laugh!' Magpie spat. 'Even if the world wasn't about to rip wide open, I wouldn't trouble my mind with you, Lady. You're less than nothing. But it aches me something sick to see Bellatrix's crown on you, and her tunic. Give them to me now, *queen*!'

Vesper laughed again. Her hair was still hidden in its layers of scarves, still wrapped in pearl strands and crowned with Bellatrix's golden circlet. Standing there with the light of dawn shimmering across her firedrake scales, tall and elegant in her headdress of silks, she did look like a queen – like a cold, vicious queen on the wrong side of a legend. 'Little guttersnipe,' she purred. 'Who are *you* to threaten *me*?'

Her eyes never leaving Vesper's, Magpie slowly unsheathed Skuldraig and held the gleaming blade up in front of her face. With her lip drawing up in a snarl, she growled, 'I'm the one who wields Bellatrix's blade.'

Vesper's eyes widened, and she stared at the knife. She looked back and forth rapidly between Magpie's eyes and the blade, and her lips contorted into a snarl of her own. Magpie could see cunning in her expression, and greed.

'Which do you think's more useful in a fight, Lady?' Magpie asked. 'A dagger or a crown?'

Vesper's hand moved in her pocket, and Magpie held Skuldraig at the ready, thinking the lady was drawing out a blade of her own. But what she held out wasn't a blade. It was a mirror.

'Fine time for vanity!' Magpie scoffed.

Vesper replied in her most lilting, musical tones, 'Whatever your will, whatever your whim, look into my mirror . . .' Unthinking, Magpie flicked her eyes toward it in irritation, and the lady finished with a hiss, '. . . *Your place is within.*'

Magpie gasped. Vesper smiled. The mirror warped, and Magpie found herself staring at her own horrified reflection as she was drawn toward the mirror by some violent magic. Her body twisted with a thrill of pain. She was wrenched from her feet as her body stretched like a cast shadow, not like living flesh. Her vision blurred and she screamed, her eyes clenched shut in agony as she was sucked into Vesper's mirror.

The lady reached out and caught Magpie's wrist before it could disappear inside the glass. She twisted, and Skuldraig dropped to the moss. When she released Magpie's hand, the strange, attenuated shape of the lass was sucked swiftly in, and the silver surface closed over her and calmed like a pond. Vesper gazed into it and smiled. Nothing peered back at her now but her own lovely face. Magpie had vanished.

Vesper knelt and picked the dagger up off the moss.

At Rathersting Castle, Talon and the crows took the steps to the dungeon three and four at a time, arriving breathless before Batch's prison cell. 'What is it, Prince?' asked the faerie on guard.

'You can go, Hesperus. I'll see to this wretch.'

With a shrug, Hesperus left, and Talon turned to Batch, who was leering out at them with his beady black eyes, seeing their distress, already weighing it and calculating.

'Blessings of the morning, good-imp,' said Calypso.

'Suck lint,' said Batch.

Talon unlocked the cell and went over to the imp reclining in the straw. He knelt and said, 'Now listen, imp, I won't tell you what big things are happening in Dreamdark; sure you know already. But your master's worse a thing than even you know, and if you don't help us it could mean the end of everything.'

Batch carefully inserted his big toe into his nostril and rummaged.

Talon went on. 'Not just the end of faeries, you ken, the end of everything!'

Batch yawned.

'Listen!' Talon cried. 'We need you to find Magpie, do you hear? I know you find things. It's got to be you. You've got to help!'

Batch withdrew his toe from his nose and commenced to gnaw on his thick toenail. In exasperation Talon cried, 'Answer me!'

Calypso stepped forward. All too well he remembered the scavenger Lick and the events of Amitav Ev, and he knew the motives of imps better than Talon did. He said, 'Look, ye blighted soul, what's it going to take?'

And Batch released his toenail from between his teeth and looked at the crow with a gleam of interest.

'What's it going to cost?' demanded Calypso. 'What is it ye want?'

'Well,' said Batch with a wicked grin. 'I always been keen to fly.'

Vesper had slid her mirror back into her pocket and was feasting her eyes upon the elegant designs engraved on Bellatrix's blade. She laughed softly at her own good luck and wondered what that twig of a lass was doing with such a knife. Her mind turned to what Magpie had said about Gutsuck and she wondered, where was he? Well, she could only hope that whatever had happened to the cur, he'd at least dispatched that scavenger first. There was no place for Batch Hangnail in the world, not with what he knew.

She was just rising on her wings to return to Never Nigh when the crows plunged through the pines, caught sight of her, and began to caw. 'It's that wormy queen!' she heard one of them shout.

She turned with a sneer to retort but caught herself when she saw the Rathersting prince was with them, and carefully she rearranged her face into the look of lovely tranquility for which she was known. 'Young Lord Rathersting,' she said sweetly when he drew nigh, riding astride a crow.

'Lady Vesper,' he returned, his eyes narrowed with suspicion.

A small falcon flew at his side and Talon asked it, 'Are you certain?' to which it nodded and spiraled down to land in the temple courtyard, seeming strangely clumsy for such a hunter of the skies.

'Lady,' said the crow with the cracked beak, 'won't you tarry with us a moment?'

'Though it would be a pleasure, I must be on my way, my fine birds—'

'Ha!' one of the crows interrupted. 'More like "low creatures," en't we, Lady?'

'Certainly not,' she said with a sweet, sweet smile.

'Then please, join us,' said another, and by the way they surrounded her and the hard looks in their eyes, she knew they weren't asking. She took a good look at their scars and cracked beaks, their eye patches and peg legs, their scorched feathers and bandages, and thought better of trying to outrace them. With a quiver of anxiety, she tightened her grip on the handle of the dagger in her pocket and dropped back down into the rubble of broken statues. The crows landed noisily and perched all around her, and the Rathersting prince leapt from his mount and joined the peculiar falcon at the clearing's edge. They spoke under their breath together. She heard the lad whisper 'Her pocket? How can that be?', and she tensed. *They couldn't know!* she thought as they turned and approached her.

'Lady Vesper,' said the lad. 'We're looking for our friend, and good gossip tells us she's here with you.'

'Here with me?' Vesper asked, spinning and surveying the wastes of Issrin. 'As you see, there is no one else here.'

'Aye, 'tis mysterious strange,' said the crow with the cracked beak. 'But who among us hasn't seen stranger things in the wide world, eh?'

'I must ask you to empty your pockets,' said Talon.

Vesper laughed. 'You think I've your friend stuffed in my pocket?'

Talon didn't laugh. The crows drew tighter around Vesper. The falcon just watched. When the lad moved toward her as if he would empty her pocket himself, she hastily withdrew the mirror and held it up. ''Tis only a mirror,' she said, struggling to hide her fury beneath her mask of sweetness.

The falcon scurried forward – it didn't move like any bird – and she heard it chuckle. Her eyes narrowed. That chuckle . . . 'More pretties in the pocket than that,' it said, and she knew. She knew the voice. She stared.

The falcon shimmered before her eyes, and it was like a veil parting to reveal the leering face that haunted her dreams, the one who knew, the only one. The scavenger, Batch Hangnail, from whom she'd stolen the priceless tunic and crown in the alley behind a junk dealer's shop in Auld Reekie. He, who Gutsuck had sworn was dead, was here, alive and leering! Choking on her rage, she dropped the mirror onto the moss and delved deep in her pocket, coming up with the knife and raising it high. Screaming a stream of profanities that made even the crows' eyeballs bulge, she plunged it toward the imp.

Batch squealed and cowered.

Vesper's voice choked off. A strange thing happened. The knife swerved and swung wild, veering through the air even as she clung to it and plunging in a powerful arc into her own back. Her mouth made an *O* of surprise as she dropped to her knees.

The noise of the crows was deafening. Talon stared, knowing the knife at once. Cursed, Magpie had said it was. Cursed, indeed! Vesper wobbled on her knees, her face draining of color. The knife had bit between her shoulder blades, but it was no mere gown or cloak she wore. Bellatrix's knife had met Bellatrix's own firedrake tunic, and the knife had not sunk deep enough to stick. It fell to the moss and a thin spray of blood arced from her shallow wound.

Several droplets fell upon the surface of the lady's mirror.

Talon and the crows saw the glass suddenly warp. A hand broke through its surface, and they cried out in surprise. A whole arm reached forth, then a head emerged. 'Magpie!' cried Talon as she wrenched herself free of the enchanted mirror, emerging whole from the impossibly small space to lay curled on her side, gasping. Talon leapt to her. The crows squawked and screamed. Vesper sat stunned, staring at the bloodied knife on the moss.

'What happened?' Talon asked, helping Magpie to sit up. 'How did you get here?'

Magpie was pale. She carefully flexed her shoulders and looked around as if waking from a dream. She spotted Skuldraig lying on the ground and reached for it, wiping Vesper's blood from its tip and sliding it back into her sheath. Then she looked at Talon and around at the crows' anxious faces. 'I went back to the well . . .' she began.

'Without us? 'Pie, why would ye go off without us?'

'It was . . . I . . .' She shook her head. 'The Blackbringer had been there,' she said. 'The Magruwen is gone.'

They stared at her, speechless. 'Ye mean . . .' began Pup, but he couldn't find the words.

'I don't know,' said Magpie quietly.

Nearby, Batch had folded the falcon skin neatly and tucked it into his satchel. He prowled slowly toward Vesper, a look of malicious delight on his face.

'We meet again, m'lady,' he said, whisker stubs twitching.

'Hoy!' boomed a voice from the sky, and they all looked up. A flurry of wings swept over Issrin Ev. Faeries. 'What's happening there . . . Lady Queen!' Gasps and shouts went round in the sky, and the Never Nigh search party – for such it was, still hunting for Poppy – descended upon the scene, two dozen strong at least.

'Lady, my lady!' cried Kex Winterkill, falling upon Vesper. 'My petal, my blossom, you're bleeding! How came you here? Who did this to you?'

With a wild look, Vesper lifted a trembling hand and pointed it in turn at Batch and Magpie. 'Seize them!'

The gents who leapt at Vesper's command had never experienced anything like the squall of crows spitting fury around the lass who lay on the moss. None could get near her. They weren't warriors, these Never Nigh gents. Most were Manygreens or Winterkills or Shineleafs, faeries more accustomed to ferns and wheelbarrows than weapons.

'Wait!' cried one gent who had hung back from the start. 'Stop! Fellows, cousins! Stop this!' The faeries drew back and the crows hunched in a tight knot around Magpie and Talon. The gent went on. 'As we're not barbarians, we'll hear what this is about first, nay?'

Vesper's lips pinched white. 'Lord Manygreen, that's noble of you, but I assure you this lass tried to kill me. And as I hear, she was the last soul seen with your daughter before she went missing!'

Magpie peered out between Mingus and Bertram. The gent who had spoken had copper hair and brown eyes, just like Poppy's. Magpie rose unsteadily to her feet. 'Lord Manygreen,' she said. 'It's true I was last with Poppy. I know what happened to her. I'm sorry I couldn't come to tell you before.'

The cluster of faeries murmured and Poppy's father drew nearer, his face wretched with anxiety. 'Little Magpie, isn't it?' he asked. 'Please, where is she?'

'You've heard . . .' began Magpie. 'You know what hunts Dreamdark?'

'The Blackbringer,' he whispered.

Magpie nodded slowly and swallowed. 'Aye, and it's true, and he took Poppy right here in Issrin Ev, though I fought to save her—'

Lord Manygreen's face contorted with sadness and the murmur of the faeries rose to a clamor.

'And I'm still trying to save her! But the reason Poppy was even here' – Magpie turned to Vesper with a look of cold rage in her eyes – 'is because your fake queen set a devil on me, and Poppy flew all the way to warn me—'

'Lies!' Vesper cut her off, flicking open her wings and rising into the air between Magpie and the faeries. 'This guttersnipe sneak is wild with lies!'

Lord Manygreen gave her a penetrating look and said, 'I've a potion of Poppy's that turns liars' noses blue. Perhaps we should all have a sip.'

Vesper blinked at him and hesitated.

'I'll gladly have a sip,' said Batch, shaking off the gents who gripped his arms. 'And I'll tell you more about my old friend Vesper Siftdust.'

'Siftdust?' repeated Kex Winterkill.

'Hear me, citizens of Dreamdark—' Vesper hurriedly declaimed, but she was silenced by a sudden trembling in Issrin Ev. Everyone looked urgently around.

The slope quaked and rocks began to loosen and tumble, and those ruined pillars that remained standing began to sway. Magpie watched as the column from which Talon had leapt to save her life leaned and came tumbling toward them, and they all scattered as it crashed to the ground. They took to their wings. Bertram bumped Talon on to his back, and Mingus seized Batch by the tail and lifted him into the fork of a tree. They all watched transfixed as the pocked, mossy face of the temple burst from within and rumbled down the steep slope, crushing the long stair and leaving behind a ragged hole in the rock.

And there, in the hole, stood the Magruwen.

38

A TERRIFIED SILENCE HUNG OVER THE FAERIES. FEW NOW alive in the world had dreamed a day when the Djinn might again walk the earth, and no faerie present, save Magpie and Talon, knew him for what he was.

Even knowing him, Magpie and Talon were as awestruck as the rest. This was not the Magruwen as they had seen him in the bottom of the well. Here was the Djinn King in splendor in a new golden skin, and he was magnificent. His gleaming mask bore full lips and broad cheekbones engraved with a filigree not unlike the design of the Rathersting tattoos. A rim of ebony lined his almond-shaped vertical eyes, and many rings of gold looped from the lobes of his golden ears. His horns curved like molten scimitars, fire-bright, sparking, and alive, and from his shoulders flared immense bat wings of the thinnest burnished gold.

The last ruins of his old temple fell away at his feet, and he looked out at the faeries in the sky, spread his great wings, and rose into their midst.

It was Calypso who first lowered his head in a midair bow and cried, 'Hail, Lord Magruwen!' and Magpie, Talon, and the crows quickly followed suit.

Suppressed gasps and cries could be heard among the Never

Nigh faeries, who only now realized who and what they were seeing. With shaky voices they echoed the cry: 'Hail, Lord Magruwen!'

'Faeries,' said the Magruwen in his smoldering crackle of a voice. 'The last stones of Issrin Ev have fallen, and tomorrow the first stone of a new temple will be quarried and cut. Hai Issrin – *new* Issrin – Ev shall rise on this site. But that is the work of tomorrow, and tomorrow is a luxury you have too long believed your birthright. You have lived blind and dumb at the edge of darkness, and if not for the restless schemes of the dead, you would already have subsided into it. You little know how close you've come, and how even now you teeter at the brink!' His voice rose to a roar, and all trembled to hear it.

Among the encircling pine trees, Rathersting faeries were arriving from across the Deeps, and with them came the hamlet clans of East Mirth and Pickle's Gander, drawn by the great noise. They faltered onto branches and gaped at the scene before them.

'Like these stones, so much from the Dawn Days has fallen away. And like this temple, the world may be rebuilt or left to crumble. One of your kind had pled for you that you might prove what you can still become. If there *is* to be a new age born on the morrow, it can have but one beginning . . .' He paused and peered closely at all the faeries, his ebony-edged eyes lingering on Vesper a little longer than the others. 'The only beginning is a new champion, one who might this night vanquish the king of devils who hunts your wood!'

Murmurs of 'new champion' and 'Blackbringer' stirred among the faeries. Stalwart warriors puffed out their tattooed chests and envisioned themselves as champion. Among the Never Nigh folk, eyes turned to Vesper. Her own eyes widened in fear. She heard Kex Winterkill clear his throat, and before she could stop him, he cried, 'Hail, Lady Vesper, Queen of Dreamdark, descended of Bellatrix, champion!'

The Magruwen turned to Vesper, flames licking out from his eyes, his horns flaring high and bright, and he growled, 'Bellatrix has no descendant but the child that dreams made real!'

Emitting a squeak, Vesper spun to flee.

With one swift wing beat the Djinn surged through the air and swung around her to cut off her retreat. She flinched from him and seemed to shrink. 'My lord,' she whispered, 'I beg you let me go!'

'How came you by Bellatrix's ornaments?' the Magruwen demanded.

Whimpering, Vesper couldn't answer, and the only other who could have told had scuttled down from the fork in the tree at the first sight of the Magruwen and made his whistling way into the obscurity of the forest, his new falcon skin safe in his satchel.

The Djinn snatched the golden circlet from its perch on Vesper's headdress and the scarves fell away, too, revealing to all the clumps and masses of writhing worms that grew from her scalp. Her hands flew to her head. As faeries gasped and some of the Rathersting warriors jeered, Magpie felt her cheeks flush with shame for the lady, even in spite of her hatred. She almost wished to unwork the spell, but then she thought of Gutsuck's gaping gore-streaked mouth and hardened her heart.

'You are banished from Dreamdark, never to return,' the Magruwen pronounced, and Vesper, sniveling, wheeled in the air to flee. 'But wait,' said the Djinn, and she found herself frozen in place. 'Such a garment as that can never be remade, now that firedrakes are extinct. I'll have it, faerie.'

Vesper made no move to take it off, but the Magruwen flicked his hand and it was wrenched from her, its lacing loosening just enough to pull it over her head and off. Beneath it she wore a fine plain gown, and bereft of Bellatrix's treasures, with her wild living hair, she was nearly unrecognizable. She turned and fled Issrin Ev, leaving her Never Nigh subjects with their mouths agape.

'Fools,' the Magruwen hissed at them, clutching Bellatrix's tunic in one great gold-sheathed hand and her crown in the other. 'A crown does not a queen make, as a sword does not a warrior make . . . but for one. One blade there is, cursed to slay any who wield it but the champion. With it, Bellatrix turned the tide of the devil wars, and since then it has traveled through blood and dust, the ornament of skeletons, releasing all who claim it to the Moonlit Gardens. Skuldraig, it is called. Backbiter. You faeries believed you would know a new champion by the relics of the old one, and you were right. But you looked to the wrong relic.'

He paused and held up the circlet, and as they watched, its gleaming gold shone brighter still until it burned white-hot. It warped and melted and trickled down the Djinn's gauntlet, raining a patter of molten gold onto the tumbled stones below. 'This circlet was naught but ornament. But Skuldraig is power, and it has found a new mistress. And I, a new champion.'

Talon turned to stare at Magpie, and Magpie stared at the Magruwen, eyes wide, her lip clamped between her teeth. The Djinn said, 'Magpie Windwitch,' and all eyes swung to her. She flushed. 'Come here, little bird,' he said, and she flew to him, feeling tiny before him.

'Lord,' she whispered, 'I thought the Blackbringer . . .' She hesitated, suddenly seeing what folly it had been to think that this great being could fall so easily. 'He went down the well,' she said.

'He hears the whispers of the roots and springs. He knew I had gone and went to see what he could scavenge.'

Up close Magpie could see the new skin was wrought of many fine scales of gold interlinked in a sinuous mesh not unlike the firedrake tunic. She drank in the sight of him, recalling the wild flame that had swirled in the depths of the well, scorching and blinding her. He reached out his great golden hand. His fingertip, when it touched her forehead, was cool. No sooner did she feel it than a complex glyph sprang whole into her mind.

'This is the champion's glyph,' he said. 'It was once fused of seven sigils but with the passing of the Vritra now only six. When you hold it bright in your mind, only a Djinn can break through its protection. It will keep you whole in the darkness, but you must not let it slip, or you will be lost.'

As with any new glyph, Magpie set to work memorizing it. The whorls, angles, and patterns were more intricate than any glyph she had ever learned, and it was three-dimensional, an object in space. A glyph like this could never be recorded in a book but only pass from mind to mind. She concentrated fiercely, tracing its glowing lines until she was certain she knew it by heart. With a tremor of anxiety she nodded, and the Magruwen drew away his hand. The glyph faded. Magpie hoped her memory would serve her to call forth so fierce a spell when the time came. 'Thank you, Lord,' she said.

'Give me the dagger,' he commanded her, and she unsheathed Skuldraig and handed it to him. She bowed her head as he touched the blade to her shoulders, saying, 'I dub you, Magpie Windwitch, Magruwen's champion.' Then he took her hand and turned her to face the silent crowd.

Such a ceremony was a thing of legend, and the faeries gawked, unnerved, until Calypso once again broke the silence with a joyous squawk. 'Hail, Magpie Windwitch, Magruwen's champion!' he cried. The words were taken up by the faeries, but their voices were weak and their faces stunned. Talon's voice rang out above the rest, and his face was alight with joy. Magpie's eyes fastened on it in the crowd and their eyes held, shining.

Turning to the Magruwen, she said solemnly, 'It's my great pride and honor to serve you, Lord.'

'And you know what your first service must be.'

'Aye, I know.'

He held out the firedrake tunic. 'Put this on,' he instructed, and with reverence she took it. The scales felt cool, like enamel, and light, and she knew no better protection could be forged on any anvil. She slipped it over her head, easing her wings out through the apertures designed for them. The tunic was large on her, but she cinched her belt around it and looked back up at the Magruwen.

With a soft sparkle he conjured something in each hand. He presented first a seal bearing his sigil and glinting with dense magicks, and then a bundle wrapped in a familiar tatter. It was a scrap of the Djinn's burst skin Talon had seen abandoned beneath the smoke of the Magruwen's cave. Fireproof, as any Djinn's skin must be, it was rolled tight to contain the precious thing Magpie knew must burn within it, a seed from the mystical pomegranate. A star to light her way through the darkness and, she hoped, to spark the other lights to life.

'I hope you're right, little bird,' the Magruwen said gruffly.

'Me too.'

'Blessings fly with you, Magpie Windwitch.' The Djinn inclined his golden head and moved away, back toward the hole that would become his new temple. As he disappeared within, Magpie thought of the great place it had once been and would be again, if she succeeded.

She turned back to the crowd, and all those eyes just blinked at her. The faeries gathered here would later recount the Magruwen's return as a day of exaltation and boast of having witnessed it with their own eyes. They would forget the stunned stupor with which they had regarded their new champion, remembering instead the cheering and celebration that *should* have occurred.

At present, celebration was the last thing on Magpie's mind. She flew back toward the crowd, pausing before Poppy's father to tell him earnestly, 'I'm going to bring her back, sir.'

He reached out his hands, palms outfaced, and she pressed hers against them. They nodded to each other, and Magpie withdrew. To the crows and to Talon she said, 'At dusk we meet the Blackbringer,' and taking a deep breath, she added, 'in the Spiderdowns.'

39

MAGPIE STOOD IN THE DYING LIGHT AT THE EDGE OF THE Spiderdowns. Nothing grew in this poisoned place. The trees had long ago choked on the spiders' venom and warped into the tortured corpses they were now. Their bare branches twisted into a dense canopy from which hung sheets and clots of sticking web, and the earth beneath was split into ragged cracks.

'The light couldn't be worse,' Nettle was telling Magpie. 'The webs will be nigh invisible. We only ever go in at brightest dawn, when the dew shines and we can see every filament. This is . . .' Her words trailed off.

'Madness?'

'Aye, though sure it would be a greater madness to seek him belowground in the spiders' lair. Listen, you got to be quick. They'll drop down on you from above and spin you right up, and their venom kills flesh and curdles blood.'

'The light's going,' said Magpie. 'It's got to be now.' She glanced over her shoulder to where the full force of Rathersting might was mustered and ready for her signal. The crows clustered together around the Blackbringer's bottle, as wily and tattered as alley cats.

'Magpie,' Talon said. 'Wait. Last night I made something.' He pulled it out of his pocket, and when she saw its shimmer she thought it was a skin, but it wasn't. It was a single long cord of finely woven spidersilk, coiled like a rope. 'It's a tether,' he told her. 'To tie round yourself, so you can find your way back out of the dark.'

'Lad!' croaked Calypso and smacked him on the back. 'Blessings, but that's a fine thing! I'm shivered to think we mightn't have thought of it at all, and then what? Thanks to ye!'

'Aye . . .' Magpie spun the end of it between her fingers. It was thin as a whisker. 'Will it hold?' she asked.

'Try to cut it.'

'Eh?'

'Go ahead.'

With a frown of skepticism she unsheathed Skuldraig and touched it to the strand, expecting the blade to slice right through. It did not. She tried again harder but it only glanced off. 'Jacksmoke!' she said, slashing at it harder and smiling in wonderment. 'How'd you do that?'

'Knitted it with glyphs for strength,' he told her.

'You should use those on your next skin too.'

'For true,' he agreed. 'For you never know when a lass may try to slit your throat.'

'Ach!'

'Tie it round you. Go on. I'll be holding the other end, you ken, until you come back out.'

She bowed her head and tied the cord round her waist over Bellatrix's tunic, and when she looked back up, her smile was gone. 'I've never had such a shiver,' she told him quietly.

'Nor I.'

They shared a solemn look until Magpie broke it, chasing all anxiety from her eyes and saying abruptly, 'Here we go.' She tugged the tether hard to test her knot and said, squaring her shoulders, 'Hang on to me, Talon.'

'I will. Blessings, Magpie.'

Then, with the warriors following silently, she turned and walked in among the dead trees. She felt the presence of many spiders lying in lurk. Very many. She hadn't gone far before one plunged down at her on a silk tether of its own. She dived and had to scramble aside as it nearly landed on top of her. She stabbed at it and it burst like the bagful of venom it was. As its eight spindly legs danced a frenzied death, she stood and prowled on, deeper into the Downs.

The fissures in the dead earth widened, their edges crusted with congealed poison and the bones and wings of dead things. The Blackbringer was down in one of those cracks while spiders boiled up and out to do his bidding.

Dark deepened.

Magpie dodged another spider, and it skittered past her toward the advancing Rathersting. She heard a pop and gush as it was dispatched. Another came and she slew it and watched its fat bag of a body shrivel as its venom drooled out. She shuddered in disgust. It seemed impossible she owed her own wings to these vile things, but so it was, and for that reason the Rathersting suffered them to live, century after century.

But not this night. Looking back, Magpie saw many dark shapes spring down onto the warriors, and a frenzy of slaying ensued. She killed two more herself, felt the sizzle of their poison on her hands and arms, and whirled back toward the black cracks in the ground, her senses reeling wildly, trying to stay alert to everything, all around, as night fell.

A warrior screamed somewhere behind her and the hairs pricked up on her neck. More spiders came boiling up out of the ground and shambled forth. So many! She visioned a hasty spell for light as she leapt and dodged them, trying to keep clear of the sly filaments of web stretched from tree to tree. She heard another faerie cry out.

This would never do! The faeries couldn't possibly dodge all these spiders and the Blackbringer, too, once he showed himself, and that was sure to be soon . . .

He rose.

This time he came as no slow fume. He jetted from the earth in a dark spew, churning through the air and sucking his skin into the shape of a horned beast. It was but a mockery of the Magruwen's form, a pathetic imitation by a creature with no dreams of his own. He landed crouched, his darkness pooling and shifting. Squinting, Magpie could just detect the dense thatch of traceries alive over the skin of him, tightly woven of many, many glyphs. It was a calculus of magic such as she had never dreamed, a prison wrought of the Djinns' highest craft.

He turned to Magpie, fixing her with savage eyes. 'You,' he purred. 'I've been hunting for you.'

'And I for you, Blackbringer,' she returned, then bellowed, 'Warriors! Now!' and the Rathersting leapt, whooping their war cries, veering in the air, slashing down spiders and web as they drew round to encircle the Blackbringer.

He laughed at them. 'Do you think you can slay me, faeries? Or have you come to spare me the trouble of hunting this night?'

'We'll spare you the trouble of hunting ever again!' spat Magpie.

He laughed once more, and from within him his ghastly tongue suddenly unspooled and shot at her. She leapt against the side of a tree just as a spider rappelled down it. Its fangs missed her face by a hair's breadth. She flung it to the ground. The Blackbringer drew his tongue back and hurled it again. An old warrior heaved himself clear of it and fell within reach of a spider. The spider reared and struck, and the warrior screamed.

Magpie knew it was time to conjure the champion's glyph and dive into the darkness, but she hesitated. She couldn't leave the Rathersting like this! She glanced back at Talon, who held a knife in one hand and her tether tight in the other, leaping and slashing as more spiders came at him and more. There were just too many!

With a great thrust of will, Magpie forced open the inner eyes the Magruwen had revealed to her, and even in the heart of that terrible place the sight of the Tapestry dazzled her. A thread glinted and caught her eye, and she recognized it at once. The Magruwen had named it for her; it was the thread for spider. With ferocious concentration, she reached for it now. The pulse roiled around her like rapids as she conjured beside it one of the simplest of glyphs, the symbol for sleep. Urgently she intertwined them. It was a desperate move. Fusing glyphs was a precise art, and joining the same symbols into different patterns could result in wildly unpredictable magicks. For all she knew, she could be casting a spell that would make the spiders' bite induce a deep sleep from which there was no waking.

But then she heard the rain of thick bodies hitting the earth and she knew she had gotten it right. The ground in the Downs, lit intermittently by the spells of the warriors, was littered with heaps of the stunned spiders. Magpie held the new glyph in her mind. She would have to maintain it even as she conjured the champion's glyph, or the spiders would awaken. She didn't know if she was capable of such a thing.

She would have to be!

Gathering all her will, she summoned the champion's glyph forth in her mind, and it bloomed there great and shining and spun beside the smaller spell. She felt the strain of it at once, as if an hourglass had been turned and her strength was beginning to slip away. How long could she hold it? She little knew.

In her fierce concentration, she didn't see the tongue coming. Straight at her it struck. But before she could even gasp, a flare of light exploded and the slithering gray thing was slapped aside with a sizzle. It fell limp to the ground.

The champion's glyph had protected her.

The Blackbringer reeled his tongue back, dragging it through the strewn spiders. Magpie felt his surprise. He released the absurd shape he had been affecting and became again a loose clot of deepest dark.

'Who—?' he started to hiss.

Then Magpie sprang. Holding the two spells side by side in her mind, she dived into the darkness of the Blackbringer and disappeared.

Talon saw her leap and gave her tether slack. He tried to catch a glimmer of her inside the beast but saw only blackness. He shivered, and hoped. He felt a slow tug at the silk line. Magpie had gone into a deep and endless place, and she was moving away from him. He slowly fed the slack to her, kept his eyes on his foe, and waited.

The Blackbringer paused in shock. He'd reached for the faerie, tasting her power on the air, eager to unskin her spark and drink her light and surge with stolen strength as she ebbed into the emptiness.

Instead he was stung, stunned. It had been thousands and thousands of years since last he'd felt it, but instantly he knew the force that thwarted him. The Magruwen. *Traitor.* And this lass with Skuldraig in her grasp – she was the Djinn King's champion. A new champion!

Yanking back his stunned tongue, the Blackbringer remembered the other, the huntress who had undone his armies and finally himself. His bane, Bellatrix. He had believed the world fallen and all such power with it, but he'd been wrong. He experienced a pang of fear as he looked at the small fierce lass.

And then she stunned him again. She dived into him.

Her power didn't surge instantly into his own as with all the other, weaker faeries, but he knew it wouldn't. She wielded the champion's glyph, and as long as she could vision it, she would be whole. The Ithuriel's champion, that Ifrit warrior with coffee-black skin who'd been his final victim in the Dawn Days, had held himself whole far longer than the Blackbringer would have thought possible. Into the bottle and into the ocean, Kipepeo had clung to that glyph inside the Blackbringer, adrift in the emptiness and not knowing he had already gone beyond all rescue. He had held on fiercely to life, some power beyond magic feeding him strength. But it was useless. He was a prisoner within a prisoner within a prison. When he had at last faltered and failed, the Blackbringer had tasted his power and raged inside his bottle, frenzied with strength and unable to spend it.

This new champion, too, would fail. It was only a matter of when.

Magpie struggled to hold the glyphs bright in her mind and peered around. Darkness without end. It was like falling outside of time, outside the world. As in her memory and in her dream, dim lights flickered in the black. She groped for the bundle the Magruwen had given her and with utmost care unwrapped it. Heat pulsed within, and bright traceries spun from its folds. She pulled away the tatter and unveiled it.

The pomegranate seed. A single star plucked from an ancient sky. Its brilliance pierced the darkness, and Magpie had to shut her eyes. But even behind closed eyelids she saw something was happening. Traceries exploded like fireworks! A feeling swelled in her, not of hollowness or warp or absence but *life*. And all around her the dying lights began to flicker and flare.

In her wonder she felt the glyphs begin to slip in her mind, and she quickly thrust all her energy back to maintaining them. The effort left her numb, and tendrils of exhaustion began to steal into the core of her being. With great care, and taking comfort in the tug of the tether around her waist, she began to move deeper into the darkness, holding aloft the blazing star.

In her wake the sparks shifted, and followed.

In the Spiderdowns a fierce, swooping battle was under way. The spiders still lay scattered, but the Blackbringer raged. His essence oozed and pooled from one hideous shape to the next as he chased the whooping warriors. They were fleet and evasive, but it didn't matter. They were tiring, and he was not. He grabbed one by the beard and sucked him in. He caught a lad by the ankle, but another, a lass, slashed clean through the end of his tongue, and the lad leapt free while the severed tongue tip twitched and oozed into the black ground.

Talon's heart pounded. The Blackbringer had almost had him. Nettle and Hiss had kept close ever since they set foot in the Downs, guarding him and the thread in his hands. He'd been uncoiling the thread steadily since Magpie disappeared, and he had now come to its end. He wrapped it several times around his fist and clenched it tight. He hoped he'd made it long enough. He'd made it as long as one night's knitting permitted. Magpie could go no farther. He gave it a tug and waited, hoping he would feel it slacken. Hoping she would soon emerge.

A very long time seemed to pass.

His old uncle Caelum, who'd drawn his tattoos, was seized, along with Hesperus, whose first babe had been born this year. The warriors were falling.

The darkness was winning.

The Blackbringer bucked and bellowed. Talon felt the tether pull taut and tug him forward. He planted his feet and strained against it, feeling his heels skid over the dead ground. He strained with all his strength, and the tether cinched tight around his fist, biting into his flesh and drawing blood. Slowly, grimacing, Talon was drawn toward the beast.

'Nettle!' he hollered, trying to dig in his heels.

His sister dashed to his side, sheathing her knives so she could grip the silk string with both hands. Side by side, they struggled against the pull of Magpie's tether, but the Blackbringer seemed to have gone wild, swirling like storm clouds, morphing into crazed shapes, spinning, hissing. The silk bit through Talon's palm. He'd spelled the thing himself and knew it was strong enough to slice right through his hand.

His blood was making it slick and hard to hold.

Nettle stumbled and dropped the cord, and without her added strength resisting its pull, Talon was yanked right off his feet. He fell to his chest and was dragged through fetid spider bodies as the tether bit tighter and deeper into his hand.

The Blackbringer was only a few yards away.

'Talon!' Nettle screamed, lunging to grab his feet and trying to wrestle him back from that yawning darkness. 'Let go of it!' He knew if he did, Magpie would be lost, but if he didn't, he'd be lost with her.

He didn't let go.

He thought of the surge of strength that had flowed through him as he coursed over Dreamdark on wings he had conjured with his own hands, and a bellow rose from his throat as he twisted his legs around in front of him to find some lip in the ragged ground to brace himself against, even for a moment. His heels met rock and, gritting his teeth, he took his throbbing, bleeding hand and pulled away from the darkness with all his might.

A scream choked from his throat. The bones of his hand constricted, and blood pulsed from his wound. He strained against the darkness, but it was no use. The pull was too strong. The Blackbringer contorted and spun, and Talon felt himself lifted into the air, tumbling toward it. He gritted his teeth and held on, thinking of the courage it had taken Magpie to dive into that nothingness. He wrenched open his eyes and stared into it. This was his last chance to save himself.

He tightened his grip.

He was drawn through the air in a kind of effortless flight, and the darkness was rushing to meet him. Then, suddenly, it cleaved open, and Magpie tumbled out, falling to her knees.

'Magpie!' Talon screamed as the inexorable pull released him. He fell back to the ground as, with infinite weariness, Magpie trembled and rose slowly to her feet.

Desperate with exhaustion, she turned to the Blackbringer, raised Skuldraig with a heavy arm, and brought it down against his skin of night. As the blade met the black, a pure chime rang out through the Spiderdowns and the beast froze, his tongue dropping like a dead snake to the ground. And as Magpie held her enemy thus immobile, she saw lights begin to sparkle forth from within him like fireflies dancing out of a dark wood. The beauty of it gave her a small swell of strength and she straightened her weary arm and held Skuldraig proud.

As the lights emerged, shadows seemed to peel away from the

Blackbringer in long strips. The sparks leapt to fill them, each to each, and figures bloomed within. In every shadow burst a blinding dazzle. Pale forms moved and turned, stretched wings and arms, opened long-closed eyes, awakened. On unsteady legs they staggered forth, blinking like sleepwalkers who had awakened in a foreign land. There came faeries and imps, many, many, but Magpie kept her eyes fixed on the Blackbringer, afraid if she were to turn and watch the miracle she was working, her concentration might give way to wonder. It was a sight for others to marvel at, and they did. The Rathersting stared, panting, bleeding, broken, and awestruck, as souls emerged to reclaim their beautiful skins from shadow.

Of course, not all the skins were beautiful. The Blackbringer had feasted on his share of devils, and they, too, stepped out of the darkness. Ignoble things, wheezing, slope-shouldered, and foul, on tentacles, on cloven hooves, with suckers for mouths, with double and triple mouths. One dismal creature possessed a mouth like a wound, and as it dragged its limp wings through the throng, its mistress's last command slowly rose to the surface of its muddled mind.

And there were humans! The first ever to stand so deep in Dreamdark, four hulking, barefoot mannies swayed among the rest of the creatures. There were so many souls. Hundreds! They were like a river of light pouring from the void. Magpie glimpsed a flash of copper hair and turned her head just long enough to see that it was Poppy. Relieved, she refocused her energy on her glyphs but kept watch out for one shape, one she knew well for she had seen it silhouetted in flight a thousand times at least: Maniac. But he was nowhere to be seen, so even as the flow of souls slowed and gradually stopped, she kept her trembling arm outstretched, and waited.

'Magpie.'

She heard Talon's voice through the hypnotic ringing of the blade. She wanted to look at him, to focus on his clear, steady eyes as the world lurched around her, but she didn't dare turn. She was certain Maniac had still not come forth, and it was all she could do to keep the glyphs burning in her mind, second after endless second. She was utterly depleted, hanging on to consciousness by the thinnest of threads, and when one last shadow finally peeled away from the blackness – a crow! – she let her arm fall with a bone-weary shudder, dropping Skuldraig and the veiled pomegranate seed both upon the ground.

Maniac wobbled and hurtled to earth as a trio of warriors rushed to steady his landing and Magpie gasped, 'Crows, now!' The other birds, circling in the sky, beat down to her through the branches, bearing the Blackbringer's bottle with them.

She didn't know how she could possibly find within herself the strength to cast one last spell. She would have to let the champion's glyph go and the Djinn's protection with it. No sooner did she realize this than the glyph was snuffed from her mind, leaving a ghost image where it had so long burned. As that too faded, she breathed deep, dug into her mind for her last reserve of power, and visioned a new glyph in its place.

At once a vortex whirled to life in the neck of the silver bottle, and the Blackbringer, weakened and shrunken, was powerless against it. The whipping air grasped the edge of his skin, and the king of devils lost his hold on the world. With a roaring of wind, he was seized and sucked back toward his ancient prison. As if the skin of night were truly a fabric, its edges flapped and swirled and he whirled slowly out of sight, his terrible rasp of a voice filling everyone's minds with his fury.

Magpie collapsed to her knees and frantically fumbled the

seal out of her pocket. She held it out to the vortex, and it began to spiral through the air toward the bottle's narrow throat.

So transfixed were the crows and warriors by this remarkable sight that none noticed the devil with the bloody fang-filled maw fix its black slit eyes on Magpie. None saw it slowly gather itself into a predator's crouch and flare its membranous wings. Gutsuck pounced like a wolf, and its hideous mouth closed over Magpie's shoulder with a gnashing sound.

She cried out and fell forward, her concentration broken.

Talon rushed to wrench the devil away, but in that instant, with impossible speed, the Blackbringer's tongue lashed out from within the silver bottle, whipped around Magpie and Gutsuck together, and sucked them both back into his prison. They disappeared just before the Djinn's seal settled firmly, irreversibly, in place. The vortex abruptly ceased, and all fell still.

Everyone stared. For long seconds they couldn't even gasp. Then Calypso shrieked and flew at the seal, desperately trying to gouge it off. Stunned, Talon reeled in the tether with his good hand. It had been severed clean by the Magruwen's sealing spell. His mind screamed and resisted believing what he'd just seen.

And then, in the dense mass of dazed faeries and creatures who'd stumbled back into the world after so long adrift, the spiders, released from Magpie's spell, reawakened.

40

IF ANY SOUL THAT NIGHT WAS PULLED DOWN INTO THE DARK cracks in the earth and devoured by spiders, none ever knew of it after. When the foul creatures revived, the Rathersting shook off their shock and sprang to life, relishing enemies their blades could bite, thrilling in rescue on so grand a scale. If anyone could have counted in the chaos, they would have discovered some thousand souls newly returned to the world. But it was a time for action, not counting, and by the time the Rathersting had coaxed and dragged every imp and faerie free of the Spiderdowns, most of the snags had slipped away into the forest, and the mannies were wandering lost and afraid.

Those who'd been bitten by spiders were Orchidspike's first patients when she conducted a hasty triage later in the great hall at Rathersting Castle. She administered a potion to subdue the poison that was burning in their veins and turned to see to other injuries.

There were many. Dozens of torn wings – those could wait – and wounds of such variety the healer knew they could not have happened this night. Bite wounds with jagged snag teeth embedded in them, clean slashes from sharp weapons, contusions, lashes, burns. Kneeling over a Sayash faerie with long spines from a devil's barbed tail protruding from her leg, Orchidspike realized these wounds were casualties of the devil wars and were tens of thousands of years old, as were the faeries who suffered them.

As flummoxed as she'd ever been in her life, she had to press her hand to her heart to steady herself. However much she'd hoped Magpie would succeed in her bold plan, it had never occurred to her there might be souls from the Dawn Days still alive within the Blackbringer! Orchidspike could have used Talon at such a time, but she wouldn't call for him. Not now. She'd had but a moment with him when she bandaged his hand, before the needs of the injured claimed her attention, and now her thoughts kept returning to his shocked face, and to Magpie.

'Lady, might I be of help to you?' asked a red-haired lass the healer didn't know. About to ask her if she could manage a spell to boil water, Orchidspike paused and took a closer look at her. Her beautiful face wore the same pale, haunted look as all these others, as if she'd just awakened from a nightmare. She too had come out of the darkness.

'Lass, what's your name?' Orchidspike asked her.

'Poppy Manygreen, Lady.'

Orchidspike, old eyes glistening, said a silent blessing and set Poppy to work mixing purifying balm for the many wounds that surrounded them.

Calypso and Mingus dragged the Blackbringer's bottle into the ragged hole in the mountain that had once been the face of Issrin Ev. The other crows followed, with Talon astride Bertram. All dread the Djinn King had once inspired in them was forgotten as they cried out for him.

'Lord Magruwen!' they cawed, their voices muffled by the dust of four thousand years that blanketed the ancient corridors.

They emerged into a great chamber, where Talon's light spell glittered over a trove of treasure. They swooped around the room, distraught and shrieking for the Djinn.

'Is it done?' he demanded, emerging from a doorway. 'Where is the lass?'

Calypso and Mingus beat down to him, lowering the bottle. 'Lord!' cried Calypso. 'Ye got to unseal it!'

'What?' he hissed.

Talon leapt off Bertram's back to the ground. He held Skuldraig in one hand and the shrouded star in the other. He laid them both before the Magruwen and said, 'Just before the seal settled on, a devil attacked Magpie, and the Blackbringer reached out and sucked them both in with him! You got to get her out!'

The Magruwen looked at the bottle, and the blade, and the bundle of old skin pulsing with starlight. No expression played over the sculpted planes of his mask, but flames spewed from his eyes and horns. 'Nay!' he choked, and seized the bottle, his golden gloves clashing against its silver. But he didn't pry off the seal that bore his sigil. He only said, 'The seal is fixed. The faerie is lost.'

Until he heard the Magruwen's words, Talon had not for a moment considered that Magpie might be lost. The absurdity of it! That single second when this thing had happened – it was barely as long as the blink of an eye, and he just couldn't believe that so small a moment could wreak so terrible a change. A sense of crazed outrage welled up in him, as if a mistake had been made in the arrangement of the moments and he should be able to reach back in time and correct it. It would take so little, just seeing the devil in time or skewering the tongue on his knife as he'd done once before.

But there was not now and never had been magic for reaching

back in time. Past moments lay as they fell, and nothing would stir them.

Talon collapsed to his knees as his stubborn disbelief was stripped away, and with it vanished a feeling he hadn't even known was growing in him, a new sense that the world was wild with possibility, that the whole of life was not a castle rampart or a single forest, but a mesh of pathways waiting to be forged.

Magpie . . .

The crows were sobbing themselves hoarse, and it was the most desolate sound Talon had ever heard.

'What's all this noise?' he heard someone ask, and looked up into the imp-marm's black eyes as she suddenly appeared.

'Good-imp Snoshti . . .' he said, his heart clenching at the thought of giving her the news.

'I had a time finding ye lot, what with the crush out there. All them souls. Blessings! She did it, neh? My lass!' Her furry little creature face was bright with joy that hurt Talon's heart to see.

'Good-imp—' he started to say, but she cut him off.

'But what's all this snoolery? Feather!' She tugged at Calypso's wing. 'What's happened to ye?'

Calypso couldn't even answer. He pressed his head against the silver bottle and wept.

'It's Magpie . . .' Talon said quietly.

'Eh?' Snoshti's whiskers twitched. 'What of her?'

'The Blackbringer . . .' he told her. 'He . . . he got her, mistress. She's in there.'

Snoshti looked at the bottle, then at Talon, then back at the bottle, puzzled. 'Lad,' she growled, her face ferocious. Then she chuffed and snorted. It sounded almost like a laugh. 'What blither!' she declared. 'Magpie's not in there!'

'Aye, for I saw it myself.'

'Neh, lad! Foolish faerie! And ye birds, who should know her better! Magpie's not in there!'

Talon looked at her, wide-eyed and confused.

'She's in the Moonlit Gardens!'

Magpie was dreaming of the Tapestry. She lay on a soft white cushion in a little room in the peak of an impossibly tall spindle of rock. It rose from the floor of the dragon's canyon like a needle standing on end, and at its very tip Fade had hollowed out this little room just for her. A dreaming place of her own. In it were many high windows – a panorama of moon – and the single deep cushion on which she slept.

She had never known such exhaustion.

When she'd found herself yanked suddenly back into the dark, she'd been too weak to think and far too weak to summon the devilishly complex champion's glyph. It had failed her utterly. But as she felt her edges begin to melt, another, simpler glyph flickered in her mind. Threshold, moonlight, garden, just like Snoshti had taught her. With an effort that felt like an explosion behind her eyes, she'd visioned it, and everything went black as the moth wings took her.

When she arrived on the riverbank she was already unconscious. She'd sunk to her knees and slumped to the grass and she hadn't opened her eyes since, not when Fade gathered her up in his paw and carried her through the sky, not when Bellatrix treated the wound on her shoulder, visioning healing glyphs, cleaning off the spatter of spider venom and plucking Gutsuck's teeth out of her torn flesh. And not now, with Bellatrix by her side singing a ballad in Old Tongue and feeding teaspoons of cool water between her lips.

She was deep in dreams, her inner eyes open and tracing the miraculous patterns of the Tapestry's weave. Her mind found rest as her body healed. It would be days or weeks before she'd wake.

Hungry for news that Magpie couldn't give her, Bellatrix had sent Snoshti to Dreamdark to learn what had happened. The lady's voice sounded peaceful as she sang, but her eyes darted anxiously to the windows, watching the sky shapes for one that might be Fade ferrying the hedge imp back across the canyon to her. But Fade didn't come, and Bellatrix began to think that in all the desperately slow years she'd passed in this timeless place, these moments were the longest.

Her head was throbbing with anxiety when suddenly Snoshti bustled through the door.

'Good-imp,' said Bellatrix, surprised. 'I didn't see Fade coming. Did he carry you?'

'Neh, Lady, I've had a lift from another,' said Snoshti, and Bellatrix saw that her black eyes were sparkling.

'What is it, Snoshti? Have you brought news?'

'Aye. The Blackbringer is captured.'

'Blessings be!'

'And the Magruwen has returned to Issrin Ev.'

Bellatrix fell silent, eyes gleaming as a rush of emotion swept over her face. 'He has?' she whispered, and when the imp nodded, she clenched closed her eyes to hold back tears. A single shining drop escaped and slid down her cheek. 'Then there is hope,' she said quietly.

'And Lady Bellatrix?' said Snoshti.

Bellatrix opened her eyes. Snoshti stepped aside and through the door came a faerie. The spoon in Bellatrix's hand clattered to the floor.

The Ithuriel's champion was an Ifrit prince, tall and beautiful and dark as ebony, with immense white moth wings and black braids crowned with a circlet of silver. In the doorway he stood absolutely still and stared at his bride.

A sound – a laugh, a sob – escaped Bellatrix's lips, and Kipepeo cried out. They met in the air and clung to each other as the force of their flight spun them up toward the ceiling of the vaulted room. They laughed and sobbed, and their wings fanned and held them aloft and spun them as their cheeks pressed, tears mingled, and lips met.

Snoshti beamed and chortled. Circling the spire, Fade peered in through the moon windows and exhaled a cascade of fireworks. And in the vault of the sky the seraphim gathered to watch, and even such souls as they who had gone beyond all earthly concerns were moved by the embrace, and began to weep.

Kipepeo wasn't the only one who came to the Moonlit Gardens that day. The elders of Dreamdark had managed to explain to all the gathered souls what had befallen them and had welcomed any who chose to stay. Some did, but many more chose the Gardens, unable to face a world from which their loved ones had been gone already for thousands of years.

A week passed, and the throng in Dreamdark thinned. The Rathersting hunted down escaped devils in the dark corners of the forest and found many of the sniveling, mild snags from the catacombs in Rome. These they put in the dungeon and fed on leftovers while they decided what to do with them, but as for the more fiendish devils, these they recaptured in bottles the Magruwen crafted for that purpose. They didn't know how many still lurked in the great wood, and kept searching.

Talon, returning after dark from a day spent casting a human phantasm to guide the lost mannies to the hedge, found the crowd in the great hall composed mostly of Rathersting for the first time since the battle. He piled a plate with mushroom sandwiches and blackberry pie and plunked it down at the chief's table. His father wrapped his arm around him and left it there, periodically squeezing his son's shoulder or tousling his hair. Talon beamed and told his father stories as he ate, but as soon as he was done, he pushed back his chair and went to his room. All night his knitting needles could be heard clicking unsteadily as he maneuvered them with his bandaged hand. The dawning of the new age might occupy his days, but his nights were for creating, and he worked in secret with a single-mindedness that was driving him to exhaustion.

Orchidspike and Poppy worked side by side day after day, mending old wounds from the devil wars, administering potions and poultices, and reweaving all shapes of wings. The healer was each day more astonished by the lass's gifts and each day more delighted with her sweet nature and surprising twinkling of mischief.

As for the young Rathersting warriors who took to offering the healer their help – something that had certainly never happened before – Orchidspike attributed that to Poppy's uncommon loveliness. But her new apprentice seemed to have no mind for flirtation and paid the lads no heed at all.

At Hai Issrin Ev, the great work had begun. A tent camp had sprung up at the mouth of the Deeps as faeries and imps from across Dreamdark came to throw their energies into building the new temple. And folk and creatures began to arrive from farther afield too. The Magruwen had given a message to the web-toed, eyeless imps who swim the labyrinth of dark springs underlying the world, and they carried word to hundreds of faerieholds that the Djinn King was returned to his temple. Each day the news spread farther. From one hidden village and clanhold to the next, all across the world, wonder was blooming in the hearts of faeries.

They came day by day, pilgrims and artisans from other forests hauling the tools of their trade, the masons' hammers and chisels, glaziers' kilns, weavers' looms, and many other things, too, and the new temple began to rise on the ruins of the old.

The Magruwen himself was often away. He'd forged two new pairs of knitting needles, one for Talon and one for himself, and with his own he'd followed the lad's example and knit himself a disguise to cloak his fireproof skin. Now as a great horned owl he explored his world, learning it anew.

The falcon skin, meanwhile, was far from Dreamdark. The world's only flying imp was skulking steadily back toward Rome to fetch his wheelbarrow from the catacombs, and he spread his own legend at every opportunity. He sang, *'All through the silvery treetops he twirled, the first, and the only, winged imp in the world . . .'*

Every creature he'd met throughout Dreamdark and Iskeri had been treated to wheezy songs of his flying adventures, though the songs, truth be told, were more numerous than the adventures. Though he'd never admit it, deep in his crusty heart Batch missed the faerie's floating spells and being hauled through the air by crows, and the Djinn's silver bat wings had not been forgotten, either. The falcon skin was a keen disguise, but the flying wasn't working out exactly as Batch had hoped. Even if it hadn't been unraveling, it was too much for his poor arms. After just a few short minutes of wing flapping they hung so heavy at his sides he could scarcely lift them to pick his nose! Mostly he scampered along, wheezing his glorious songs and dreaming of silver wings.

*

Still camped on the green above Snoshti's village, the crows were no use to anyone. They didn't even hunt down snags with the Rathersting but just huddled miserably around their fire, puffing smoke rings and waiting for their lass to come back to them.

They weren't the only ones waiting. The Magruwen visited his champion in her dreams, but her friends weren't so lucky. Like the crows, Poppy and Talon could only wait, though they put their energies into work instead of smoking and did a little better job of hiding their longing.

41

WHEN MAGPIE FINALLY OPENED HER EYES, BELLATRIX WAS by her side. 'Child of my heart,' she whispered. 'Thank you.'

Kipepeo stepped up and placed a hand on his bride's shoulder. 'Blessings to you,' he said.

Magpie knew the traditional Ifrit greeting from her time excavating the temple of the Ithuriel, and she told him, 'And to the fire that kindled you,' her voice hoarse after such long silence.

Pleased, Kipepeo knelt beside her and took her hand. 'Thank you, little one,' he said, 'for guiding me out of the darkness.'

'I should thank you,' she told him with a weak smile. 'If Lady Bellatrix didn't love you so awful much, she'd never have meddled with the Magruwen's dreams, and I might not have been born.'

He raised an eyebrow and looked at his lady. 'Meddled with the Magruwen's dreams?' he repeated.

'I've much to tell you,' Bellatrix said, biting her lip and laughing. A look of mischief transformed her features so that she seemed very young, as indeed she had been when she'd died. Remembering the terrible despair she had seen so recently on that same face, Magpie was nearly overcome with a wave of emotion to think that she had played a part in Bellatrix's happiness and Kipepeo's freedom. Joy was bright in their eyes, and Magpie smiled, feeling warm and calm.

'Dreamdark is eager for your return, Magpie,' said Bellatrix. 'The new temple is begun, and many have come from afar who are eager to see you.'

Magpie knew of the temple from the luminous dreams the Magruwen sent her. She'd seen a tent camp and cook fires and faeries of every shade from golden to ebony to snow, gathered together to work. She'd glimpsed Poppy, laughing and alive, and Maniac, as grim and fierce as ever. Indeed, all her crows were mighty grim, and now that she was awake, Magpie felt a deep pang of yearning for her clan, both her feathered family and her parents and grandmother, and the West Wind, too. And, she realized when a tracery spinning in her vision turned out to be not a glyph but a tattoo, for Talon.

It was time to return to the world of light.

She parted fondly from Bellatrix and Kipepeo at the doorway to her dreaming place, and Fade carried her on the top of his head back across the canyon. Sitting in the same hollow at the ridge of his brow where once Bellatrix had knelt to tell Fade the stories that would bring Magpie into being, she had her first glimpse of the seraphim. Beings of the air, they seemed formed of fluid crystal, each with a brilliant spark at its core. They were singing, and it was the most glorious sound Magpie had ever heard.

'Mags!' gasped Pup, choking on a smoke ring. 'Mags!' he croaked and, still coughing, tackled her where she'd appeared. She hit the ground and rolled with him, completely enveloped in feathers. She couldn't see and could scarcely hear or breathe, but she knew when the other crows came hooting and cawing and jumped on

Pup. She felt like a sprout's dearest doll, the one that ends up with its button eyes and yarn hair cuddled off by love.

'Crows!' she gasped. 'Please!'

When at last they let her breathe again she staggered to her feet and flung her arms around Maniac's neck and didn't let go for minutes. 'I love you, blackbird,' she said quietly into his feathers.

'Ach, Mags,' he grumbled, patting her with his feathertips. "'Tis awful fine to see ye too.'

Then the same crows who had only minutes before been mauling her around on the moss commenced to fuss like biddies, clucking, examining the bandage on her shoulder, and arguing over who got to carry her across the woods to see the new temple. Calypso won, and the others griped about it all the way.

With her chin resting on Calypso's head, flying betwixt treetops and low clouds and feeling an absolute absence of impending doom, Magpie sighed contentedly. When they arced around the edge of the Spine and the face of Issrin came into sight, she sat up straight and stared. It had been only two weeks, but new columns had already been erected to brace a new pediment. Carvers stood on scaffolds or hovered on their wings, tapping with their chisels and hammers and etching an abstract pattern of wind and flames into the marble.

The Magruwen came to meet her in the marble dust of the courtyard and guided her through the scaffolding to the ancient halls and corridors within. He had left them largely undamaged when he destroyed the facade and blocked all entry, and faeries were everywhere busy cleaning and polishing. He showed her the reception hall with its obsidian throne and then, down several flights of sweeping stairs and through a massive locked door, his archives. On towering shelves down labyrinthine aisles, every book and scroll his scribes had penned since the Dawn Days was in its place, unplundered and untouched by time. And in the far reaches, in a dark niche beyond the scribes' carrels, stood the Blackbringer's bottle.

Just looking at it, every memory of Magpie's journey seemed to surge through her. The fishing boat, the Vritra's ashes, her first sight of Dreamdark in the mists of dawn, the terrifying descent down the old well with a cake in her hands, all churning faster and faster. Poppy's white face vanishing before her eyes, Bellatrix, Fade . . . until the moment she felt the Blackbringer's tongue wrap around her. She shuddered. Here he was, sealed away, this elegant silverwork giving no hint of the turmoil within.

She had done it.

The Magruwen said, 'Much lies ahead if a new age is to be built . . . on forgiveness.'

Magpie blinked. Those had been her own words. Somehow she had persuaded the Djinn King to come back to the world. He wasn't looking at her but past her, lost in his memories, and Magpie wondered again what terrible secret lay buried in the history of her folk. Of what great treachery were faeries guilty? She almost hoped she would never know, but something told her that one day the dusts of the past would be sifted and secrets long buried would be laid bare. It shivered her.

'My brethren must be awakened if the Tapestry is to be healed,' the Magruwen continued. 'And faeries must awaken, too, and learn what world they live in, or soon every forest will tumble under axe, every river will run black, and every devil will squirm free. No longer can you be alone against them. There must be other champions. This is no golden age of peace upon us, child, but it *is* a reawakening, and we will let neither devil nor dragon-killer steal the world we made.'

Standing there, a bandaged twig of a sprout, Magpie clung to the hope that she would be equal to the life that lay ahead of her. 'I'll do my best, Lord,' she said.

He reached out one golden gauntlet and Magpie saw the familiar gleam of Skuldraig in his grip. She took the knife back, and the Djinn said, 'Blessings fly with you, child.'

From Issrin, Magpie and the crows flew above the Deeps toward the healer's cottage. Poppy, of course, attuned to the web of green whisperers that made up the forest, heard she was coming and raced to meet her. They collided in a midair hug and spun laughing among the trees. They settled back down to Orchidspike's garden, and the lady and her apprentice checked Magpie's shoulder and assured themselves Bellatrix had done a fine job of it, though not so fine as the healer might have. There would be scars.

Orchidspike told Poppy to go off and enjoy her friend's company. 'I've waited hundreds of years for you, lass. I can wait a few more days. Go play.'

The lasses flew to Rathersting Castle, and every warrior on the ramparts whooped and clamored as soon as they hove into view. 'Hail, the Magruwen's champion!' they cried, and the chief came outside, eager to meet the lass who'd saved his life. When he dropped to one knee before her and bowed, Magpie blushed deep red. 'A feast!' he cried. 'We must have a feast! Come to the hall, lasses . . . Talon!' he bellowed. 'Where is that lad?'

But Talon couldn't be found, and the celebration began without him. Magpie was offered the tremendous honor of a clan tattoo. She gritted her teeth while old Caelum, one of the warriors who'd followed her out of the dark, drew it onto the back of her neck with a wasp stinger. The table was laid, whisker fiddles were tuned, and mugs overflowed with mead. Magpie's eyes kept straying to the door, but still Talon didn't come. She was dancing a whirling jig with Poppy and Nettle when she sensed a hurtling shape coming at her fast. She leapt aside just in time to see Talon land one of his wild scamperer's leaps right before her. His arms were outstretched, and too late Magpie realized he had meant to hug her. There was an awkward moment as she stumbled away, and he dropped his arms to his sides, and his hug turned into a wave. 'Blessings, Magpie,' Talon said with a blush.

'Jacksmoke, Talon! Where you been?'

'Me? I might ask you! Lazing about in the afterlife with dragons feeding you grapes, I ken? That what being champion does to a lass?'

'Neh!' Magpie laughed.

'Lad!' cried Bertram, hobbling over on his peg. 'Fine to see ye!' The crows mobbed him, and they weren't too bashful to hug him. 'Ye're a good lad, Talon, and I'll miss ye fierce when we go,' Bertram told him.

'When you go? When's that?'

'Three days,' Magpie answered with a touch of wistfulness.

'So soon?'

'Aye. We're headed for Anang Paranga to see my folk. Sure they'll be winding up their work with the shape-shifters soon, and I reckon once I tell them everything that's happened, about the Magruwen being awake and all, they'll be keen to come back here and meet him—'

'And his library,' interrupted Bertram.

'Aye,' agreed Magpie. 'I wish I could be here to see Papa's face when he sets eyes on it!'

'Won't you be coming back with them?' Talon asked.

'Neh, not so soon as that. There's work to do and plenty of it.'

'Champion work?'

Magpie blushed, still unaccustomed to her new title. 'Sure.

We got the other Djinn to find now. The dreaming places of the Azazel and the Sidi Haroun are like to be around there, maybe in one of the Yalay volcanoes, or up in the Sayash, and we might have luck. And there's always devils to catch. Guess you've seen your share of snags lately, neh?'

'Aye, the dungeon's full of 'em,' Talon said distractedly. Under his breath he muttered, '*Three skiving days?*'

But Magpie had caught sight of food being carried in and didn't hear him. 'Jacksmoke! I could eat slugs, I'm so famished,' she declared, her eyes following platters of fritters and apricots and cakes, and they all went to fetch their dinner. Magpie, Poppy, and Talon sat down to dine together, scarcely noticing the lads who fought for the fourth seat at the table. It was Hiss who won by stamping on another's foot, and he spent the meal staring at Poppy and missing his mouth with his spoon.

They'd scarcely finished dessert when Talon stood and said good night and left the great hall. Magpie watched him go with a pang. She danced and sang with the others until the moon was sliding down the far slope of the sky, but Talon didn't return.

Magpie and Poppy were inseparable over the next few days. They wandered through the tent camp meeting the faeries from foreign forests, and everywhere Magpie went, all eyes were on her. Faeries called blessings and held up babes to see her, and imps of sorts she'd never seen gave her posies of flowers. She blushed so much Swig predicted she'd be stained a permanent crimson, but she minded it less than she would have thought. To feel that she was a daughter of Dreamdark in these times, that was something.

She saw nothing of Talon in those days.

On the day of their departure, Magpie and the crows were toasting taters around a fire with Poppy and a clan of Iskeri stonemasons when Magpie looked up to see a falcon veer across the sky. Her pulse quickened. 'Is that Talon?' she asked, pointing.

By her side, Swig snorted. 'Un-skiving-likely. His skin's long gone. Sure ye heard, Mags, neh?'

'Heard what?' she asked, puzzled.

'How he traded that crusty scavenger his fine skin? Eh, birds!' he hooted. 'Mags don't know about the lad's skin!'

'Aye,' Calypso told her. 'When Vesper'd stowed ye in that mirror we were mad frantic and Batch wasn't keen to help find ye – ye know what those meats are like – but Talon made the trade quick as quick, soon as he heard what the imp wanted.'

Magpie frowned, flummoxed. What with Talon's absence these past days she'd all but convinced herself their friendship was a fancy. As for the times he'd saved her life, well, wasn't he a Rathersting? Wasn't that what they did? But to learn he'd traded his most cherished thing to find her . . . she bit her tater so she wouldn't have to speak. But there was an explanation: he'd saved her so she could save his folk. Simple as that.

'Three days have flown fast,' said Poppy sadly.

Magpie nodded. They were leaving at nightfall. The caravans were packed. Faeries had come from all around Dreamdark with baskets of fruit and casseroles for their journey, with breads, pots of jam, puddings, and casks of drink, and the crows had stowed it all away with greedy grins. Orchidspike had contributed several jars of a precious healing balm and Poppy a fresh batch of moonlight mist in a copper urn.

With all the hubbub of preparation, it hadn't really hit Magpie that her time in Dreamdark had come to an end, and now she felt a hollow little ache in her gut. 'We'll be back,' she said with a lightness she didn't feel. She'd had plenty of practice leaving folks behind, but she always knew that when she did, whatever hole her absence left would fill in fast, like a pit dug at the shore. It was just the way of things. It was her lot.

Magpie and the crows said their farewells in the new courtyard at Hai Issrin Ev. The Rathersting warriors hovered in the sky in formation with their knives held high, and as the crows crested the trees with the caravans, the warriors gave them a deep 'Hurrah!'

It was a hero's departure, and but for a small, deep pang, Magpie felt as she always did at the start of a journey, as if the world was opening before her like a window. She took a deep breath filled with eagerness, regret, excitement, anxiety, and sadness and whirled around in the air, pausing to gather herself together and dart in a burst of wild flight, out and away.

She heard a voice cry 'Wait!', and she faltered to a hover.

Talon.

She heard gasps from the faeries below before she saw him, but still she wasn't prepared for the sight of him when he did shoot up into the moonlit sky. She stared and the crows stared, but quickly turned their surprise into hoots of approval. 'Handsome wings, lad!' called Bertram.

'Fine choice!' cried Calypso.

Magpie shook her head and a slow, marveling smile spread over her face. 'Uncommon . . .' she murmured.

He was wearing a new skin, but he wasn't cloaked in falcon feathers as before. In all ways but one he was just himself, pale wild hair and blue eyes and tattoos, and the wings that seemed to grow from his shoulder blades as naturally as any bird's – feathered wings and black. Crow's wings.

'I just finished it!' he said, moving toward Magpie with the ease of a born bird. 'I was mad shivered it wouldn't be done in time!'

'In time?' she asked, confused.

'Aye, in time to come with you! I couldn't ask anyone to carry me across the whole world!'

'I'd've carried ye, lad!' croaked Bertram.

'Thanks, feather,' said Talon. 'Now you won't have to.'

Magpie looked closely. The glint and gleam of traceries wove through the wings, giving away its magical origins to her eyes alone. To any other eyes these wings were as true as the crows' own. 'This is what you been doing?' she asked, flummoxed.

He nodded. 'Night and day,' he said earnestly. 'I can't stay behind, Magpie. I've already told my father. I need to see what's out there. Look, I can keep up!' He spun on his wings and surged high like a raptor shooting after prey, then dropped back down to her in a graceful glide. 'I don't have to use my arms or anything. I used the glyph, the one from my dream.'

'You been planning to come all along?' Magpie asked.

'Sure, and you had to be in such a great hurry! I haven't slept a wink in three days!'

'But Talon, you eejit, why didn't you just say so? We'd've waited for you!'

Surprised, he said, 'You would?'

'Sure,' Magpie said gruffly. 'I guess I don't mind having you around.'

'So . . . I can come?' he asked hesitantly, and they both grew bashful.

'Skive.' Magpie scowled. 'You want me to invite you nice? Course you can come!'

Calypso swooped in and jostled Talon cheerfully with his wings. 'Good lad! Let's be off, then. The wind and world await!'

And Magpie and Talon shared a look that both could feel like a fizz of magic in the air. The sky unrolled before them like a path, and with burning cheeks and full hearts, side by side, they followed it.

ACKNOWLEDGMENTS

It's an extraordinary honor for a book to get a new life for a new audience, and I'm so grateful to the team at Hodder Children's Books for bringing Magpie and company to readers in the UK for the first time. To Felicity Alexander, Harriet Wilson, Naomi Berwin, Naomi Greenwood, Anne McNeill, Joana Reis, Laura Pritchard, Ruth Alltimes, and Katherine Agar, thank you so much for your guidance, enthusiasm, and patience throughout this process. I could not be more thrilled to begin this new chapter with Hodder and British readers, both the young and less young. Thank you.

Reading the acknowledgments for the original edition of this book was a journey into the past. All those old thanks still apply. To Alexandra Saperstein, my best friend of 30+ years: your enthusiasm has always been a kind of magical writing adrenalin. To Jim Di Bartolo, my husband, favorite artist, and action scene consultant, who brought my characters to life in the art for the old editions: you were there at every step, and none of this would exist without you. To my mom, Patti Taylor, for the word 'batch' (which, inexplicably, is my family's term for any unidentified, gross substance, especially if it's sticky), *and* for creating the solid foundation of my entire creative life: thank you for never doubting us or letting us doubt ourselves. And to Jane Putch, my magical, life-changing agent, who I met while pretending to be confident at a conference: what a journey it's been. Onward!

ALSO AVAILABLE AS AN AUDIOBOOK